BEYOND
the
BLOCKBUSTERS

Children's Literature Association Series

BEYOND
the
BLOCKBUSTERS

Themes and Trends in Contemporary Young Adult Fiction

Edited by
Rebekah Fitzsimmons and Casey Alane Wilson

University Press of Mississippi / Jackson

The University Press of Mississippi is the scholarly publishing agency of
the Mississippi Institutions of Higher Learning: Alcorn State University,
Delta State University, Jackson State University, Mississippi State University,
Mississippi University for Women, Mississippi Valley State University,
University of Mississippi, and University of Southern Mississippi.

www.upress.state.ms.us

The University Press of Mississippi is a member
of the Association of University Presses.

Library of Congress Cataloging-in-Publication Data

Names: Fitzsimmons, Rebekah, editor. | Wilson, Casey Alane, editor.
Title: Beyond the blockbusters : themes and trends in contemporary young adult fiction /
edited by Rebekah Fitzsimmons and Casey Alane Wilson.
Other titles: Childrens Literature Association series.
Description: Jackson : University Press of Mississippi, 2020. | Series: Childrens Literature As-
sociation series | Includes bibliographical references and index.
Identifiers: LCCN 2019046236 (print) | LCCN 2019046237 (ebook) | ISBN 9781496827135
(hardback) | ISBN 9781496827142 (trade paperback) | ISBN 9781496827159 | ISBN
9781496827166 | ISBN 9781496827173 | ISBN 9781496827180
Subjects: LCSH: Young adult literature21st centuryHistory and criticism. | Young adult litera-
ture, American21st centuryHistory and criticism. | BISAC: LITERARY CRITICISM / Childrens
& Young Adult Literature | LCGFT: Essays. | Literary criticism.
Classification: LCC PS490 .B47 2020 (print) | LCC PS490 (ebook) | DDC 809.3/99283dc23 LC
record available at https://lccn.loc.gov/2019046236
LC ebook record available at https://lccn.loc.gov/2019046237

British Library Cataloging-in-Publication Data available

Contents

Section 2. Expanding Boundaries

Section 3. Revealing Boundaries

Introduction

Boom! Goes the Hypercanon: On the Importance of the Overlooked and Understudied in Young Adult Literature

Rebekah Fitzsimmons and Casey Alane Wilson

In the last two decades, Young Adult (YA) literature has become increasingly popular; both the YA fan base and YA publishing imprints have continued to grow at a time when many other subsets of book publishing are shrinking (Corbitt). Consequently, fans, critics, television and film producers, and academics all have turned more attention to the YA field. While YA continues to expand, however, the corpus of texts that are most taught, studied, and critically examined regularly overlap with texts discussed in the popular media; this has created an increasingly small hypercanon of texts that are very often limited to the kinds of bestseller texts that make a huge impact on popular culture (Fitzsimmons 203). To non-experts, the category of young adult literature is often considered to be synonymous with huge blockbuster fiction titles like *Harry Potter*, *Twilight*, *The Fault in Our Stars*, and *The Hunger Games*. As a result, many experts in YA feel the need to frame their work in terms of this small collection of texts to justify their work's value: writers foreground these blockbuster texts in their essays, presenters discuss them at conferences, and teachers design entire courses around them. While the popularity of these notable books helps writers to connect with audiences and attract students and researchers to the field of children's literature, limiting scholarship to this hypercanon means many valuable and important perspectives and approaches are left out.

This collection intends to address this challenge by interrogating the depth and breadth of YA literature by bringing together essays that perform a large-scale meta-analysis of current trends and subgenres within YA. As a consequence of this aim, the collection has two major goals. The first is to provide scholars, critics, and readers of YA literature a model to move away from analysis focused only on singular popular texts and toward a broader framework of common themes, character arcs, and genre conventions present in the contemporary YA field. While close readings are a valuable analytical tool—and, indeed, are present in various forms throughout this collection—our intention is not to offer deep analyses of individual texts. Instead, we offer a bird's-eye view of the field that explores the ways genres, themes, and trends are shaped across multiple texts. This macrolevel approach allows our contributors to examine crucial intertextual references, texts with overlapping plot structures, and the social and political contexts surrounding the emergence of new subgenres that often appears only in the background of micro-level analyses. By collecting essays on broader theoretical and generic frameworks, this collection offers an exciting glimpse of a field exploding with popularity while acknowledging and examining that field's awkward limitations and categorical growing pains.

The second major goal of this collection is to expand the corpus of materials with which children's literature scholarship regularly engages and examines. As the field of YA literature grapples with its own historical limitations in terms of representation and works to feature an increased diversity of voices, YA scholarship should likewise diversify the genres and titles of texts it examines.[1] As we address in this introduction, the focus of critical and pedagogical attention primarily on blockbuster books risks limiting our understanding of young adult literature—and thereby reinscribing incomplete visions of the work being done in the field. By providing metacritical frameworks as well as extended reading lists within each subgenre, this collection opens doors for scholars and teachers alike to engage with a broader range of texts by a more extensive list of authors. While our collection is not, and cannot be, exhaustive, it nonetheless offers interventions into an extensive range of pressing conversations, such as the inescapable prevalence of dystopian fiction in post-9/11 YA literature, the impact of gender normativity on the adolescent experience, and the reenvisioning of old genres to encompass more complex, diverse, and accurate representations of twenty-first-century teens. Rather than narrowing our focus to one particular point of contention in the field, we have brought together contributors who can speak *across* the field, offering a unique insight into the breadth of conversations the study of YA makes possible. Rooting our discussion in the historical and contextual realities of young adult literature as it currently exists, our collection will open new avenues of intervention, and scholarship that is better prepared to address the diverse realities of YA in the future.

Young Adult Literature

Young adult literature—much like the audience to which it caters—is both young and profoundly complex. A product of the twentieth century, the category of young adult literature emerged as a means for publishers to capitalize on the rise of the new teenage subculture that grew out of the World War II era.² Although initially written for an adult readership, Maureen Daly's 1942 novel *Seventeenth Summer* is often credited as the first modern young adult novel; the quietly romantic tale, comparable in form and plot to many of today's contemporary YA romances, prioritized "the world of the teenage protagonist to the exclusion of the greater (adult) world" (Pattee 10).³ This focus on the teenage experience quickly became a hallmark of the category and gained more weight with the 1967 arrival of S. E. Hinton's *The Outsiders*. Both Daly and Hinton were young writers, lending veracity to their attempts to center the young narrator's perspective. Books aimed at young adult readers no longer needed the invasive, prescriptive voice of an adult on the page to be valid and successful—the teenager and her ideas sufficed. Although the "authenticity" of having young writers at the forefront soon faded in favor of adults writing in the voice of teenagers, texts like *Go Ask Alice* (1971), a book ghost-written by an adult but framed as a diary kept by an "anonymous" young girl, demonstrated that the priority of the youth perspective, however constructed, would remain.

The development of an appropriately teenage "voice" had further ramifications for the publishing category, most notably in the thematic and structural elements that quickly became hallmarks of young adult literature. Given the category's focus on characters whose age positions them on the verge of adulthood, YA literature is often associated with the coming-of-age story. As Roberta Seelinger Trites explains, however, the notion that YA literature is exclusively about coming of age—that is, the bildungsroman—has been overgeneralized (10). While some YA novels do bring their protagonists to adulthood by the end of the story, many choose instead to have their characters take only a few more steps along the path toward coming of age. As such, Trites argues that it is important to recognize that YA literature is also active within the tradition of the *entwicklungsroman*—that is, novels of development (10). As we will see throughout this collection, the role of progress—toward knowledge, toward complexity, toward adulthood— remains central to many of the conversations in twenty-first-century YA literature. Recognizing that the teenage protagonist must experience some form of growth, regardless of whether or not that growth brings them into adulthood, is a hallmark of most young adult novels currently on the shelves.⁴

One of the primary ways the teenage character experiences this develop-ment within YA literature is by disrupting the systems that define their lives.

Editor Mark Aronson suggests that YA literature by necessity reflects the space we have carved out for the real-world teenage experience, explaining that teenagers are encouraged to "test themselves against society, each other, and themselves in some mix that includes sex, thought, conformity, and rebellion" (33). Being a young adult in the way Aronson describes is a performative act in which members must "test themselves" in one of the prescribed ways in order to fully claim an identity. Sociologists like Kent Baxter point to the constructedness of adolescence itself, a phase of life invented in response to historical and cultural moments; the very concept of "storm and stress" as a defining feature of a young person's life was invented by G. Stanley Hall in his seminal text *Adolescence*, which used biological and psychological milestones to frame what would become the stereotypical, troubling traits society feared in its teenagers. While this is admittedly a perspective that presumes value in defining adolescents in relation to what Nancy Lesko calls "narratives of growing up and biologically based developmental schemas," it is the perspective that most accurately reflects the discourse that surrounds teenagers today (138). Child-saving movements and institutions, including high schools, scouting organizations like the Boy Scouts and Campfire Girls, the juvenile justice system, and even young adult literature were formed in order to prevent teens from living up to society's worst expectations; without intervention, these child-savers feared, teens would naturally become uneducated, hormone-fueled, peer-pressured, sex-crazed juvenile delinquents.

Despite the overtly constructed nature of the form, many scholars argue that the literature written for young adults must embrace the liminality of the space teenagers occupy in order to be productive. As Perry Nodelman explains, "young adult fiction might both be similar to other texts written for children and vary from them. Perhaps young adults' texts are those that begin with the standard polarities [of child and adult] of children's fiction but have the potential, at least, to deconstruct them" (58). Thus, Nodelman suggests that while children's texts are deeply rooted in the perceived separation between child and adult, young adult texts can offer a way of complicating that relationship. Trites goes further, arguing that this is, in fact, the driving pedagogical impulse behind YA literature. She writes, "The chief characteristic that distinguishes adolescent literature from children's literature is the issue of how social power is deployed during the course of the narrative . . . protagonists must learn about the social forces that have made them what they are" (2–3). As Trites notes, these social forces may take many shapes—including the layered and tangled interactions between concrete institutions like school, government, and church, and more abstract constructions like race, sexuality, and gender—but it is often the goal of YA literature to disassemble them in order to put their inner workings on display for teenage readers. Trites later points out, however, that the examination of and rebellion against these social forces often ends in a sanctioned form: "Adolescents have to fail at one form of institutionally proscribed rebellion before they find an institutionally tolerated form of rebellion that paradoxically allows them to remain within the system" (34). That is, the teenage protagonist is allowed to examine the inner workings of an oppressive system but is rarely given the tools to break free of the system entirely.

Blockbuster Books

While young adult literature has thus been built around the teenage audience and its evolving place within society, the category itself has undergone many transitions and transformations throughout its decades of existence. In part, this is because young adult literature is not a single genre but a publishing category that encompasses *multiple* genres, therefore allowing the market to more efficiently respond to the whims of reader demands. The popularity of *The Outsiders* spawned an entire decade of so-called problem novels; the immense reach of *Sweet Valley High* supported a boom in mass-market series fiction; the blockbuster arrival of *Twilight* sparked a surge in the popularity of paranormal romance. The very expansiveness of YA literature is the quality that allows it to be successful: with so many styles and writers under its giant tent, it can respond nimbly as its young readers jump from trend to trend and genre to genre.

Despite the complexity and depth of the YA category, however, much of contemporary culture still views YA literature as an overly simplistic genre filled with superfluous melodrama and silly, overused plot devices—not least because of the rise of more visible blockbuster books. While the term "blockbuster" is most commonly associated with films to mean a hugely successful popular film laden with car chases, expensive special effects, and big-name actors, the term has been increasingly applied to other forms of media such as record labels, television networks, and digital platforms like YouTube. Even book publishers have begun to rely on major hits—as opposed to a diversified list of steady sellers—as the primary source of profit.[5] For the purposes of this collection, a blockbuster book is defined as a bestselling book that exceeds conventional or expected boundaries such as genre or marketing categories. Blockbusters are the books that become so recognizable they can be comfortably featured in multiple sections of a bookstore; for example, *The DaVinci Code* could be found in Popular Fiction, Mystery, Crime/Thriller, and Historical Fiction, while *Twilight* could comfortably sit cover out in the YA,

Romance, Paranormal/Science Fiction, and Bestselling sections, and both texts could make seasonal appearances on the "Beach Reads" and "Before it was a Motion Picture" displays. As a result of their boundary-crossing nature, these books also regularly expand readership beyond traditional genre or category expectations in order to achieve a wider cultural recognition, which often leads to crossover into other forms of media (film, television, video games) that bring even more readers back to the original text.

The history and evolution of young adult literature has thus regularly been tied to the "blockbuster" book: a singular success in one genre makes room for an array of lesser-known entrants to follow. The current success of the YA market owes an immense debt to Stephenie Meyer's *Twilight* (2007), which ranked as *USA Today*'s best-selling book of 2008. The popularity of *Twilight* reinvigorated the YA publishing industry and launched a massive interest in the paranormal romance genre. This blockbuster was followed by the overwhelming success of Suzanne Collins's *The Hunger Games* (2008) and the successive flood of dystopian trilogies. Later, John Green's *The Fault in Our Stars* (2012) ignited a resurgence of the contemporary romance genre. Since blockbuster books dissolve the often arbitrary readership boundaries set up by publishing categories, such as those between teen and adult readers, these texts often draw attention to a subgenre and its regular readers in new and sometimes unexpected ways. In the case of YA, Rachel Falconer notes that the phenomenon of "crossover fiction," or books like *Twilight* that find an adult audience despite being written for younger readers, "made people acutely aware of the lack of consensus about what constituted appropriate reading for children as opposed to adults, and by extension, about the difficulty of maintaining traditional distinctions between childhood and adulthood" (3). As a result of this new widespread recognition, experts and non-experts alike produce (and subsequently reproduce) discussions about those subgenres that focus almost exclusively on the blockbuster texts. As Fitzsimmons has argued in previous scholarship, the blockbuster status of these books often usurps the authority and cultural relevance of other cultural markers, such as industry prizes, reviews, or critical acclaim (155–65). The resulting "hypercanon" often defines the children's and YA categories within the mainstream understanding, overshadowing other landmark texts and leading to misunderstanding or oversimplification of these categories.

In the case of YA, repeated conversations centered on texts like *Twilight, The Hunger Games,* and *The Fault in Our Stars* create a narrow view of YA literature both within the field of children's literature studies and within the public imagination. Fueling this misperception are articles and opinion pieces published in popular media outlets that dismiss YA literature outright, especially those chiding adults for reading these "juvenile" texts. The non-expert authors of these articles often point to specific blockbuster texts as metonymic representations of what the "genre" of YA literature looks like, highlighting the immense popularity of these texts as one of their many flaws.[6] Cultural critics are quick to reprimand (white male) adults for engaging with the vacuous frippery of stories that often feature the lives and concerns of young women, lecturing them for "reading down" by picking up an unserious "genre" of literature.

Theoretical Framework

It is this overall impression of homogeneity that this book seeks to correct by highlighting the vast array of genres, developmental patterns, and tropes that are regularly published under the umbrella of YA literature. To accomplish this goal, this collection provides scholars, critics, and readers of YA literature a critical model of metanarrative analysis, or analysis of multiple texts with similar themes, character types, tropes, or genre conventions. By focusing on distant reading techniques and constructing frameworks that illuminate conventions of these established and emerging subgenres, this collection adds to the growing body of critical work focused specifically on theorizing YA as its own category of literature. These essays provide clear evidence against the overarching reductive readings of YA as a uniform genre, while outlining avenues for future study of forthcoming texts.

Second, by pushing the conversation beyond the most commonly recognized "blockbuster" texts, the contributors to this collection present a wider, more diverse range of stories, storytellers, and approaches to the complex issues faced by teens. In exposing scholars, teachers, and readers of YA to a broader base of texts to work with, we aim to demonstrate that the texts under discussion within the hypercanon are not the only texts worthy of attention and analysis, nor are the texts chosen to be made into blockbuster films the only texts that can capture the attention of teen readers. In line with and in support of the goals of #WeNeedDiverseBooks and the #OwnVoices movements, this collection seeks to establish new theoretical frameworks for engaging with texts beyond those actively promoted by the current publishing industry. While these conversations have gained traction in recent years—including with the blockbuster status of texts like Angie Thomas's *The Hate U Give* (2017)—we recognize that they have yet to be treated with anything approaching parity within the critical environment. Therefore, this collection aims to engage with intersectional theoretical approaches that acknowledge the financial and demographic realities of the YA publishing market while still pushing toward a more inclusive picture of YA literature that accurately reflects readers, authors, teachers, and scholars from diverse backgrounds.

Bearing these factors in mind, we have encouraged our contributors to select their texts based on a few specific guidelines. First, the majority of the texts discussed within this collection have been published after 2005, a year marked by a variety of changes to the media landscape: the launch of YouTube, the expansion of Facebook to high school students, and the release of landmark YA texts like Scott Westerfeld's *Uglies* and John Green's *Looking for Alaska*. Although there are immensely valuable texts from before this time that qualify as both understudied *and* overlooked, we have chosen to use this time frame to tie our discussions to the rise of the blockbuster-book trend in twenty-first-century YA literature, which emerged most notably with the 2007 release of *Twilight*. Moreover, we have chosen to focus specifically on YA literature as a publishing category. While middle-grade fiction and texts aimed at younger readers are worthy of similar metatextual analysis, lumping them in with discussions of the teenage readership would ultimately do all texts involved a disservice, as they often have different pedagogical intent, marketing strategies, and boundary-crossing potential. Similarly, although we recognize the ongoing evolution of "New Adult" literature—that is, books aimed at a slightly older readership, often about college-age characters—we have, with minimal exceptions, opted to treat "New Adult" as a separate publishing category as well. While we do recognize the importance of crossover texts—adult literature read by teens, YA literature read by adults, books that hover right on the thematic extremes of each category—we chose to prioritize those texts that have been specifically published and marketed as YA novels, in order to maintain consistency across the collection.

Structure and Form

One of the difficulties in putting together a collection of essays that move beyond typical categories of texts and broach new approaches to YA subgenres is finding a way to group those essays together with the same spirit of defiance of traditional approaches. Each essay in this collection combines critical theory, metanarrative frameworks, and comparative readings in creative and innovative ways. However, we have put these essays together into three major sections that allow overlapping conversations to emphasize and amplify the type of work that each essay performs on its own.

The first section, Defining Boundaries, groups together essays that collectively work to provide insight into the conventions of existing subgenres within the YA category. In identifying these often under-recognized subgenres and highlighting the overarching shape and themes found in many of the novels within a subgenre, these essays expand the scope of YA literature studies, both in terms of text selection and emerging theoretical frameworks. These essays focus on representative texts within an identified subgenre but are intended to provide analysis and theoretical frameworks that can be applied productively to existing and forthcoming texts within that subgenre.

"Exploring the Genre Conventions of the YA Dystopian Trilogy as Twenty-First-Century Utopian Dreaming" by Rebekah Fitzsimmons examines the popular format of the YA dystopian trilogy and, by considering the trilogy as a unified text, outlines the plot patterns and other genre conventions apparent in this form. Through a distant comparative reading of multiple trilogies, this essay argues that their pedagogical nature utilizes the liminal position of teens in society to advocate for rebellion and institutional overthrow in the pursuit of a utopian hope for a better future.

"Oversharing on and off the Internet: Crossing from Digital to Print (and Back) in Young Adult Works Authored by YouTube Stars" by Rachel Rickard Rebellino examines the nonfiction side of YA by analyzing the generic conventions of memoirs of young YouTube content creators and the challenges those creators face when trying to cross platforms from internet video into print book. In subverting the "print is dead" narrative by moving from new media to old, Rebellino traces the complex interplay between audiences, internet popularity, and bestsellerdom, as well as the different truths that emerge in text rather than video.

"Paranormal Maturation: Uncanny Teenagers and Canny Killers" by Rachel Dean-Ruzicka examines the trope of uncanny teens using extraordinary abilities to track and stop serial killers. Using the framework of Freud's concept of the uncanny, Dean-Ruzicka unpacks the ways these teens use supernatural skills to "do what the adults cannot: identify and track a serial killer," leading to atypical forms of maturation. The essay establishes how these teens often operate outside the law and outside conventional understandings of relationships to themselves and other people, creating a more complex, uncanny version of coming of age for readers to grapple with in this subgenre.

"Fathoms Below: An In-Depth Examination of the Mermaid in Young Adult Literature, 2010–2015" by Amber Gray presents a compelling analysis of the figure of the mermaid within the subgenre of YA paranormal romances. Using a comparative framework, Gray outlines the major tropes present in these narratives and points to the value of the mermaid as a liminal figure with a fluid identity. Gray argues that these mermaid narratives often serve to demonstrate how larger political issues often affect teens, whether or not they choose to be involved in the political process, while the mermaid can serve as a valuable touchstone for teens grappling with their own multivalent identities.

"Who Are These Books *Really* For? Police-Violence YA, Black Youth Activism, and the Implied White Audience" by Kaylee Mootz analyzes the emerging subgenre that addresses police violence, Black activist movements like Black Lives Matter and #TakeAKnee, and structural racism through a youth-oriented lens. Mootz lays out the emerging conventions of this subgenre and common subject matter, such as structural racism and the power of protest. Mootz also closely examines the didactic lessons of these texts and demonstrates how many of the "teaching moments" in these texts address a majority-white audience unfamiliar with the concepts of white privilege and structural inequality. Mootz's chapter encourages scholars and educators to pay close attention to which characters are permitted to grow and change and which are called upon to speak out in the aftermath of police violence, especially as the genre continues to expand.

The second section, Expanding Boundaries, brings together essays that explore collisions of subject, theme, and character in ways that challenge the limits of long-established genres. While the essays in the previous section provide insight into the rules that define (emerging) genres, the essays in this section look at texts that question the rules as we know them. The analyses in this category include critiques of form, representation, and genre that combine to present a nuanced portrait of contemporary YA literature's capability for invention and exploration.

"New Directions for Old Roads: Rewriting the Young Adult Road Trip Story" by Jason Vanfosson maps the very American genre of road trip stories onto twenty-first-century contexts. Using queer theory to address the limits imposed on women, young adults of color, and LGBTQIA+ teens in the face of road trips, Vanfosson's essay argues that the narrative of the open road as a space for transformation and self-discovery is often reserved for cis-het white males.

"New Heroines in Old Skins: Fairy Tale Revisions in Young Adult Dystopian Literature" by Jill Coste examines YA dystopian fairy tale retellings through a feminist lens of embodiment and political engagement. Coste links the didactic nature of fairy tales and dystopias and notes the sense of agency that allows teen readers to imagine a different, more hopeful future while calling them to engage in activism in the current moment. The value in examining this popular subgenre of YA lies in its often subversive reworking of common tropes, both from fairy tales like *Sleeping Beauty* and broader problematic social conventions that perpetuate rape culture narratives.

"Manufacturing Manhood: Young Adult Fiction and Masculinity(ies) in the Twenty-First Century" by Tom Jesse and Heidi Jones examines the "crisis in masculinity" lamented in twenty-first-century popular media and the ways in which contemporary YA novels work to reimagine and redefine masculinity outside or above the toxic frameworks that came before. Framed through a critical literacy lens, this essay examines "varied portraits of what it means to 'be a man' in the twenty-first century," as depicted in contemporary YA texts. They note that previous traditional markers of American masculinity, such as physical strength, competitiveness, and self-reliance, are increasingly challenged through the denigration of old stereotypes, like the "dude bro," and celebrated new ideals, such as the "sensitive thinker."

"Mythopoeic YA: Worlds of Possibility" by Leah Phillips demonstrates how the liminal nature of YA, neither adult nor children's literature, opens a space for fantastic world building that can disrupt the hegemonic concepts of traditional fantasy. Phillips argues that contemporary mythopoeic YA, written by women primarily for girls, "offers unparalleled avenues for increasing diversity and inclusivity." Phillips traces the evolution of mythopoeic YA from its "founding mother" Tamora Pierce, who challenged the notion of the typical male hero and quest in her series. Phillips locates and analyzes a number of newer series that further challenge the typical pseudomedieval European fantasy setting by locating stories in fantastic worlds based on Nigerian, Middle Eastern, Japanese, and Southeast Asian cultures and including characters from a wide range of races, religions, classes, sexualities, and physical abilities.

The third and final section, Revealing Boundaries, works to critique existing categories by tracing often unspoken genre norms and pushing back against expectations. Some of these essays offer much-needed updates to the critical treatment of existing genres, while others point to explicit gaps in both the texts themselves and the critical treatment of those texts. While the first section explores conventions and tropes that help fit YA texts into various subgenres, and the second section argues for the expansion of restrictions that have previously been taken for granted, this section works to illuminate boundaries that previously may have been hidden or overlooked by previous analyses. These essays seek to place unspoken assumptions into a theoretical framework that will enable future critical conversations.

"'Tell Me Who I Am': An Investigation of Cultural Authenticity in YA Disability Peritexts" by Megan Brown uses a disability studies framework to examine the ways in which peritextual elements like biographies, dedications, and author's notes can build a narrative of authenticity, on a spectrum from personal experience to carefully researched to minimal exposure. Brown argues for the importance of authentic representation of disability as well as an increased recognition of the importance of accurate representation of not only the experience but also the meanings of the lived experiences in order to avoid the perpetuation of negative stereotypes and inaccurate understandings.

In "Reimagining *Forever* . . . : The Marriage Plot in Recent Young Adult Literature," Sara K. Day examines the trope of early marriage in YA romance novels, maintaining the concept of permanence of young and even first love as the desired outcome of adolescence. Using a postfeminist lens, Day analyzes the conversations and cultural contexts surrounding marriage in the twenty-first century. She notes that many YA novels (mis)use classic "marriage plot" novels such as *Jane Eyre*, *Middlemarch*, and *Pride and Prejudice* as templates, while ignoring or erasing the subversive elements of those narratives in order to privilege a traditional upper-class heteronormative understanding of marriage as the natural "happy ending" of a romance.

A timely essay, Roxanne Harde's "No Accident, No Mistake: Acquaintance Rape in Recent YA Novels," examines the subgenre of YA texts detailing the rape of the main character and the aftermath. Harde examines the pedagogical messages of novels with regard to speaking up about versus staying quiet about the assault, tracing the narrative tropes from Laurie Halse Anderson's seminal *Speak* through to more recent additions to the subgenre. The essay also examines narratives that touch on the point of view of the rapist and the important work of addressing the messages rape culture instills in young men as a means of combatting the ongoing issues of acquaintance rape and sexual assault.

"Eliminating Extermination, Fostering Existence: Diverse Dystopian Fiction and Female Adolescent Identity" by S. R. Toliver engages in a much-needed exploration of the popular subgenre of dystopian texts with female main characters; her intersectional examination of female protagonists of color provides readers with a valuable resource for introducing diverse texts to readers and classrooms. By disrupting the hyper-canon of YA dystopian texts that focus largely on white protagonists, Toliver moves conversations about identity and the treatment of marginalized populations in future societies into a more central space in the discussion surrounding these texts.

"Sharpening the Pointe: The Intersectional Feminism of Contemporary Young Adult Ballet Novels" by Sarah E. Whitney examines contemporary ballet novels that focus on young women of color in the traditionally white universe of ballet. She argues that these texts, largely authored by women of color, add layers of postfeminist and queer analysis to ongoing discussions about the physicality, rigor, body image disorders, racism, and rape culture behind the "music box ballerina."

Boom! Goes the Canon: Moving beyond the Blockbusters

While this collection covers a great deal of ground and opens up discussion into a wide array of important and underappreciated subgenres, it also falls far short of encompassing all the subgenres available under the YA category. While we, as editors, have sought to include a balance of viewpoints, topics, and tropes, we have done so with a recognition that any claim to totality is impossible. It is our hope that this collection will set the stage for more metacritical readings of YA texts and theoretical discussions of these subgenres as organic, evolving areas of study.

We invite readers, then, to read this collection with three major takeaways in mind.

First, we assert that YA is a diverse publishing category that is often misunderstood or miscategorized as a singular genre. While there are some who may intentionally misrepresent YA in order to make larger cultural critiques lamenting the "downfall" of American culture, the larger misperception is often due to a limited exposure to YA texts. As this collection of essays clearly demonstrates, a vast forest of YA texts exists beyond the first few major blockbuster trees. Further, we hope to add additional voices to a growing movement of literature scholars calling for a study and theory concentrated on YA literature in its own right. YA scholarship has been steadily built around the work and theories within the children's literature framework; it may be time to begin to study and theorize YA in its own space, as historians like Paula Fass and Steven Mintz and sociologists like Lesko and Mike A. Males have done in those adjacent fields. We hope these essays will help to frame the kinds of broader genre and thematic conversations that an autonomous YA literature studies would address.

Second, while the blockbusters that have come to represent YA in the larger cultural imagination have merit and are worthy of study, there are often multiple texts that address similar themes, tropes, character arcs, or genres in useful, interesting, or problematic ways. Therefore, our collection argues that there is value in looking beyond the blockbusters and toward texts that have been overlooked and undervalued as a result of the field's preoccupation with the "next big thing." Our contributors offer frameworks for study and analysis that can be put to work by all those who interact with YA literature. The essays that follow make suggestions for texts that teachers at all levels might incorporate into their syllabi and present arguments for citing or examining books still in need of deep analytic study. Prize committees may find broader categories of texts to consider in their deliberations; librarians will find titles with similar themes and structures to offer during readers' advisory. The texts this collection discusses are varied and often have little overlap from one essay to the next, but we believe this to be a feature, not a bug. What unites these texts is their value in representing a field that has exploded in popularity so quickly it has proven nearly impossible for critical discussions to keep apace. While these texts may not all rank among the most popular, the essays in this collection nonetheless demonstrate their collective influence on discourse about twenty-first-century adolescence and the continuing evolution of YA literature. In many cases these understudied texts elaborate, expand, deepen, or diversify the issues raised by blockbuster texts. Our hope is that this collection can shine the spotlight at texts that have not been brought to center stage before, therefore bringing a more complete story to the study of YA literature.

Third, as scholars, teachers, librarians, and patrons of YA literature, we have influence over which texts become blockbusters—with reviews, awards, social media signal boosting, and our purchasing dollars, we can help to influence the next set of blockbuster texts, which in turn can help influence the appeal and impression of YA literature to a broader audience. The growing success of titles featuring authors, characters, and plotlines that better reflect the YA population of readers may further the call for more diverse texts, but that success is not guaranteed. Taking inventory of the makeup of our own syllabi, scholarly citations, and individual purchases can help ensure that our students, patrons, and friends are exposed to the rich scope of literature published under the umbrella of YA literature. The work we have done here is designed to open the door to reading more diversely; with that in mind, we have included an extended reading list curated by our authors at the end of the collection. This reading list collects texts that informed the choices each author made in their analyses—and we hope it will also inform your choices as you design your courses, develop your presentations, and deepen your scholarship. The future of YA literature and its readership belongs not just to the blockbuster books but to all the texts that we choose to study, teach, and read. We hope this collection will be one step among many toward making the field of YA literature studies a more representative and complete place.

Notes

1. As we write this essay, the children's literature community is processing serious allegations of sexual misconduct by several well-known authors. While the fallout from this #MeToo moment will take time to process, we would argue that the allegations against Sherman Alexie, in particular, support the argument against relying on singular "representative" texts in our collective teaching and scholarship. Calls to remove the works of problematic authors from syllabi and reading lists add to the urgency for the broader analysis of children's and YA lit genres and trends we propose in order to support more diverse reading throughout the field.

2. In the interest of space, we offer here only a brief gloss on the development of young adult literature. The history of the publishing category has been covered in more detail in many other texts, including most notably Michael Cart's regularly updated *Young Adult Literature: From Romance to Realism*.

3. Certainly, there are arguments to be made for and against using Daly as a marker of YA's origins; novels for young readers existed before Daly's book, and books marketed explicitly

as "young adult" novels came later. However, given the YA market's emphasis on a specifically "teenage" readership, the 1942 release of *Seventeenth Summer* coming just a year after the first in-print usage of the word "teen-ager" in a 1941 issue of *Popular Science* offers a useful parallel.

4. Admittedly, the notion of "progress" as the defining feature of YA literature is not without its flaws. As Nancy Lesko argues, this preoccupation with progress reflects remnants of recapitulation theory, which presupposes that childhood development "progresses" toward an evolutionary ideal; therefore, these novels of progress are based on a presumption of the teenager as an inheritor of colonialist, white, masculine, able-bodied ideals (25–27). We use this framing not as an endorsement of its implications but as a reflection of the field's predominant view of the role of the teenager as always moving toward adulthood.

5. For a more detailed breakdown of this "blockbuster strategy" and the effects it has had on a wide variety of entertainment venues, from sports to opera, music to Hulu, see Anita Elberse, *Blockbusters: Hit-Making, Risk-Taking, and the Big Business of Entertainment* (New York: Henry Holt, 2013).

6. Significant examples of these opinion pieces include Ruth Graham's "Against YA," and Joel Stein's "Adults Should Read Adult Books." More recently, Lizzie Skurnick's *New York Times* article "In Y.A., Where Has All The Good Sex Gone?" faced criticism for addressing only recent YA blockbuster books in order to make generalizations about YA romance as a whole.

Works Cited

Anonymous. *Go Ask Alice*. New York: Simon Pulse, 1971.

Aronson, Marc. *Exploding the Myths: The Truth about Teenagers and Reading*. Scarecrow Press, 2001.

Baxter, Kent. *The Modern Age: Turn-of-the-Century American Culture and the Invention of Adolescence*. U of Alabama P, 2008.

Cadden, Mary, et al. "New Star Authors Made, Old Ones Rediscovered in 2008." *USA Today*, Gannet Co, 1 Jan. 2009, usatoday30.usatoday.com/life/books/news/2009-01-14-top-sellers-side_N.htm.

Cart, Michael. *Young Adult Literature: From Romance to Realism*. American Library Association, 2010.

Collins, Suzanne. *The Hunger Games*. Scholastic, 2008.

Corbitt, Sue. "Editors, Agents, and Authors Take the Pulse of Today's YA." *Publishers Weekly*, 20 Oct. 2017, https://www.publishersweekly.com/pw/by-topic/childrens/childrens-industry-news/article/75172-editors-agents-and-authors-take-the-pulse-of-today-s-ya.html.

Daly, Maureen. *Seventeenth Summer*. Dodd, Mead, 1942.

Falconer, Rachel. *The Crossover Novel: Contemporary Children's Fiction and Its Adult Readership*. Routledge, 2009.

Fitzsimmons, Rebekah. "Prizing Popularity: How the Blockbuster Book Has Reshaped Children's Literature." *Prizing Children's Literature: The Cultural Politics of Children's Book Awards*, edited by Kenneth Kidd and Joseph Thomas. Routledge, 2016.

Graham, Ruth. "Against YA." *Slate*, 5 June 2014, http://www.slate.com/articles/arts/books/2014/06/against_ya_adults_should_be_embarrassed_to_read_children_s_books.html. Accessed 2 Feb. 2018.

Green, John. *The Fault in Our Stars*. Penguin, 2012.

Hinton, S. E. *The Outsiders*. Speak, 1967.

Lesko, Nancy. *Act Your Age! A Cultural Construction of Adolescence*. Routledge, 2012.

Meyer, Stephenie. *Twilight*. Little, Brown, 2005.

Nodelman, Perry. *The Hidden Adult: Defining Children's Literature*. Johns Hopkins UP, 2008.

Pascal, Francine. *Double Love*. Random House, 1983.

Pattee, Amy. *Reading the Adolescent Romance: Sweet Valley High and the Popular Young Adult Romance Novel*. Routledge, 2010.

Skurnick, Lizzie. "In Y.A., Where Has All the Good Sex Gone?" *New York Times*, 9 Feb. 2018, https://www.nytimes.com/2018/02/09/books/review/sex-young-adult-fiction.html.

Stein, Joel. "Adults Should Read Adult Books." *New York Times*, 23 May 2012, https://www.nytimes.com/roomfordebate/2012/03/28/the-power-of-young-adult-fiction/adults-should-read-adult-books.

Trites, Roberta Seelinger. *Disturbing the Universe: Power and Repression in Adolescent Literature*. U of Iowa P, 2004.

We Need Diverse Books. WeNeedDiverseBooks.org, 2018.

BEYOND
– the –
BLOCKBUSTERS

1

Exploring the Genre Conventions of the YA Dystopian Trilogy as Twenty-First-Century Utopian Dreaming

Rebekah Fitzsimmons

Young adult (YA) dystopian literature has been an inescapable feature of the YA book market since the beginning of the twenty-first century.[1] From the early 2000s, trilogies like The Hunger Games and Divergent have dominated the YA best-seller list, the box office, and many conversations about YA literature. This essay argues that the YA dystopian trilogy is a multibook storytelling formula that establishes a new form of twenty-first-century utopian writing. The historical didactic intent of utopian/dystopian literature as a form of societal critique combined with the pedagogical role of YA literature creates a new genre in the utopian/dystopian tradition that follows a three-book format. What's more, as a growing number of trilogies conform to this emerging generic form, much as emerging utopian literature followed the form of Thomas More's inaugural text, the lessons that encourage teens to think beyond (some) institutions are reinforced in readers' minds and reinscribed on the subgenre through repetition. In examining the genre conventions and pedagogical strategies of YA dystopian trilogies, this essay outlines a helpful framework for analyzing the wide range of trilogies that exists within this subgenre, allowing scholars and students to move beyond the best-known trilogies in order to examine the utopian impulses of all these texts.

As noted in the introduction to this volume, YA literature is widely invested in teaching children about social forces and the ways in which institutions—church, government, school—reinforce more abstract social constructions like race, gender, and sexuality. Roberta Trites argues that teens are expected, even encouraged, to rebel against these limits, failing at inappropriate or childish forms of rebellion before locating the "institutionally tolerated form of rebellion that paradoxically allows them to remain within the system" (34). Rebellion is encouraged—possibly even required—in YA literature because it teaches protagonists (and, by extension, readers) how to find the limits of the institutions they must inhabit. Perhaps it is no surprise, then, that YA literature has become so invested in dystopian worlds. Teenagers make natural protagonists for dystopian novels because they are expected to rebel and push boundaries, which is a necessary plot device for a dystopian narrative to perform its critical work. Stereotypically, teenagers feel that they are outcasts in society, that they are not understood, and that adult society is repressive, unfair, and built on outdated or arbitrary rules. Dystopian fiction magnifies those unjust, repressive elements and pushes them to the extreme, building a fictional world devoted to critiquing aspects of society that seem fundamental and unchangeable, and exposing the teen reader's place in the real-world equivalent of that system.

History of YA Dystopias

Early examples of the YA/dystopia generic blend can be seen in novels from the late 1980s and 1990s; books like *Ender's Game* by Orson Scott Card (1985) and *The Giver* by Lois Lowry (1993) play on traditional dystopian fears of overly structured societies and repressed free will, even while addressing typical teen fears about growing up, puberty, bullies, and high-stakes tests.[2] The rise of the twenty-first-century YA dystopian marketing juggernaut is often linked to the 2002 publication of M. T. Anderson's novel *Feed*. Due in part to its status as a finalist for the National Book Award for Young People's Literature that year, *Feed* soon became a favorite of high school and college instructors as a critical dystopian text focused on technology, consumerism, and environmentalism.

Following Anderson, YA dystopian texts spent the next decade as the bestsellers du jour, thanks in no small part to the overwhelming success of Suzanne Collins's The Hunger Games trilogy (2008–2010). Collins popularized the trilogy format along with the YA dystopian subgenre, and the blockbuster series is credited with spawning a wide range of imitators. However, in tracing the genre conventions in trilogies published between 2005 and 2015, it is clear Collins was not the first to write in this three-book format.[3] Much of the existing criticism of YA dystopian trilogies focuses on The Hunger Games and Divergent series; this essay outlines the genre conventions that apply broadly to YA dystopian trilogies but uses the Chaos Walking trilogy by Patrick Ness as the analytical focus.[4]

In mapping out this generic metanarrative on a broader scale, I demonstrate that these novels represent not just a teen fad but a broader cultural moment and an emerging subgenre. These trilogies draw upon the literary traditions of critical utopian literature to create a space for (some) teen readers to imagine and potentially enact social change, even as the subgenre privileges that utopian dreaming for white, heteronormative, cisgendered, able-bodied characters. In chapter thirteen of this collection, S. R. Toliver's essay clearly outlines the limitations of the YA dystopian subgenre in addressing the place of young people of color and queer youth in shaping and saving the future world(s). I acknowledge this limitation within the scope of my own argument and use it as an opportunity to call on teachers and scholars to engage with YA dystopian trilogies beyond the most common blockbuster series. I claim that the pedagogical strategies of these trilogies empower (some) teens to look beyond the obvious forces that shape their society to critically examine the limits placed upon them and to channel their (overwhelmingly white) teen rebellions into socially and politically impactful movements.

Utopian Traditions

While the utopian impulse existed in myths, legends, and religious reassurances that a more perfect world is possible, it was Thomas More who invented the word *utopia* to describe his carefully structured island society in 1516 (Elliott 3–24). Since the word is a play on the Greek, meaning both "the perfect or good place" and "no place," "utopia necessarily wears a Janus-face. The portrayal of an ideal commonwealth has a double function: it establishes a standard, a goal; and by virtue of its existence alone it casts a critical light on society as presently constituted" (22). To narrate an alternative world that improves on reality is to suggest that reality is imperfect but improvable. In the midst of the industrial era, modern warfare, and the ruthless side of capitalism, John Stuart Mill coined the word *dystopia* in 1868 (Vieira 16). At the same time, the highly structured, proscriptive utopias of More's tradition shifted toward the futuristic, borrowing elements from science fiction and apocalyptic narratives to articulate fears about the growing role of science in creating weapons of mass destruction, surveillance technologies, medical advancements, mechanized labor, eugenics, and climate change (Clayes 115–22). The twentieth century led to an understanding that one man's utopia, such as Hitler's Aryan nation, was other men's and women's dystopian nightmare; as such, dystopias of different eras often reflect the general fears of that time (108–22).

The generic qualities of dystopias reflect a few specific criteria. Like a utopia, a dystopia often exists in an isolated or insulated place, separated from other societies either by space (an island, a distant planet) or political reality (wars, closed borders, censored communication technologies). Dystopias detail the social structure, governing body, and daily life of an isolated society in a way that invites comparison to the reader's contemporary society, which Darko Suvin refers to as "cognitive estrangement" (*Metamorphoses* 4). Unlike utopias, dystopias are described by insiders, since visitors are generally not allowed into these closed-off societies (Moylan 148). The protagonist often harbors outsider feelings, as a result of either tragic circumstances or an encounter with a knowledgeable individual or rebellious figure who exists outside full control of the dystopian society. Since the protagonist cannot unsee the truth of the injustices or hypocrisies that the outsider has revealed, these insider narratives allow the reader to identify with the protagonist "by means of the thoughts and feelings of the characters in that new society who are involved in the daily struggle to build a world of human freedom and self-fulfillment" (Fitting 148).

Just like utopian fiction, dystopian novels have at their heart a pedagogical mission; critical utopias and dystopias use the genre as a space from which to criticize the author's own world in order to encourage change (Moylan 186–94). While dystopias are often considered bleak stories filled with dark nightmares built on the most pessimistic vision of human nature, more-contemporary dystopian narratives are not without a spark of hope or the promise of escape. They are meant to provoke fear and dread in the reader in order to spark the "utopian hope" that will impel the reader to seek a better way forward. "[D]ystopias that leave no room for hope do in fact fail in their mission" (Vieira 17). The goal of these "critical dystopias" "is to make man realize that, since it is impossible for him to build an ideal society, then he must be committed to the construction of a better one . . . they are, in fact a variant of the same social dreaming that gives impetus to utopian literature" (17). Building on this argument, I locate the YA dystopian trilogy within this critical dystopian tradition and argue that these trilogies paint rebellion as heroic and celebrate the disruption of corrupt systems, through violence if necessary. Therefore, unlike the lessons Trites identifies in school fictions, these YA texts advocate for the overthrow of existing institutions within the dystopian systems in favor of a more perfect society.

Mapping the Genre Conventions of YA Dystopian Trilogies

By identifying the YA dystopian trilogy as a distinct subgenre and mapping its phases, it becomes easier to see the common pedagogical strategies and didactic missions of these texts.

After analyzing over a dozen YA dystopian trilogies, I have determined that this subgenre has three phases.[5]

Phase 1 establishes the rules and realities of the dystopian world and places the protagonist in direct conflict with that system through a ritualized rite of passage symbolizing coming of age.[6] Phase 2 expands the world of the dystopia beyond the protagonist's home to show that the protagonist's problems are only a small part of the larger dysfunctional system; given the size and scope of these inequities, conflict with the ruling forces of the dystopia becomes inevitable. Phase 3 forces alliances to shift as new forces (re)appear to realign the balance of power; these forces often demonstrate alternative societal structures that appear to offer an alternative to the status quo. At the heart of the rebellion, the protagonist makes difficult choices that often result in self-sacrifice, in order to overthrow the ruling forces and defeat the main antagonist. Each trilogy then concludes with a gesture toward Ernst Bloch's "utopian hope," where society begins to reassemble itself, moving toward more-democratic, justice-oriented structures.

Phase 1: Rules and Realities

Like most speculative fiction, each YA dystopian trilogy is built around "a strange newness, a *novum*," or a specific element that marks where the dystopian system has deviated from our own (Suvin, *Metamorphosis* 4). This estranging principle often serves as the hook for the trilogy's marketing (such as *The Hunger Games*'s premise of "in a world where children fight to the death on TV") and affects the shape of the trilogy's plot and social critique. The resulting "cognitive estrangement" transforms the remaining recognizable elements of everyday life into the unusual or foreign, which Suvin argues allows the reader to view our own society with fresh eyes (*Metamorphosis* 10). In *The Knife of Never Letting Go* (*Knife*), the first book in the Chaos Walking trilogy by Patrick Ness, Todd lives on a distant planet where a native "germ" causes the thoughts of all men to be audible and visible. Todd describes this phenomenon, called "Noise," as:

> a flood let loose right at me, like a fire, like a monster the size of the sky come to get you cuz there's nowhere to run . . . Never mind plugging yer ears, it don't help at all . . . the voices talking and moaning and singing and crying. There's pictures too pictures that come to yer mind in a rush, no matter how much you don't want 'em, pictures of memories and fantasies and secrets and plans and lies, lies, lies. (20–21)

This estranging principle of Noise has created an utter lack of inner privacy, and the resulting panoptic atmosphere has driven the all-male settlement of

Prentisstown to cultlike behavior, alcohol abuse, and violence. Additionally, the pages of the text explode with alternative fonts and text sizes that push beyond the typical margins in a visual representation of Noise, estranging the reader from the traditional visual expectations of a novel.

Phase 1 begins by focusing on a particular subset of society, the home of the protagonist. This allows the reader to become immersed in the world of the dystopia and to understand the rules and realities of the society through the focus of the protagonist. These subsets, like Panem's District 12 or *Divergent's* Dauntless faction, serve as miniaturized examples of the dystopian system. In *Knife*, Prentisstown (we're told) is the last surviving settlement on New World, consisting of 146 men; supposedly, all of the women and most of the men died in the war with the native species, the Spackle.

The motivating action of Phase 1 is a ritualized rite of passage, where the dystopian system initiates the protagonist's transition from childhood to adulthood through proscribed practices. Though the protagonist is a part of the dystopian system, he or she often feels pushed to the margins as a result of personal circumstances. At the start of *Knife*, Todd, the only boy remaining in Prentisstown, is isolated by rules that forbid men from speaking to boys. Todd flees the settlement before turning thirteen, when the ritual is scheduled to take place. During his flight he learns that this ritual entails hearing a version of the true history of the town and being made complicit in that history (397). The real reason there are no women in Prentisstown is that human women are unaffected by Noise, and so the men, led by Mayor Prentiss, killed them all thirteen years earlier. After the mass murder, Mayor Prentiss ritualized the process of coming of age so that the "way that a boy in Prentisstown becomes a man . . . It's by killing another man. All by theirselves" (448). Like the rites of passage in other dystopian novels, such as the faction selection in *Divergent* or surviving the Reaping and the Hunger Games, this ritual marker of adulthood initiates the coming-of-age process, ultimately leading the young men in Prentisstown to become full participants in the dystopian system. Surviving the coming-of-age process requires the young adult protagonists to navigate their own loss of innocence or ignorance as to the form and function of their society, while the dystopian structure drives them toward becoming complicit in upholding the dystopian system in which they live. The choices each protagonist makes to accept or disrupt different steps in the ritualized rites of passage shape the conflict with the dystopian system throughout the trilogy.

The dystopian trilogies at large paint adults as passive participants in the structure and maintenance of the dystopian system. While previous generations of adults are responsible for the current shape of society through inattention, irresponsible behavior, intentional scientific advancements, or poor choices, these trilogies demonstrate how adults also abdicate their responsibilities to fix the system. To become an adult, these books teach the reader, is to become an integral part of the system and to perpetuate the cycle of oppression. This creates a ticking clock for the young protagonist, who must race against the aging process in order to complete rebellion before her or his coming of age.

This incitement to rebel can be brought about by an impossible conflict with the system itself, like Katniss's sister being chosen for the Hunger Games, or by an encounter with an outsider, like Todd's discovery of Viola, the first girl he has ever seen. Viola's presence and her lack of Noise shake Todd's understandings of what is and the "truths" espoused by the Mayor; she also introduces new variables as to what is to come. Viola crashed on New World in a scout ship in advance of an incoming convoy of thousands of new settlers. Once Todd knows this information, he and Viola must flee Prentisstown, or his Noise will certainly reveal her. Ben, Todd's foster father, helps them to escape but cannot go with them; all grown men from Prentisstown have been exiled, on pain of death, by the other New World settlements. Todd has the option to flee because he has not yet "become a man" and therefore is not yet considered complicit in the mass murder.

Phase 1 places the protagonist, armed with new knowledge, in direct conflict with the dystopian system. By refusing to complete the coming-of-age ritual, Todd disrupts the Mayor's "prophecy" of a perfect army with no weak links, a complete army purified by hate (450–51). The fallout that follows this disruption of the rite of passage develops into the main conflict of the series, and as such the protagonist's status as enemy of the state—whatever that dystopian state might look like—is cemented at this early stage in the series. Katniss is pitted against President Snow; Todd and Viola against Mayor Prentiss. However, at the end of the first phase, the reader and protagonist(s) alike are unaware that this initial disruption has already established the path toward overthrowing the dystopian system in the remaining books. A small teenage rebellion becomes the spark for a larger societal rebellion that eventually brings down the ruling power.

Phase 2: Sizing Up Dystopian Systems

Phase 2 begins when the author opens the world from the enclosed dystopia of Phase 1 to a more complete picture of the society. In Phase 1 a close examination of a smaller subset of society is required in order to fully realize the physical, emotional, and psychological stakes for the main character(s). Phase 2 determines the stakes beyond the protagonist's inner circle: for civilization and, in many cases, the human race. In some trilogies the larger world is known but inaccessible; in other trilogies, including Chaos Walking, the existence of additional settlements is a revelation that disrupts the dystopian system itself. No matter the circumstance, the importance of this expansion of the world cannot be overlooked. Phase 2 confirms the protagonist's—and the reader's—worst fears about the true extent of the dystopia. While each subset of the society is being oppressed by the same force, the wider view of the world reveals the different ways in which groups of people seek to cope with that oppressive force, and the uneven application of that oppression in certain subsets of society. It is by expanding the scope of the dystopia and opening the larger world to readers' exploration that the protagonist's privileges are emphasized: in many trilogies, the race, gender, class, and able-bodiedness of the protagonist provide a relative but previously unrecognized security to the protagonist, especially when compared to other, less privileged subsets of the dystopian society. For example, in The Hunger Games trilogy, readers recognize the inequitable enforcement of law and the harshness of punishments across the various districts, depending on the race and class of the inhabitants.

In their flight across New World in *Knife*, each settlement that Todd and Viola encounter responds to Noise differently. One town isolated all of the women away from the main settlement; another placed women in charge. In touring each of these towns, Viola and Todd come to realize that the oppressive force of Noise has created a new, overwhelming, gendered power dynamic, resulting in flawed systems of adaptation or resistance, though none appear equitable or ultimately sustainable. Todd and Viola intend to warn the citizens of the city Haven and the approaching convoy of settlers of the Mayor's world domination scheme but are thwarted by the Mayor's advancing army. By the end of book 1, the Mayor captures Haven, declares himself president of New World, and imposes his dictatorial, misogynistic views on the remaining living residents of the planet. In book 2, *The Ask and The Answer* (*Ask*), both protagonists get up-close experience with various factions within Haven, including the resistance movement, The Answer.

By examining the oppressive forces beyond her or his home, the trilogy changes the fundamental questions driving a teenage protagonist's rebellion. Initially, the protagonist's main concern is with the survival of her or his closest friends and family. As the series opens into a wider view of the oppressed landscape, the protagonist's concern spreads outwards to encompass society as a whole. It is through this development that the trilogy shifts from individual survival to systemic change. It is at this stage that the books' pedagogical strategy makes it clear that participants in the revolution will have to completely rethink their own worldview, including questioning their own privilege within that space. Traditions, family, notions of home, safety, place—all of these become disposable in the making of a better society. In *Ask*, Viola initially acts as an apprentice healer in Haven but becomes an active participant in The Answer when she realizes that Prentiss's policies endanger all the women of Haven and will harm the lives of the new settlers she is meant to protect. Despite her objections to The Answer's violent techniques, such as bombings and destroying resources, Viola realizes neutrality is essentially the same as acquiescence to Prentiss's vision of New World.

While the trilogies make it clear that those teens who join the fight against the unjust ruling faction will often have to sacrifice much or even all, the books universally condemn those individuals or sections of society who sit on the sidelines of the revolution until they can join the eventual winner. Active participation (either you are with us or you are against us) is the only allowable choice, these books instruct. Wishy-washy individuals or those people who focus on their own survival over the well-being of those they love are often brutally maimed, tortured, or killed. For example, the mayor of Haven, who surrendered and collaborated with Prentiss rather than fight, is blown up by a booby-trap intended for Prentiss. As a result, teen readers who have been privileged enough to avoid active participation in politics are taught that disengagement is complicity at best, enabling of dystopian oppression at worst.

Phase 2 concludes by setting up the stakes for the final conflict with the dystopian powers, then upending those stakes by introducing new, unexpected players into the existing power dynamics. *Ask* is caught up in the dual perspectives of Viola, in The Answer's resistance movement, and Todd, who, under the influence of Prentiss, is forced to commit atrocities against the native species and the women of Haven. However, book 2 concludes dramatically by introducing a massive army of the native species poised to invade Haven and eliminate all of the human settlers. The surprise reemergence of this unexpected power causes a realignment of priorities as Prentiss, the leader of the resistance, and newly arrived scouts from the settler convoy form a tentative alliance out of necessity.

Phase 3: Emerging Utopian Hope

This realignment of power dynamics also heralds a new change in scope for the trilogy. Phase 2 of the YA dystopian trilogy deals with the wider world *within* the dystopia; the transition to Phase 3 reveals the world(s) *outside* of the dystopian system. In essence, Phase 2 expands the boundaries of the dystopian system, and Phase 3 breaks those boundaries open in order to suggest other possible systems and solutions to the estranging principle responsible for the dystopia in the first place. The existence of these outside forces drastically realigns the protagonist's worldview and causes political and military shifts in the ongoing small-scale conflict. Whereas the danger for protagonist and allies had previously come from within the dystopian system itself, the outsiders bring their own threats to bear. A new level of urgency to repair the broken political system within the dystopia comes from the potential world-ending fallout should the dystopia come into a direct conflict with these outside forces.

The revelation of the mysterious outside force can initially serve as a beacon of hope—a sign that life outside the dystopian system is, in fact, possible—but the outsiders offer equally problematic solutions to the existing system. On New World, the native species that calls itself "the Land" has evolved a form of merged consciousness enabled by the Noise, making communication instantaneous and multimodal. Initially, the Land is presented as a harmonious society with no secrets, lies, or outsiders; however, as the conflict with the humans continues, it becomes clear that members of the Land, including the leader, the Sky, have the capacity to hide the truth, disguise thoughts, and betray promises, just like the human settlers.

The protagonist comes to realize that throwing off the dystopian system may be for the best but that replacing that system with another existing one might be just as bad. Adding this final layer of an external threat is the final move the trilogy has to make before reaching the ultimate resolution of the series, in no small part because it reiterates that all of the current political options available to the protagonist are fatally flawed in some way. As Mayor Prentiss notes, the leader of The Answer, Mistress Coyle, is just as problematic a leader as he is. "You'll be swapping one tyrant for another, Todd. I'm sorry to be the one to tell you" (*Ask* 507). In *Monsters of Men* (*Monsters*), the newly arrived convoy scouts demonstrate their own extreme reactions to the new overload of information via Noise, dramatizing why the newly arrived settlers are unprepared to assume leadership. Todd and Viola realize that none of these adults can lead New World out of its current failed system of perpetual conflict and into a new, peaceful one. This echoes the same development in other trilogies, such as when Katniss comes to realize that a militaristic totalitarian regime led by President Coin would be just as bad as the current system led by Snow. Every phase of development in the trilogy pattern leads to the realization that repairing the current system is impossible and that it should be wholly discarded. Despite this revolutionary impulse, the protagonists come to realize that the replacement form of government closest at hand is not itself always inherently revolutionary.

The last part of the YA dystopian trilogy comes in the form of a large-scale battle between the main character(s), his or her assembled allies, and the forces of control. No matter whom the protagonist is fighting against (government, tyrant, corporation), the end result is nearly always the same: a complete, violent overthrow of the system and the destruction of the dystopian figurehead (and other looming authoritarian figures). *Monsters* ends with the violent deaths of the leaders of all three major factions; the Sky is blown up when Prentiss bombs the peace talks; Mistress Coyle self-immolates in a suicide-bombing attempt to kill Prentiss; Prentiss is driven mad by Noise and walks into the ocean, where he is devoured by literal sea monsters. This vacuum of leadership allows the teen protagonists and their allies to assert a new system of assimilation and hybridity, based on what they have learned over the course of the trilogy.

Strikingly, each of these trilogies emphasizes the importance of breaking the cycle, teaching the protagonist (and thus, the readers) the importance of recognizing the causes of a dystopian situation and undermining that potential through action. The protagonist(s) also must come to recognize that achieving the overthrow of the damaged system will be neither graceful nor peaceful; things are going to get worse before they get better. There will be a loss of coherence in society, divisions among and between family members, violence, and sacrifice. Resistance is often violent, overthrow quick, and the results brutal, both for the protagonist and the society. The protagonist suffers severe injuries, loss of loved ones, destruction of home, and even, in some cases, death. At the end of *Monsters*, Todd, who was shot in the final conflict with Prentiss, remains in a medically/mystically induced coma, nurtured by the Land. This is the same "technology" that saved Todd's foster father, Ben, and transformed him into a hybrid figure capable of merging his consciousness with other humans through Noise. If Todd survives, he will have sacrificed part of his humanity in order to help solve the systemic issue of Noise through a new utopian system.

Across all of these YA dystopian trilogies, however, the didactic message remains the same: undermine, break, or otherwise eliminate the previous dystopian system and establish in its place a new, more utopian scaffolding upon which to build the future. However, what is left after that overthrow should not yet be interpreted as a utopia. That is, the "ideal" system that replaces the old is often predystopian rather than postdystopian; many of these trilogies revert to a democratic system that closely resembles that of the current US. However, there is an acknowledgment of the imperfection of humanity and society, and an acceptance that whatever system eventually replaces the recently overthrown one, it is better than what came before. Within the narrative, questions remain to indicate that the new system is not perfect. From outside the narrative, readers can also point to problematic social and political implications that echo and/or critique our own society, such as a reinvestment in whiteness and heteronormativity in this "new" system. The conclusions to these trilogies resemble Ernst Bloch's utopia-in-progress, gesturing toward the dream of a better, more justice-oriented society, but the frequent recapitulation of contemporary structures causes the utopian vision of this subgenre to fall short.

There are legitimate criticisms (both fictive and literary) that the proposed utopian systems may not work. As Toliver notes in chapter thirteen, LGBTQIA+ characters and characters of color rarely survive the violent overthrow portion of blockbuster dystopian narratives and therefore are often excluded from the utopian dream of the future. The end of *Mockingjay* mentions a democratic system of government being instituted, but there is little discussion about how regional differences or the vast income inequality of different districts might be resolved. *Monsters* gestures toward a new cooperation between the Land and the existing settlers, as well as a potential human/alien hybrid better adapted to the overwhelming Noise. However, the novel does not fully acknowledge the real-world precedent in which the Indigenous populations of North America made treaty after treaty with unceasing waves of new settlers, which were routinely broken. Given that Viola has absented herself from leadership while she waits for Todd to wake up, and Todd, who narrates the final chapter, remains unconscious, the reader is left with a feeling of hope without specific details as to how this new truce will be different from the last one (or the next one). In this way, all of the authors of the dystopian trilogies echo the adult abnegation of responsibility from within their own novels; the authors, being firmly integrated into our existing system, cannot imagine beyond its overthrow. The future of utopia is left to the imaginations of the teen reader; however, that reader is still overwhelmingly assumed to be white, able-bodied, cisgendered, heteronormative, and financially privileged.

While the endings of these trilogies are complex and worthy of more scholarly attention, they are often satisfying because they resolve the tropes and plot points that are important to (Western) readers: fascist totalitarian governments are overthrown, and the "evil" leaders are appropriately punished. Democratic notions of citizen input into government are acknowledged, and groups marginalized by the totalitarian regime are reintegrated into society. Equality becomes the overarching theme of society, and relative economic stability (everyone has a place to live, food to eat, and a meaningful task to complete on any given day) becomes the status quo. While the surviving protagonist(s) and the remaining rebels bear the scars of battle, society comes through the war generally improved. There is hope for a better future, but there is also general acknowledgment that restoring society is an ongoing process, one that may falter (Suvin, "Locus" 120). However, the reader can rest assured that if history does choose to repeat itself, teenagers are a renewable resource.

Reading the Metanarratives: Patterns and Meaning

From a storytelling perspective, the effectiveness of any YA dystopian trilogy is dependent upon the extent to which it executes this pattern. All of the trilogies analyzed for this chapter attempt to fulfill this utopian impulse, pushing the reader toward a hopeful conclusion; however, not all follow through on this project in a successful or believable manner. For example, the critical success of Chaos Walking is tied to the inevitability of its outcome: there is no way to turn the settler ships around, and the reader is told about the native species from the first chapters. In contrast, the Divergent series delays Phase 3 until the later portions of book 3, *Allegiant*, so that the external source (a shadowy government agency running experiments on the city) is a surprising reveal rather than a driving force of the narrative. Whereas other trilogies foreshadow their external forces, having spent so much of the trilogy time within the small, well-defined factions of Chicago, Veronica Roth's readers resist the messiness that comes with the shocking introduction of this outside world. Combined with the death of Tris and the disruption of the traditional "happy" ending to the love story, the conclusion of the Divergent trilogy feels rushed at best, unbelievable at worst.[7]

After elucidating this metanarrative pattern, it is possible to draw conclusions about the didactic stakes of this subgenre of YA literature. The first conclusion is that this pattern marks an interesting and potentially useful movement in the progression of utopian/dystopian literature itself. Early utopian novels were prescriptive, laying out every element of a city-sized society, often structuring the "perfect" society on slave labor, highly regulated class and gender roles, and the elimination of the disabled. As a result, the early utopias of the sixteenth and seventeenth centuries became impossible to enact, and even to imagine (Frye 326). Today, in the wake of fascist regimes and modern technology, the very idea of a strict order being enforced by a government feels oppressive to readers (329). However, in Bloch's concept, utopian thought is about progress: the moment it solidifies into a static system, utopia is lost (Elliott 10). The YA dystopian trilogy captures this idea of process: the dystopia develops out of a crisis, devolves into a latent dystopian state, then is overthrown, and reemerges as a utopia-in-progress. Tom Henthorne, who asserts that genre conventions require adult dystopias to end in despair, declares that "the [Hunger Games] trilogy may begin like a dystopia, but it does not end like one" (34). The conclusion of each trilogy is a gesture toward utopia, with the necessary acknowledgments that the new system is fragile but under the control of young people who continue to seek something better during a historical moment of upheaval and reconciliation.

The second conclusion is that these novels are specifically relevant to a contemporary YA audience, as traditional rites of passage become increasingly disrupted by economic realities and shifting social norms. Teens who live in an age of "fake news" can readily identify with dystopias set in a future where the internet/Noise rules the lives of young people (Uglies, Chaos Walking). Young people concerned with climate change recognize its reflection in dystopian narratives based in worlds ravaged by these forces (Under the Never Sky, Delirium). The trilogies may be metonymically named for the first book in the trilogy, in which the dystopia is articulated, but each ends with a third book that points to a utopian possibility of improvement and change based on the actions of young adult protagonists. This structure appeals to a contemporary teen reader, who is unlikely to believe in a storybook happy ending but who may also reject the bleak dystopian endings of Orwell's *1984* or Zamyatin's *We*.

The third conclusion is that the repetition of these themes compounds. For the past decade, trilogies like The Hunger Games, Divergent, and Chaos Walking have dominated the best seller lists. Millions of children, young adults, and adults have read these books and watched the film adaptations. Once a teen has read or even looked at these trilogies online, helpful algorithms embedded in popular book-buying sites like Amazon.com will recommend similar titles as popular, best-selling texts that match that young adult's preferences. Put another way: for the past decade, a broad subgenre of popular YA novels has been teaching teens that the only way to truly avert dystopia is through complete and violent overthrow of corrupt systems, led by young adults. Critics often dismiss YA literature as "trash," with added disdain for these trilogies, given their intersection with similarly "lowbrow" genres like science fiction and fantasy. However, in identifying the metanarrative pattern behind a new subgenre of utopian fiction, the YA dystopian trilogy, I assert that the vast majority of these trilogies contain a similar pedagogical message of rebellion that deserves closer study. Even as I write this essay, young people are engaged in acts of #resistance, using social media to bring attention to police violence, gun violence, and voting rights. If, as Trites argues, YA novels are meant to instruct or provide moral guidance to teens as they come of age, it merits serious attention that these trilogies have been instructing young readers in a pedagogy of resistance, overthrow, and utopian hope for the past decade.

Notes

1. This theory and essay are deeply indebted to Dr. Casey Wilson for her thoughtful critiques, encyclopedic knowledge of contemporary YA literature, and strong feelings about *Allegiant* by Veronica Roth, the three-hour conversation about which launched this book collection.

2. These two novels also rode the twenty-first-century dystopian wave into theaters, with a film adaptation of *Ender's Game* released in 2013, and *The Giver* in 2014.

3. Texts include: Scott Westerfeld's Uglies (2005–2006), Patrick Ness's Chaos Walking series (2008–2010), James Dashner's The Maze Runner (2009–2011), Veronica Roth's Divergent (2011–2013), Marie Lu's Legend (2011–2013), Lauren Oliver's Delirium (2011–2013), and Veronica Rossi's Under the Never Sky (2012–2014).

4. I chose Chaos Walking as the analytical focus for this chapter in order to move the discussion beyond the highly recognized and discussed trilogies; the series is critically recognized but less often taught or written about critically. However, as I write this essay, a movie adaptation of *The Knife of Never Letting Go* is in post-production, so the series's popularity may drastically shift in the near future.

5. Please see the "Further Reading" section for a more complete list of trilogies I analyzed in order to distill this pattern as well as more recently published trilogies that also conform to it.

6. While some of these trilogies equate Phase 1 with book 1 and so forth, this is not always the case. Therefore, I will discuss the phases as the genre conventions and, where relevant, locate the start and end of these phases within discussions of the trilogies themselves.

7. As a result, the film adaptations of this series changed substantial parts of the story, but the second and third installments were commercial and critical flops, and the fourth is unlikely to be filmed.

Works Cited

Anderson, M. T. *Feed*. Candlewick Press, 2002.

Bloch, Ernst. *The Principle of Hope*. MIT Press, 1986.

Card, Orson Scott. *Ender's Game*. Tor Books, 1985.

Claeys, Gregory. "The Origins of Dystopia: Wells, Huxley and Orwell." *The Cambridge Companion to Utopian Literature*, edited by Gregory Claeys, Cambridge UP, 2010, pp. 107–32.

Collins, Suzanne. *The Hunger Games*. Scholastic, 2008.

Dashner, James. *Maze Runner*. Delacorte Press, 2009.

Elliott, Robert C. *The Shape of Utopia: Studies in a Literary Genre*. U of Chicago P, 1970.

Fitting, Peter. "Utopia, Dystopia and Science Fiction." *The Cambridge Companion to Utopian Literature*, edited by Gregory Claeys, Cambridge University Press, 2010, pp. 135–53.

Frye, Northrop. "Varieties of Literary Utopias." *Daedalus*, vol. 94, no. 2, 1965, pp. 323–47. *JSTOR*, http://www.jstor.org/stable/20026912.

Henthorne, Tom. *Approaching the Hunger Games Trilogy: A Literary and Cultural Analysis*. McFarland, 2012.

Lowry, Lois. *The Giver*. Houghton Mifflin, 1993.

More, Thomas. *Utopia*. Unabridged ed. Dover, 1997.

Moylan, Tom. *Scraps of the Untainted Sky: Science Fiction, Utopia, Dystopia*. Perseus, 2000.

Ness, Patrick. *The Ask and the Answer* (Chaos Walking trilogy). Walker Books, 2010.

Ness, Patrick. *The Knife of Never Letting Go* (Chaos Walking trilogy). Walker Books, 2008.

Ness, Patrick. *Monsters of Men* (Chaos Walking trilogy). Walker Books, 2010.

Oliver, Lauren. *Delirium*. Harper, 2011.

Orwell, George. *1984*. Signet Classic, 1961.

Rossi, Veronica. *Under the Never Sky*. Atom, 2013.

Roth, Veronica. *Divergent*. HarperCollins, 2011.

Suvin, Darko. "Locus, Horizon, and Orientation: The Concept of Possible Worlds as a Key to Utopian Studies." *Utopian Studies* vol. 1, no. 2, 1989, pp. 69–83. *JSTOR*, https://www.jstor.org/stable/20719001.

Suvin, Darko. *Metamorphoses of Science Fiction: On The Poetics and History of a Literary Genre*. Yale UP, 1979.

Trites, Roberta Seelinger. *Disturbing the Universe: Power and Repression in Adolescent Literature*. U of Iowa P, 2004.

Vieira, Fátima. "The Concept of Utopia." *The Cambridge Companion to Utopian Literature*, edited by Gregory Claeys, Cambridge UP, 2010, pp. 3–27.

Westerfeld, Scott. *Uglies*. Simon Pulse, 2005.

Zamyatin, Yevgeny. *We*. Penguin Twentieth Century Classics, 1993.

Further Reading

Aguirre, Ann. *Enclave*. (Razorland Book 1). Feiwel and Friends, 2011.

Aguirre, Ann. *Horde* (Razorland Book 3). Feiwel and Friends, 2013.

Aguirre, Ann. *Outpost* (Razorland Book 2). Feiwel and Friends, 2012.

Cass, Kiera. *The Elite* (Book 2). HarperCollins, 2013.

Cass, Kiera. *The One* (Book 3). HarperCollins, 2014.

Cass, Kiera. *The Selection* (Book 1). HarperCollins, 2012.

Condie, Allie. *Crossed* (Book 2). Dutton Juvenile, 2011.

Condie, Allie. *Matched* (Book 1). Dutton Juvenile, 2010.

Condie, Allie. *Reached* (Book 3). Dutton Juvenile, 2012.

Dashner, James. *The Death Cure* (Book 3). Dell, 2011.

Dashner, James. *The Maze Runner* (Book 1). Dell, 2009.

Dashner, James. *The Scorch Trials* (Book 2). Dell, 2010.

DeStefano, Lauren. *Fever* (Chemical Garden Book 2). Simon and Schuster, 2012.

DeStefano, Lauren. *Sever* (Chemical Garden Book 3). Simon and Schuster, 2013.

DeStefano, Lauren. *Wither* (Chemical Garden Book 1). Simon and Schuster, 2011.

Lu, Marie. *Champion* (Book 3). Penguin Books, 2013.

Lu, Marie. *Legend* (Book 1). Penguin Books, 2011.

Lu, Marie. *Prodigy* (Book 2). Penguin Books, 2013.

Mafi, Tahereh. *Ignite Me* (Book 3). HarperCollins, 2014.

Mafi, Tahereh. *Shatter Me* (Book 1). HarperCollins, 2011.

Mafi, Tahereh. *Unravel Me* (Book 2). HarperCollins, 2013.

O'Brien, Caragh. *Birthmarked* (Book 1). Roaring Brook Press, 2010.

O'Brien, Caragh. *Prized* (Book 2). Roaring Brook Press, 2011.

O'Brien, Caragh. *Promised* (Book 3). Roaring Brook Press, 2012.

Oliver, Lauren. *Delirium* (Book 1). HarperCollins, 2011.

Oliver, Lauren. *Pandemonium* (Book 2). Harper Collins, 2012.

Oliver, Lauren. *Requiem* (Book 3). Harper Collins, 2013.

Ryan, Carrie. *The Dark and Hollow Places* (Book 3). Random House, 2011.

Ryan, Carrie. *The Dead-Tossed Waves* (Book 2). Random House, 2010.

Ryan, Carrie. *The Forest of Hands and Teeth* (Book 1). Random House, 2009.

Wasserman, Robin. *Frozen* (Cold Awakening Book 1, formerly known as *Skinned*). Simon Pulse, 2008.

Wasserman, Robin. *Shattered* (Cold Awakening Book 2, formerly known as *Crashed*). Simon Pulse, 2009.

Wasserman, Robin. *Torn* (Cold Awakening Book 3, formerly known as *Wired*). Simon Pulse, 2010.

Zhang, Kat. *Echoes of Us* (Hybrid Chronicles Book 3). HarperCollins, 2014.

Zhang, Kat. *Once We Were* (Hybrid Chronicles Book 2). HarperCollins, 2013.

Zhang, Kat. *What's Left of Me* (Hybrid Chronicles Book 1). HarperCollins, 2012.

2

Oversharing on and off the Internet: Crossing from Digital to Print (and Back) in Young Adult Works Authored by YouTube Stars

Rachel L. Rickard Rebellino

In late 2014 Simon & Schuster launched Keywords Press, billed as a "new pub-lishing home for a new kind of storyteller" (*Keywords Press*). While the phrase "a new kind of storyteller" is intentionally vague, the imprint's releases reveal a specific definition: YouTube stars. Since its founding, Keywords has pub-lished books penned by YouTube sensations and marketed primarily, though not exclusively, toward youth audiences. Young adult literature and YouTube have been long intertwined through the overlapping fame of John Green as both celebrated author and cofounder of the YouTube channel vlogbrothers[1]; however, 2015 and 2016 saw a new manifestation of this connection. Works by young people who garnered fame on YouTube such as Tyler Oakley, Joey Graceffa, and Zoe Sugg sold tens (and sometimes hundreds) of thousands of copies and frequented *New York Times* best-seller lists (Robehmed).[2]

YouTube itself has taken a prominent place in youth culture. A 2015 study by Defy Media found that 96 percent of teens watch free online videos at an average of 11.3 hours a week (*Youth Video Diet* 4). In addition to its role as a platform for watching free videos, YouTube also archives media and func-tions as a social network (Burgess and Green 5). As Burgess and Green point out, the core of YouTube as a business is participatory culture, a term Henry Jenkins created to refer to a shift in how consumers and creators of media interact (*Convergence Culture* 2). Fitting with Jenkins's definition of participa-tory culture, YouTube has relatively low barriers to creating and sharing videos;

facilitates and, in order to achieve more widespread viewership, requires social connection; and traditionally has been a space where informal mentorship exists between more experienced creators and less experienced ones (Jenkins, "Confronting the Challenges" 5–6). YouTube has been described as a kind of (Yo)uTopia for media creators wherein there is "no hierarchy of discourse," and "clips of ordinary people, media people and celebrities are interlinked, in a single network" (Tolson 285). That ideal is flawed for many reasons, including the fact that today many top creators are sponsored by media conglomerates through partnership programs that give those creators access to more monetary support and more-professional-looking content.[3] Unlike traditional media, though, YouTube does provide a space where young adults can produce, distribute, and respond to texts, relatively free of adult intervention, and the creative products of an individual can be spread in ways that were once limited by gatekeepers in control of more traditional media distribution.

In light of the possibilities that differentiate YouTube from more traditional media and the commonplace belief that as a society we are shifting away from print and toward digital platforms (Kelly), the recent trend of YouTuber memoirs may seem surprising. The fame of these content creators is rooted in YouTube's connectivity and community, raising the question of what creators gain by turning to traditionally published books. The obvious answer is, of course, financial. Since fans do not pay to access most YouTube videos, these creators must monetize their fame in other ways, including ad revenue, sponsorships, or merchandise. I believe, though, that there is more at work in the YouTube memoir trend than purely economic gain. Sites of participatory culture have been prized for the connectivity that they allow. However, I argue that the repeated choice among YouTube stars to create print memoirs, as well as the consistent narrative around the creation of those memoirs, suggests a surprising perceived affordance of traditionally published literature: increased intimacy.

Rachel Berryman and Misha Kavka have argued that in order to become YouTube celebrities, creators must establish a relationship with their viewers, as their success relies upon viewers being drawn both to the creators' content and to the creator as a person. The authors define intimacy on YouTube as constructed across four different capacities: "the spatial (evoking closeness), the temporal (evoking immediacy), the social (produced by patterns of direct address and self-revelation) and the medial (evinced by small-screen techniques such as cinematography, mise-en-scène, editing rhythms, etc.)" (310). Despite the possibilities for evoking intimacy on YouTube through these techniques, though, the authors of the texts I explore in this chapter utilize print memoir as a means to disclose information they have not shared online. In this way, they suggest the limitations of the construction of intimacy on YouTube from a creator's perspective. The dimensions Berryman and Kavka elucidate may allow the consumer of a video to experience a sense of narrative intimacy, or the feeling of a personal relationship created "through the disclosure of information and the experience of the story as a space that the narrator invites the reader to share" (Day 3). However, those same consciously constructed ways of evoking closeness create distance from the perspective of the text's author, leading to the use of an alternative medium for disclosures that are perceived to be more vulnerable or that carry a degree of risk.

Within the following pages, I examine several recently published memoirs by YouTube stars in order to articulate the converging and diverging roles of connectivity and intimacy across media platforms.[4] First I turn to specific examples from the books themselves, identifying features of the subgenre of YouTube memoirs and tracing how their authors attempt to replicate the participatory culture of YouTube through creating connectivity within print texts. In the next section, I interrogate the YouTubers' stated rationales for creating print memoirs in order to consider the possibility that print offers an individual intimacy disallowed by the larger online community of YouTube. Finally, I turn to the intersections of YouTube and YA literature as a whole, exploring the ways that the blurring of narrative forms created by these memoirs necessitates an increasingly expansive conceptualization of young adult literature.

Creating Connectivity: Layering Participatory Culture into Print

YouTube memoirs seem intentionally created to connect an author's print book to her or his online presence and, in turn, to tap into the affordances of participatory culture. For example, the title of Tyler Oakley's memoir *Binge* (2015) calls to mind the way that Oakley's nearly eight million YouTube subscribers might choose to consume the videos he creates.[5] It also offers an imperative for how readers ought to interact with the book, which is divided into a series of short chapters—almost all less than ten pages—mimicking the abbreviated length of most YouTube videos. The brevity creates the potential for readers to gain a sense of satisfaction as they complete each chapter, potentially leading them to binge-read Oakley's stories just as they may watch dozens of Oakley's over five hundred online videos in one sitting. In many cases these chapters could easily be connected into longer essays, as they tend to revolve around similar themes. However, the structural choice seems intentional in its connection to the expected conventions of YouTube videos, and, indeed, each of the YouTube memoirs examined here eschews more extensive narratives in favor of bite-sized essays.

Authors of YouTube memoirs also attempt to capture the "feel" of their online personalities through formatting reminiscent of digital content and an overarching tone fitting with a YouTuber's particular brand. For example, a mainstay of Jenn McAllister's YouTube channel is her top-ten lists, which combine earnest advice with silly visuals. McAllister's *Really Professional Internet Person* (2015) features brief chapters that detail moments from her young life and include sometimes relevant lists, such as "Things Nobody Will Care About When You Leave High School." This explicit connection to existing content positions McAllister's book as a print extension of her online presence, rather than as a separate undertaking. Similarly, the memoir's format mirrors a digital experience: it is oversized, with chapters featuring page design elements marking the book as different from traditional memoirs, which primarily use plain, prose text on a white page. Instead, the book is decidedly multimodal, including throughout each chapter page designs featuring text and pictures in browser windows or bubbles reminiscent of iPhone messages, and non-prose content such as photographs and screenshots.

The format of Dan Howell and Phil Lester's *The Amazing Book Is Not on Fire* (2015) strives even more openly to replicate the online reading experience. Unlike other YouTube memoirs, Howell and Lester's book features no substantive sections of prose text; instead it includes primarily images, dialogue, and found materials. Virtually every page is different from the next, and print representations of digital media—Howell's first website, Lester's chat logs, and screenshots of iPhone messages—abound. In short, the book calls to mind the internet itself, full of a seemingly endless variety of content. While *The Amazing Book Is Not on Fire* is the most decidedly untraditional in format, each YouTube memoir includes visual elements, suggesting that, at least in the minds of the books' publishers, such visual material is essential to successfully translate a YouTuber's online presence to print. Although, of course, much youth literature, and particularly youth nonfiction, includes visual material (Coats, *Bloomsbury* 292), the frequency with which the format of YouTube memoirs veers toward the nontraditional implies a pervasive belief that print, prose text needs augmentation in order to connect with readers.

The memoirists have also largely replicated the tone of their online personas, perhaps despite simultaneously seeing the print format as an opportunity to break from some of those conventions. For example, Shane Dawson, the author of *I Hate Myselfie* (2015), is known online for his self-deprecating humor, frank discussions of topics like sex and relationships, and unfiltered language. With over twelve million subscribers and almost 3.5 billion collective video views, he is the most popular of the stars whose books I am examining. His memoir almost immediately takes on a tone similar to his YouTube videos as Dawson tells readers, "In this book, you'll get to see the real me, not the 'me' you see on YouTube. You will get to know what's really in my head, and I'm warning you it's not pretty. It's a twisted land of self-hatred, sadness, and lots of repressed anger toward every person who's ever hurt me. ENJOY!" (4). Dawson's written prose largely mirrors how he speaks in his videos, raising questions about the extent to which either his videos or his memoir allow readers to connect with what Dawson terms "the real me." Throughout the text, his "tell-it-like-it-is" style and tendency toward bawdy humor is evident as he explores personal details of his life, attempting to balance disclosure (discussing, for instance, his eating disorder) with consistent self-deprecation and a heavy lean toward vulgarity.

Beyond this attention to format and tone, in order to reproduce the participatory possibilities that YouTube facilitates, these YouTube memoirs incorporate past and possible future interactions with fans. For example, Ricky Dillon, who has been posting videos since 2009 and has amassed a following of over three million subscribers, frames his book *Follow Me: A Memoir in Challenges* (2016) as an opportunity for participation from readers. He explains that this book, like YouTube, is a chance to share and collaborate: "The beautiful thing about YouTube," he writes "is that it's all about sharing! Collaborating and group participation are what we thrive on, and in that spirit, this book that you're holding in your hands is not just me telling a bunch of little stories about my life. It's also a chance for us to do some fun stuff together" (1). Dillon's book offers a series of very short chapters in which he reveals nuggets of personal information. Before each chapter is a "random" challenge—something silly and fairly easy to complete—and after each chapter Dillon includes another challenge related to the chapter's theme. Although sometimes these second challenges tend toward the trivial, many function as pseudo-self-help action items. For example, after a chapter in which Ricky discusses sharing something difficult with his family, he encourages readers to "#ConfessForRicky" by "[c]onfess[ing] something to your parents or a friend that you've never told them" (35). Ricky asks readers to share their response using a hashtag so that he can, in turn, respond to them.

Although Dillon's book is the most directly interactive, other YouTube celebs include their fans in different ways. McAllister's book features fan letters, and Oakley released pieces of *Binge* to fans on the free website Wattpad prior to its release date. Dawson begins each chapter of *I Hate Myselfie* with fan artwork. Early in his book, he explains this decision, stating that he has "a lot of really talented fans" (2). Their art, based on excerpts of the book chapters, creates a text in which the narrative is constructed both by Dawson's explanation of events and by his fans' interpretation. Not unlike the existing practice of creating fan art or fan fiction, Dawson's book brings the act of fan responses to print, and, in doing so, complicates the barrier between author and audience, fitting even more closely with ideas of transmedia storytelling.

Joey Graceffa, another popular YouTuber, has been one of the most commercially successful authors emerging from this trend with both a memoir, *In Real Life* (2015), and a series of dystopian young adult fiction. Graceffa's understanding of his relationship with his fans, numbering at over 8.5 million YouTube subscribers, plays a substantive role in his book. Early on, he reflects on his own relationship *as a fan*, commenting that he would post on a beloved band's social media in similar ways to how his fans try to reach him. "Basically [the band's] MySpace page was just me geeking out, raving about them and begging them to post on my own page, but I never got any sort of response (I find this extremely funny now, because some of you reading this have done the exact same thing to me on Twitter. You know who you are!)" (57). The reflection on his experience and use of direct address to speak to the fans reading his words is coupled with explicit references to meeting and interacting with fans. Further, Graceffa, like Dawson, mixes fan-created content with his own. *In Real Life* contains two sections of photography—one of photos of Graceffa growing up, and one made up of brief profiles of various fans, all of whom are girls between the ages of 13 and 17. The girls answer questions that prompt personal reflection, including "What scares you?" or "How's life been lately?" (n.p.). Though this section feels a bit exploitative, as some of the revelations are extremely personal for people who, unlike Graceffa, are not profiting financially from their disclosure, the attempt to showcase fans and link their stories to Graceffa's own exemplifies the interactivity that YouTube and, in turn, YouTube memoirs attempt to foster.

In a final example of the effort to replicate participatory culture in these print books, each of the YouTube memoirs includes some kind of content imitating the informal mentorship that is a definitional aspect of participatory culture. Within their memoirs the authors cast themselves as mentors for future YouTubers, offering details of the steps they took to achieve success in both general and specific ways. While all of the memoirists trace their paths from being unknown creators of online videos to YouTube stars, many also detail specific "behind the scenes" information about what it means to find success online. For example, Joey Graceffa discusses the concept of collaborations (or collabs) in depth. In these collabs two or more creators film videos together, and then each posts a video on his or her own channel while encouraging fans to watch the video(s) posted by the other collaborator(s). Graceffa reveals that the motivation for these collaborations is not just genuine affection for the other creator(s): "I'd like to say [the collaboration] was done purely in the spirit of supporting other talent, but although we all genuinely liked each other, there was an unspoken understanding that by collaborating, we'd be spreading our own brand across new platforms; we hoped everyone would gain more subscribers" (77). These instructional aspects of the books suggest that the memoirs function as part of the participatory culture of YouTube; they are yet another way for readers to access and learn from more experienced content creators.

Emphasizing Intimacy: Unveiling the Affordances of Print

The myriad ways in which these YouTube memoirs appear intentionally structured to replicate the experience of YouTube intensifies the question of why the authors decided to publish print narratives in the first place. Much of the initial discourse about these books has focused on financial motivation. Texts for young people frequently expand into other forms of media, with toys becoming television series, television series becoming comic books, and toys and books being sold simultaneously (Mackey; Seiter). Indeed, the financial motivation for these memoirs seems clear: the authors' millions of subscribers constitute a ready-made fan base, and nearly all of the YouTube memoirists explicitly acknowledge that their readership is likely made up of their extant fans. Most authors operate under the assumption that readers are already fans, and, anecdotally, as someone unfamiliar with many of these creators prior to pursuing this project, simply reading the books often became a multimodal, multiplatform experience. I frequently returned to the authors' YouTube channels and social media or to web searches in order to understand the videos or online controversies the books mention.[6] The authors largely seem to envision an audience that possesses a quasi-encyclopedic knowledge of their social media history and YouTube creations. Interestingly (though perhaps unsurprisingly), despite the fact that most of the creators/authors explain some of the business of YouTube within their books and defend the choices they have made along their YouTube journeys that led to financial gain (e.g., endorsing certain products), the experience of writing a book is never disclosed as a money-making endeavor. I fully acknowledge that financial motivations contribute largely to this trend, but I also believe that there is a more substantive reason for turning to print books. After all, these YouTube creators can (and oftentimes have) turned to other methods to make money. For example, many of the stories told in these memoirs could just have easily been packaged as pay-to-access videos. Instead, I argue that this trend of YouTube memoirs suggests that print, while understood to be not as conducive to direct interactivity as online platforms, is simultaneously perceived by the memoirists as offering a unique opportunity for intimacy, allowing for the perception of an individual relationship between creator and consumer.

Most of the YouTubers reference their decision to write a book somewhere within the memoir itself. This decision is often framed as a chance for the creators to impart wisdom to the book's presumably young audience. Ricky Dillon overtly describes his book as didactic: "You'll learn stuff about . . . my worries, insecurities, greatest memories, and tons more. Most important, I hope that by doing the challenges you'll learn something new about yourself, too" (2). The following chapters navigate several repeated themes, including physical and mental health, creative exploration, and comfort in one's own skin. Dillon aims to be a role model for those just beginning to explore their creativity and encourages readers to embrace constructive criticism while ignoring those who unfairly doubt them. Joey Graceffa similarly frames his book as instructive, concluding each chapter with guidance ranging from tips on how to study to his favorite places in Los Angeles to examples of digital apps that can be useful for children with autism. Meanwhile, Shane Dawson's narrative is less direct in its framing of Dawson as a role model. While he does not directly state his intent to help readers, he writes extensively about issues related to the lives of his teen audience: body image, sexuality, gender expression, and the high school experience. He often comments on the youth of his presumed readership, consciously casting himself as an older, wiser adult, despite the fact that at the time of writing the book he was only twenty-five. For example, he states at one point that "Mitchel Musso was a thing in 2007. I know most of you have no idea who that is but trust me, he was a thing" (64).

This positioning of the author as someone from whom the reader can learn suggests the need for the consumer of the text to trust its creator. These authors are not experts on most of the topics about which they give advice; instead, their credibility as advisors comes from their willingness to be vulnerable about their own experiences. This vulnerability, which is defined by Brené Brown as "uncertainty, risk, and emotional exposure" (34), is central to the narratives constructed around the YouTube memoirs as a whole. Each memoir is presented as a space for the authors to increase the amount of intimacy between themselves and their fans by exposing something about themselves. YouTubers have become famous for oversharing. They film vlogs that trace the details of their lives and routinely divulge details about romantic relationships. However, each YouTube memoir promises something more: more disclosure, more intimacy, and more information. At least one editor working at Keywords specifically posited that print offers an increased intimacy, stating that "fans see books as a more intimate means of connecting with their favorite online stars than watching and commenting on a video" (Palmer). Oftentimes, the paratexts both adjacent to and separate from the books themselves advance this rationale, positioning the memoirs as offering a unique intimacy not available through YouTube. The back cover of Shane Dawson's book advertises that the book "takes us deep into the experiences of an eccentric and introverted kid," and in the introduction to her book, Jenn McAllister states that "this book is full of things you don't know about me" (McAllister 11). Oakley's first chapter begins with the revelation that his real name is Mathew, not Tyler (Oakley 3). It is clear that print is seen as connected to disclosure.

In their definition of the construction of intimacy on YouTube, Berryman and Kavka theorize the platform's immediacy as an affordance in the creation of a sense of intimacy from the viewer's perspective. However, that sense of immediacy may not operate in the same way for the creator. Instead, the *lack* of immediacy that comes with the format of the book appears to serve as a catalyst for YouTube memoirists to offer more disclosure within their writing. Graceffa's memoir offers an especially interesting example. In its opening pages, he hints at a surprise to be revealed: "I have kept a giant part of my life hidden for many reasons, and in this book I'm finally going to let it all hang out" (11). He goes on to discuss his experiences being placed in a special education classroom, and his mother's alcoholism. The "giant part" of Graceffa's life that he reveals, though, is his sexuality. Chapter 14, entitled "Surprise," consists of two words: "I'm gay." Graceffa initially envisioned the book as his way of coming out publicly. Three days before the book's release, though, he released a music video on YouTube called "Don't Wait." In the video he fictionalizes many of the subjects in his memoir: his tense relationship with his mother, his difficulties growing up, and, most directly, his sexuality. The video ends with Graceffa kissing another man. In a vlog-style afterword, Graceffa claims that it is "one little small glimpse into what you will get in my book *In Real Life*. Which comes out on this upcoming Tuesday." The day before the book's release, Graceffa published a follow-up video entitled "Yes I'm Gay" in which he elaborates his decision to openly discuss his sexuality, stating that this was "one of the first times ever" that he was going "to really talk and be open" on YouTube. Though he ultimately did reveal his sexuality online, writing his memoir was the impetus for his vulnerability with his fans.

Oakley's *Binge* concludes with a chapter that raises questions about the limits and possibilities of intimacy within print and digital spaces. Oakley reveals the problems that he sees with faux digital intimacy: "[M]y addictive personality lives on, and my game of choice is still online. The major difference is, now, @tyleroakley is my character. The level-ups come from real-life hustle—collaborating, attending events, working on projects, and always, always chasing the numbers" (295). Oakley describes feeling empty as a result of creating an online persona, and he uses *Binge*'s conclusion to call for authenticity. Rather than seeing YouTube as a competition wherein participants seek to gather the most followers, he declares a desire for more intimate connections: "I want to take only the opportunities that make me feel alive. I want to meet people who want to meet Mathew Tyler Oakley, not @tyleroakley. When I do meet them, I want to have plenty to tell them about what makes me happy while I'm not on the Internet" (301). Within this conclusion, Oakley draws attention to the lack of intimacy that he perceives online: fans watch and interact with a performance of Oakley (@tyleroakley) that is constructed specifically to garner digital success. Contrastingly, he suggests that readers who have purchased his book have, in some way, met "Mathew Tyler Oakley," the more authentic version of himself.

This suggestion obscures the fact that the author version of Oakley is no less of a performance than the YouTube version. Whether or not creators perceive publishing a print book to offer more intimacy than filming a YouTube video, in reality, both in their videos and in their memoirs, each YouTuber carefully selects which aspects of their lives to conceal and reveal, as well as the manner in which to disclose those details. Their authorial voice is no less of a performance than their YouTube persona. Further, if we understand intimacy to be connected to vulnerable disclosure, and, in turn, vulnerability to be connected to risk, perhaps intimacy is an impossible goal for cultural products. The very process of editing, or reforming and remaking a text to appear a certain way in an attempt to appeal to a certain audience, suggests a lack of risk and, in turn, a lack of intimacy.

Resisting Hierarchies: YouTube and/as Young Adult Literature

Attempts to create a hierarchy for the levels of intimacy available within the digital and print formats with which YouTubers have created content quickly unravel. This impossibility is partially due to the fact that both the YouTubers' online content and their print memoirs are edited, polished texts operating as examples of what Jenkins terms transmedia storytelling. The lives of these YouTube stars are conveyed to their fans in a variety of mediated narratives across myriad digital and traditional platforms. The memoirs exist in conversation with the videos, social media profiles, and other mediums through which these YouTube stars share aspects of their lives. This experience of engaging in a cross-platform reading experience is, of course, not unique to this subset of texts. Writing in 1999, Eliza Dresang coined the term "radical change theory" to address the ways that youth literature was changing to "promote interactivity, connectivity, and access" in a world where literacy means far more than just reading and writing print texts. What the cross-platform life writing characteristic of YouTube stars does offer, though, is a continually changing text, formed as the creators turn to a variety of platforms to tell their stories.

The use of the print young adult memoir as just one of many forms of life writing that these YouTube stars produce calls attention to larger hierarchies that exist in the study of youth literature. As Karen Coats points out, most of the texts studied by YA literature scholars are written by adults, and, in turn, many of those texts reify a conception of adolescence that is acceptable to adult gatekeepers ("Young Adult"). The focus on an adult authorship has led scholars to interrogate whether children's or young adult literature can actually exist (Rose), and, if it can exist, what the separations between author and audience mean for how it is written, published, and read (Nikolajeva; Trites). The presence of young authors, ranging from nineteen to twenty-six in the books discussed in this chapter, narrows the distance between author and reader, raising questions about what YA literature looks like when it includes texts produced by actual adolescents.

In her 2017 article on the state of YA scholarship, Caroline Hunt suggests the importance of considering nontraditional reading experiences: "We need to be aware of *how* adolescents are reading as well as *what* they are reading" (214). Karen Coats similarly urges youth literature scholars to "rebel against established theoretical orthodoxies and adult-inflected expressions of value, to be constantly attentive to innovation, to follow cool, to take risks, to be unapologetically presentist, to reach strong but always provisional conclusions, to adapt our critical identities to the objects we study, to be fickle in our pleasures" ("Young Adult" 322). Traditionally published texts, including these memoirs, are, rightfully, a substantive focus of our field. However, if we are to attend to what and how teens are reading and to "follow cool," we must also be willing to wade into the constantly shifting digital stream of texts and to explore the fascinating symbiotic relationship between traditional print literature and digital youth culture.

Notes

1. Vlogbrothers, which Green founded alongside his brother Hank, was one of the earliest YouTube channels. Initially it featured a project called Brotherhood 2.0, wherein the brothers communicated with each other exclusively through vlogs, which they alternated posting online daily for one year. Since their first video in 2007, the Green brothers have gone on to found several YouTube channels, including Crash Course, which releases educational videos, and were the founders of VidCon, a conference for YouTubers.

2. Oakley's *Binge* remained on the "Hardcover Nonfiction" list for eleven weeks as well as the monthly "Celebrities" list for six months, and Sugg and Graceffa's novels appeared on the newspaper's "Young Adult Hardcover" list.

3. Media behemoth Disney, for example, runs the Disney Digital Network, which, according to their website, "creates high quality, digital-first stories and delivers them globally to Gen Z and Millennial audiences through the platforms and influencers they know best." For a more in-depth exploration of the complicated place YouTube holds as a media platform and social network, see Burgess and Green's *YouTube: Online Video and Participatory Culture*.

4. This study draws upon a wider exploration of books written by YouTubers, but, for the purposes of this chapter, I focus on six books marketed as memoirs or essay collections that either were explicitly published and sold as young adult books or, in the case of Tyler Oakley's *Binge*, were obviously written toward a youth audience. For example, Oakley explains how T9 word texting works, something that readers in their early twenties would likely know. It is worth noting that the vast majority of YouTube memoirs written for teen audiences are authored by young men, whereas many YouTube memoirs directed at twenty-somethings are written by women YouTubers.

5. All of the YouTube-related statistics mentioned in this chapter are current as of March 2018.

6. For example, Joey Graceffa devotes a chapter of his book to the apparently well-known controversy of him making a YouTube video complaining of his car being towed that was eventually refuted by another, less well-known YouTube personality who had photo evidence of the fact that Graceffa's car was parked illegally.

Works Cited

Berryman, Rachel, and Misha Kavka. "'I Guess A Lot of People See Me as a Big Sister or a Friend': The Role of Intimacy in the Celebrification of Beauty Vloggers." *Journal of Gender Studies*, vol. 26, no. 3, 2017, pp. 307–20.

Brown, Brené. *Daring Greatly: How the Courage to Be Vulnerable Transforms the Way We Live, Love, Parent, and Lead*. Gotham, 2012.

Coats, Karen. *The Bloomsbury Introduction to Children's and Young Adult Literature*. Bloomsbury, 2018.

Coats, Karen. "Young Adult Literature: Growing Up, in Theory." *Handbook of Research on Children's and Young Adult Literature*, edited by Shelby A. Wolf, Karen Coats, Patricia Enciso, and Christine A. Jenkins. Routledge, 2010, pp. 315–29.

Day, Sara. *Reading Like a Girl*. UP of Mississippi, 2013.

Dresang, Eliza T. *Radical Change: Books for Youth in a Digital Age*. H. W. Wilson, 1999.

Hunt, Caroline. "Theory Rises, Maginot Line Endures." *Children's Literature Association Quarterly*, vol. 42, no. 2, 2017, pp. 205–17.

Jenkins, Henry. *Confronting the Challenges of Participatory Culture: Media Education for the 21st Century*. The John D. and Catherine T. MacArthur Foundation Reports on Digital Media and Learning. MIT Press, 2009.

Jenkins, Henry. *Convergence Culture*. New York UP, 2006.

Kelly, Kevin. *The Inevitable: Understanding the 12 Technological Forces That Will Shape Our Future*. Viking Press, 2016.

Keywords Press. 2014–16, thekeywordspress.com.

Mackey, Margaret. "Spinning Off: Toys, Television, Tie-Ins, and Technology." *Handbook of Research on Children's and Young Adult Literature*, edited by Shelby A. Wolf, Karen Coats, Patricia Enciso, and Christine A. Jenkins. Routledge, 2010, pp. 495–507.

Martens, Marianne. "Transmedia Teens: Affect, Immaterial Labor, and User-Generated Content." *Convergence: The International Journal of Research into New Media Technologies*, vol. 17, no. 1, 2011, pp. 49–68.

Nikolajeva, Maria. *The Rhetoric of Character in Children's Literature*. Scarecrow Press, 2002.

Palmer, Alex. "Follow the Influencers: Social Media Stars 2016." *Publishers Weekly*, 5 Feb. 2016.

Robehmed, Natalie. "For Many YouTube Stars, Next Step Is an Old-Fashioned Book." *Forbes*, 16 Oct. 2015, https://www.forbes.com/sites/natalierobehmed/2015/10/16/for-youtubers -books-still-hold-influence/#34bd954d7de6.

Rose, Jacqueline. *The Case of Peter Pan, or the Impossibility of Children's Fiction*. U of Pennsylvania P, 1984.

Seiter, Ellen. *Sold Separately: Children and Parents in Consumer Culture*. Rutgers UP, 1995.

Tolson, Andrew. "A New Authenticity? Communicative Practices on YouTube." *Critical Discourse Studies*, vol. 7, no. 4, 2010, pp. 277–89.

Trites, Roberta Seelinger. *Disturbing the Universe*. U of Iowa P, 2000.

Youth Video Diet. Defy Media, April 2016.

Further Reading

Butler, Marcus. *Hello Life!* Headline, 2015.

Dawson, Shane. *I Hate Myselfie: A Collection of Essays*. Atria/Keywords Press, 2015.

Dawson, Shane. *It Gets Worse: A Collection of Essays*. Keywords, 2016.

Dillon, Ricky. *Follow Me: A Memoir in Challenges*. Keywords Press, 2016.

Franta, Connor. *A Work in Progress*. Keywords, 2015.

Graceffa, Joey. *In Real Life: My Journey to a Pixelated World*. Keywords Press, 2015.

Howell, Dan, and Phil Lester. *The Amazing Book Is Not on Fire: The World of Dan and Phil*. Random House Children's Books, 2015.

Howell, Dan, and Phil Lester. *Dan and Phil Go Outside*. Random House Children's Books, 2016.

Lee, Caspar, and Emily Riordan Lee. *Caspar Lee*. Hachette, 2016.

McAllister, Jenn. *Really Professional Internet Person*. Scholastic, 2015.

Oakley, Tyler. *Binge*. Gallery Books, 2015.

Sundquist, Josh. *We Should Hang Out Sometime*. Little, Brown, 2014.

3

Paranormal Maturation: Uncanny Teenagers and Canny Killers

Rachel Dean-Ruzicka

Paranormal teenagers capable of stopping a serial killer? Surely this can't be a subgenre to itself? Yet it is, stretching across the boundaries of historical fiction, fantasy, boarding-school narratives, Black speculative fiction, and traditional high school novels.[1] The female detectives featured here can be read as descendants of the twentieth century's most famous teen detective: Nancy Drew.[2] This subgenre, in fact, updates Nancy's abilities and the crimes she solves to twenty-first-century audiences. While the initial Nancy Drew mysteries largely focused on property and misplaced persons, the books here have higher stakes and are more in line with a contemporary serial-killer-saturated popular culture. The protagonists in this chapter have various extraordinary skills that enable them to track serial killers successfully, from "hunches" to visions. Michelle Abate makes an effective case for Nancy's "hunches" as a psychic ability in her book *Bloody Murder: The Homicide Tradition in Children's Literature*. As she notes, "A central but commonly overlooked feature of the title character's crime-fighting prowess is her psychic ability. In narratives throughout the series, Nancy's famous hunches, her powerful sense of intuition, and her unfailingly accurate gut feelings play as vital a role in her ability to solve cases as her use of reason, logic, and material evidence" (120). While the true nature of Nancy's hunches is not explored in depth in her long-standing series, she is undoubtedly the site from which the tradition of the uncannily brilliant girl detective springs. Like Nancy, the characters in this chapter appear at first to be typical teens and experience many hallmarks of adolescence: first loves, job training, and new "schools." Normalcy is quickly challenged by two uncanny developments, however, as they negotiate a serial killer's presence and their unique ability to stop him or her.

This essay examines the characters' maturation through the multivalent terms *canny* and *uncanny* in relationship to both the novels' protagonists and antagonists. While the characters have average adolescent experiences, their uncanny abilities disrupt reader expectations for what it means to become a mature adult. Freud notes, when discussing the uncanny and fiction, that authors can "trick us by promising us everyday reality and then going beyond it," which is exactly what we see in this subgenre (157). The essential element of Freud's *unheimlich* (uncanny) is its connection to the *heimlich*, or something we generally find comfortable or homey. We are unsettled because the uncanny is so close to home, so nearly normal as to frighten subtly and perniciously. Here I trace the development of the teens' paranormal powers, their need to master their special abilities, and the eventual justice meted out on serial killers. The subgenre's larger appeal lies in the mastery and self-possession the characters gain, as they can do what the adults cannot: identify and track a serial killer. Ultimately, the uncanny detectives often become killers themselves, dispatching the serial murderers they have set out to find. This mirroring between protagonist and antagonist leaves readers wondering whether the books have merely created a new kind of killer, one armed with extraordinary abilities they can now successfully deploy.

The relationship between the terms *canny* and *uncanny* is essential to my analysis, in addition to Freud's *heimlich* and *unheimlich*. I consider Anna Jackson's "Uncanny Hauntings, Canny Children" to explore this less often considered binary, where

> Canny is a word which has increasingly come to mean a cleverness that is not just about knowing things, but is about a particular sort of capability, the capability to manipulate people and events in your own self-interest. It has to do with self-possession—a self-possession that makes you capable of acting powerfully in and on the world. And if we understand canny as a type of self-possession, suddenly it makes perfect sense that issues of identity would be explored through narratives of hauntings, narratives about being *possessed*. (159, original italics)

The teenagers here are seeking self-possession, a desire to come into their own, as readers find repeatedly in YA novels. However, this subgenre includes characters possessed by uncontrolled impulses, abnormal skills, and even the occasional haunting, all paranormal happenings that wedge themselves into the narrative regardless of genre. YA readers expect certain conventions as markers of maturation. This is a common element seen in articles throughout *Beyond the Blockbusters* as well, in liminal spaces occupied by mermaids, the hunt for individual power in dystopian fairy tales, and engagement in heterosexual relationships leading to "mature" marriages.[3] Characters gain knowledge, but especially important is the ability to distinguish between knowing and not knowing, according to Eric Tribunella's *Melancholia and Maturation*. He explains, "Proper adults are supposed to know and think about certain things, but they are also supposed to remain ignorant or unthinking about others" (55). Yet the protagonists' uncanny abilities unsettle a knowing/not knowing narrative resolution. Because the characters must face both terrible deaths and paranormal intervention, they engage with things that many mature adults would prefer not to know. Because of this, they are not able to fulfill the second aspect of Tribunella's claim: "Knowing and not knowing are also related to maintaining one's predefined position in the social order, remaining undisruptive, and being subdued and law abiding" (55). Characters *must* know things that make sure they disrupt normalcy, and that keep them from being law-abiding. This is where the uncanny disrupts reader expectations, across genres.

Here I analyze twelve books featuring uncanny teenagers and serial killers published within the last ten years.[4] Listed according to genre, they are as follows. Libba Bray's *Diviners* series features an ensemble cast with paranormal abilities; I focus on Evie, a 1920s flapper who receives visions from the objects she holds. Mindy McGinnis's historical novel *A Madness So Discreet* takes place in a nineteenth-century asylum, where Grace hones her uncanny memory to profile and stop a serial killer. William Ritter's *Jackaby* series is set in the 1890s and features Abigail, who hunts supernatural serial killers with her unusual boss's help. Kristin Cashore's fantasy novel *Graceling* pits Katsa's supernatural ability to survive against the sadistic King Leck in a nearby land. Sarah Beth Durst's *Conjured* bridges the fantasy and boarding-school genres, as it takes place in the confines of a government agency where Eve, a former ragdoll made human, is in witness protection. She must recover her memories to testify against "the Magician," a powerful serial killer from another world. Maureen Johnson's heroine Rory in *The Name of the Star* must stop a Jack the Ripper copycat killer while mastering her ability to interact with ghosts from her new boarding school in London. Jennifer Lynn Barnes's *Naturals* series takes place in an elite FBI boarding school, where Cassie and other teenagers train to use their uncanny abilities. This plot device is also the basis for Susanne Winnacker's *Imposter* series, where Tessa learns to use her shape-shifting abilities to impersonate a victim and stop a killer. Sunny, in Nnedi Okorafor's *Akata Witch*, must use her Leopard Person juju to stop Black Hat from killing local Nigerian children. Kimberly Derting's *The Body Finder*, Jill

Hathaway's *Slide*, and Gregg Olson's *Envy* take place in average high school settings, as the protagonists must learn to deal with their unstable abilities while appearing normal to their peers. Every character here must use their extraordinary abilities to defeat an uncanny murderer, whether the killer is a ghost or a deranged aunt.[5]

Uncanny Necropedagogies

The process of maturation in this subgenre is directly tied to what the characters learn about death and murder. These books, like many others for young adults featuring trauma and death, serve a particular pedagogical function. Necropedagogy requires "individuals to grapple with questions of trauma, mourning" and "moral claims about progress, the universal human, and the ordering of time itself" (Abate 224). Readers find death and trauma represented repeatedly in children's and young adult literature, ranging in severity from stories about dying pets to the Holocaust. While this subgenre may seem far-flung from the personal and historical significance of these two examples, the characters here still must face losses. Instead of losing a close friend or an entire community, they lose a sense of normalcy and safety. The "universal human" becomes a threatening presence, as serial killers hide in plain sight. Tribunella argues that engagement with loss creates a particular portrait of mature adulthood, an end goal for the characters who experience loss and death. The question, then, is what type of maturation is highlighted through the necropedagogy found in this murderous subgenre. According to Tribunella, mature adults are serious, knowing, responsible, experienced, law-abiding, hardworking, and heteronormatively gendered (xxi–xxii). Through discussions of their training, socialization, and romantic entanglements, we can see how the characters grow to be more serious, have new knowledge and experience, must be hardworking in order to capitalize on their skills, and engage in heteronormative relationships. However, these books leave some important characteristics of mature adulthood behind. The characters are not terribly responsible, but most importantly, they are not law abiding. They seem to lack responsibility, in part due to the fact they appear in a first book in a series, and thus the authors are invested in drawing out that process of maturation through multiple books. The characters still need room to grow and must return to spaces where they are cared for by others as they move on to the next book, where they will continue to mature. The primary difference is a willingness to function outside the law, utterly without any sense of guilt, which ultimately creates uncanny adults.

The version of uncanny maturation presented in this subgenre is a near-universally white one. The ability to function cannily outside of the law is extended to the white characters and killers, as well as to the middle-class, heteronormative protagonists. The law both protects and allows for the transgressions of the paranormal teens, either actively in the form of FBI training or passively when accepting inexplicable tips from the teens. The subgenre aligns canniness with whiteness, repeatedly. This is problematic on multiple levels, including the suggestion that the categories of maturity Tribunella illustrates are more available to white characters in this subgenre. The marker of maturation these characters lack, to be law abiding, is also a privilege of whiteness. A multitude of examples in recent American culture point to the criminalization of brown bodies, from real-world examples like the shooting deaths of Philando Castile, Tamir Rice, and Michael Brown to YA literature addressing the topic, like Angie Thomas's *The Hate U Give*, Nic Stone's *Dear Martin*, and Kekla Magoon's *How It Went Down*. One can imagine how differently a subgenre dealing with the realities of police, race, and innocent deaths would handle the "law-abiding" issue of maturation. Certainly, the pedagogical takeaway would not be that one can operate outside the law with impunity, particularly for the nonwhite protagonists seen in the examples listed above. The exception to the rule is the Black speculative fiction represented by *Akata Witch*. Because Sunny's story takes place in Nigeria, she is growing her uncanny abilities in a considerably different racial and judicial structure than the other protagonists seen here.

Regardless of where the books take place, either in the real world or in a fantasy land, all the characters begin the stories with unstable and untrained powers. As uncanny teens transition between the familiar and the frightening space of their new abilities, their narratives become unfamiliar or unknowable places. Sylvia from *Slide* experiences this early in the novel as she thinks, "I can never get used to the feeling of looking through someone else's eyes. It's as if each person sees the world in a slightly different hue. The tricky part is figuring out who the person is" (4). When Sylvia passes out from her sleep disorder, she slides into another's mind. This power is uncontrolled and unfocused as the book begins, often causing her harm as she passes out unexpectedly. Lack of control, or use of powers for frivolous purposes, exemplifies many of the teenagers' experiences and immaturity at the beginning of their stories. In *The Diviners* the heroine notes, "There were few things worse than being ordinary, in Evie's opinion. Ordinary was for suckers. Evie wanted to be special. A bright star. [. . .] If Evie had been sober she might have stopped. But the gin made her foolishly brave," as she psychically reads an object and then spills someone's secrets in order to "be special" at a drunken party (Bray 17–18). Evie has uncanny abilities yet lacks the ability to deploy them maturely. In some cases, like *Imposter* or *The Name of the Star*, characters have help from official organizations to guide them in using their powers effectively. In others, like *Slide* and *The Diviners*, the protagonists must learn to handle their powers on their own. Regardless, the characters face questions about trauma and death that are the basis for their process of maturing.

Paranormal detectives and serial killers occupy *both* the canny and the uncanny in this subgenre, where the killers have already matured into their abilities. Serial killers are often associated with a particular shrewdness, a skill at manipulation that leads to a series of deaths, not terribly far from Cassie's training to manipulate marks through her observational powers in *The Naturals*. The young detectives learn to negotiate their abilities, gaining skills and expertise, a familiar process of growing up. Yet their abilities are also clearly extraordinary. In Jackson's article, her example from *The Haunting* ends with "the book [raising] the spectre of the uncanny only to resolve the complicated plot with a celebration of canniness, and an alignment of canniness with maturity, with growing up" (163). Throughout the narratives, characters must learn to manage their uncanny abilities with canny acumen. The characters' canniness is celebrated, and some new level of maturity reached by the books' conclusion, building on the normalcy the authors establish early in the texts. Yet the question of whether justice is served lingers, as readers repeatedly watch serial killers shot, stabbed, slashed, trapped, burned, and poisoned to death by the "good guys," who express no guilt about the deaths they have caused.

Establishing Generic Normalcy

The authors begin their texts with an attempt to establish their characters as average teenagers within genre expectations. Relying on two touchstones of adolescence, puberty and group socialization, they begin by creating characters with whom readers easily identify. Largely this happens in two ways: through a romance subplot or through an experience where the characters must adjust to a new social group dynamic (and sometimes both). Even in the case of Eve, the world-hopping rag doll, her introduction comes through the normalcy of a first job. Like many teenagers on summer vacation, she is faced with this parental logic: "You can't sit in the house by yourself all day [. . .] You need structure to your day," and "interaction and experiences" will be good for her (Durst 16). The books seem to insist paranormal teens are "just like us"—*look, they have crushes too!* Yet the characters must figure out how to deal with their first crush and hide their visions from him. When an elite investigative body chooses them, they still need to negotiate where they fit in, just like any student on the first day of high school. The novels orient readers along generic expectations: mean girls and high school dances in the contemporary texts, establishing strong and unusual women for the time in historical fiction, and orienting readers to different languages and customs in Black speculative narratives, world-building in fantasy novels. Regardless of genre conventions, all twelve texts establish a level of *heimlich* before or alongside the *unheimlich* readers discover. To revisit Freud's earlier quote, this impulse is the authors' attempt to "trick us by promising us everyday reality and then going beyond it," where the everyday reality we experience is the normalcy of genre conventions (157).

The authors often use a romance subplot to present average teenagers, relying on the norms of puberty and sexual exploration to make their characters identifiable. Certainly, the heteronormative nature of this subgenre could also be read through a postfeminist lens, such as Sara Day offers in her contribution to this volume. However, unlike the paranormal romance plots of *Twilight*, *Shiver*, or *Fallen*, the romance is not the central focus, as that honor goes to hunting a killer. The presence of a killer and the young women's growing paranormal powers regularly disrupt their romances. Cassie from *The Naturals* struggles to decide between Dean and Michael in her new FBI home. Sylvia eventually figures out her best friend has been in love with her for ages in *The Body Finder*. Violet questions just why, exactly, the incredibly hot Zane would go for her in *Slide*. Their relationship eventually leads to questions about whether Zane himself is the killer, a primary point of tension in the novel and uncanny interjection. Abigail falls for a cop/werewolf in *Jackaby*, adding to her ability to manipulate the criminal justice system of 1890s New England in her favor. Katsa's protection of the secret of Po's Grace ultimately defeats King Leck in *Graceling*. Tessa uses her shapeshifting abilities to impersonate Alec's girlfriend in *Impostor*, which he for some reason forgives her for doing. It is an uncanny version of trying to dress up to impress the coolest guy in school and is deeply distressing, as it extends to Alec's nonconsensual kiss. Tessa's choice here is another example of how the stories begin with characters' immature use of their powers, powers they must learn to hone and mature by the end of each book.

These examples highlight how the familiar becomes uncanny, stressing the unnatural situations the characters experience. Rory from *The Name of the Star* finds herself in the middle of a Jack the Ripper copycat crime spree, thinking, "[I]t finally dawned on me that he hadn't brought me in here for the sole reason of watching a video of someone being murdered (though that was probably *part* of the reason)" (Johnson 133). For Rory and Jerome, the normalcy of a first kiss is coupled with the killer's ghostly visage on a surveillance camera, the uncanny injecting itself into a normative girl-likes-boy plot. In fact, the heteronormative plot here is nearly universal, again mapping onto Tribunella's qualifications for mature adulthood. Only *Akata Witch* and *A Madness So Discreet* lack a heteronormative romance plot, as Sunny's age and Grace's sexual abuse exclude these as effective plot devices. No character expresses any desires outside of heteronormative ones, as explorations and crushes locate the stories within the realm of the non-queer *heimlich*, exemplifying the familiar and comfortable teen narrative, but ultimately twist it into something quite *unheimlich*. This heteronormative focus also implies to readers that one can mature into a killer, as long as one follows other societal expectations for maturation, such as heterosexual crushes.

For the books not focusing as heavily on romance, the authors use the trope of fitting into a new social space to orient readers. The adjustment to societal structures is one of the hallmarks of YA literature; as Roberta Trites points out, "YA novels tend to interrogate social constructions, foregrounding the relationship between the society and the individual" (20). Readers find this most clearly in the books where the protagonists must leave home, moving to a training facility for their abilities, a boarding school, or a nineteenth-century madhouse. In *A Madness So Discreet*, Grace needs to adjust to her social standing in a new mental hospital. Despite her apparent muteness and lobotomy scars, she makes friends with Nell and Elizabeth, who help her settle into her new Ohio asylum. Of course, what neither of her friends realizes is that she is there only to hide from her abusive father, is perfectly capable of speech, has had a fake lobotomy, and now spends her nights profiling serial killers with her doctor. For all the normalcy the books attempt to pursue through romance and social structures, the uncanny nature of the protagonists' powers disrupts that familiar space; whether in the shape of first kisses while considering a murder or hiding one's nightly adventures at murder scenes.

There are a variety of standard plot points throughout this subgenre, which assures that the books feel comfortable to readers. However, the characters in these novels grow and develop into uncanny versions of the maturing adolescent, often aided by a process of formalized training or education. Ann Pellegrini's "What Do Children Learn at School? Necropedagogy and the Dead Child" notes that "the child uneasily straddles past and future, death and life" as it "summons the fantasy of a future" (103). Lee Edelman's *No Future* and Rebekah Sheldon's *The Child to Come* refer to this fantasy of a future as reproductive futurity, where the figure of the child is a nest for political power and promise. Edelman and Sheldon discuss the child in texts hatched for an adult audience, such as Alfred Hitchcock's *The Birds* or Cormac McCarthy's *The Road*. However, the subgenre in this essay deals with adolescent figures created for a teen audience. This shifts the child (or teen) from a position of imagined futurity to one of imagined maturity, an important distinction when considering the necropedagogies at work here. Mature adulthood is refigured for the paranormal teens as a space that negotiates and perpetuates violent deaths. The characters must master their uncanny abilities to mature, but that maturity also means ending the lives of others.

Uncanny Mastery as Maturation

What each character must figure out is how to cannily use their uncanny abilities to fight evil. In some cases, state-sponsored organizations clearly use the teens' abnormal powers to solve crimes.[6] In Jackson's essay on uncanny children, she notes that the boarding-school narrative allows characters to explore "an intellectual uncertainty that comes from not being at home, not on familiar territory" (169–70). As the characters' lives have been destabilized by an unhoming, a transition to new space and new family structures, they have the opportunity to explore and master their new powers. This is the case in a more traditional boarding-school tale, like *The Name of the Star*, as well as those characters who are taken from their homes by a government agency like those in *Imposter, Conjured*, and *The Naturals*. YA readers are familiar with the narrative of the extraordinary child who leaves home to train their abilities, of course. The uncanny intervention is the figure of the serial killer, one whom the paranormal teen *in particular* must stop.

Mentors, but never a parent figure, sometimes help the teenagers master their powers, emphasizing that intellectual uncertainty of the *unheimlich*. Only two characters are orphans, Cassie in *The Naturals* and Katsa in *Graceling*, resisting the narrative of forced independence often found in YA novels. Instead, parents largely function as a site of normalcy and must be kept in the dark about their children's unusual powers. This could be read as a step toward the responsible nature of mature adulthood, one that remains unfinished at the end of the first-in-a-series novels. Many mentors tend to have uncanny or eerie powers themselves, yet still need the teenagers to solve crimes. Sunny, in Okorafor's *Akata Witch*, must use her juju to sneak out of her house in order to find the Leopard People, who teach her to use her powers. She and her friends must defeat the Black Hat; a task more experienced Leopard People failed at in the past. Even the characters who learned their knowledge from a parent, like Cassie in *The Naturals*, need training to take up their positions as serial killer hunters. Cassie eventually uses her ability to manipulate others in order to distract the killer: "I was speaking her language, telling her what she wanted to hear: that I was like *her*, that we were the *same*, that I understood this was about anger and control and having the power to decide who lived and who died" (Barnes 287, original italics). While her aunt wants her to become a natural killer, Cassie instead manipulates her to a standstill, allowing fellow "Natural" Michael to regain his gun and shoot the killer. This is one example of how, at the end of their training, characters can venture into the world to defeat a killer. Rory does it as a ghost hunter in *The Name of the Star*, knowing she must act as "[s]omeone who held no threat. Someone he'd talked to before. Someone like me" (Johnson 339). Rory has learned to talk to ghosts with enough confidence to coax the killer away from her colleagues, relying on the training she received at the hands of Scotland Yard's ghost squad.

When the protagonists do not have a mentor figure, they must gain canniness on their own. The ultimate goal is to defeat a serial killer in these books, meaning there is always something at stake for the characters. They must master their uncanny powers to save themselves or others, but never to merely turn the killers over to the authorities. In *The Body Finder*, Violet finds herself cornered by a serial killer and must focus her abilities to identify him under his police officer exterior: "The shrill vibrations. The ones that had nothing to do with the pulsating beat coming from the dance. The same high-pitched, ear-piercing resonance she'd felt before. [. . .] She'd run into him that day, right before she'd located the killer, when she'd been following Brooke's bells" (306). Violet uses her psychic vibrations to realize that the *first* serial killer she tracked had a partner, one disguised as a familiar, comfortable police officer. She hones her ability to identify the psychic noises and smells she identifies as *killer* and *victim* in order to defeat two killers. Similarly, Sylvia masters her ability to slide, choosing particular objects and relaxing her mind in order to see through another's eyes. This allows her to purposefully track the killer, rather than the random sliding she experienced at the novel's beginning (Hathaway 228–29). Both characters have to trust their instincts to master their powers, perhaps not so differently from how Nancy Drew learned to listen to her hunches decades earlier. No longer possessed, Sylvia and Violet take control of their abilities and exhibit a self-possession that gives them the confidence to defeat murderous cops and jealous ex-mistresses, respectively.

The Canniness of the Serial Killer

Serial killers, like abnormal teen investigators, are both canny and uncanny. The mirroring sets up troubling parallels, particularly when considering the extrajudicial killings that often are sold as just resolutions. Because maturity is ultimately aligned with the ability to circumvent the law in this subgenre, the teens end up with many of the same capabilities as the killers by the end of the novels. For the teens to grow and embrace the uncanny nature of their powers, they must become canny killers themselves. The psychopathic killer may be crazy, but he is crazy like a fox, able to use his or her abilities as "a canniness so far at the edge of canniness as to border on the uncanny" (Jackson 163). When discussing uncanny *individuals*, Freud states, "We can also call a living person uncanny, that is to say, when we credit him with evil intent. But this alone is not enough: it must be added that this intent to harm us is realized with the help of special powers" (149). Roger Lane gives a concise definition of the serial killer's "special powers" in his book *Murder in America: A History*:

> Serial killers, defined as those who kill three or more people over thirty days or more, are also typically white and often middle class, but they are often quite different from mass murderers, and even more frightening. [. . .] Unlike mass murderers, while serial killers may be psychotic they are also secretive, clever, often charmingly seductive. (319)

Lane's definition reflects Freud's concept of the uncanny individual: a particular type of harm coupled with the special powers of cleverness (or perhaps *canniness*) and charm. In many ways the killers have fully grasped the uncanny maturation process the teens themselves are experiencing. They master societal expectations to hide their evil intent under a charming façade, like the archetypical Ted Bundy. The killers also avoid the lawfulness Tribunella discusses as one characteristic of a mature adult. They work within societal systems but fail to recognize the "individual and common good of observing laws and customs" (Tribunella xxii). Instead they twist systems to their own advantage, becoming uncanny adults hiding in the social order.

While Lane defines serial killers as typically white and male, Scott Bonn argues against this trope in this excerpt from his book, published in *Scientific American*:

> The racial diversity of serial killers generally mirrors that of the overall U.S. population. There are well documented cases of African-American, Latino and Asian-American serial killers. African-Americans comprise the largest racial minority group among serial killers, representing approximately 20 percent of the total. Significantly, however, only white, and normally male, serial killers such as Ted Bundy become popular culture icons.

Archetypical serial killers in American culture are the Ted Bundys, John Wayne Gacys, and Dennis Raders of the world. They represent the inscrutable white male figure; they are beyond scrutiny, as their white, middle-class nature allows them to hide in plain sight. Much less often do we find references to nonwhite serial killers, although they do exist. Bonn lists Coral Eugene Watts, Anthony Edward Sowell, and Ángel Maturino Reséndiz (aka Rafael Resendez-Ramirez) as examples. They were all prolific killers, yet are hardly household names. These (mis)representations of race imply canniness as a white quality, both in the killers and the paranormal teens. Again and again, this subgenre encourages readers to see whiteness aligned with a rejection of behaving lawfully. The focus on white serial killers hiding in plain sight, and the absence of such narratives about nonwhite serial killers, has an underlying message that brown male bodies are expected to transgress the law.

One argument for why Americans are so fascinated with serial killers is that they have "become the container and symbol for a contemporary understanding of evil in popular culture, one that posits evil as hidden, persistent, and spectacularly gruesome" (Murley 5). Serial killers hide their "evil" under an ability to cannily manipulate their victims, which is what makes them uncanny monsters. They are also reliable villains across popular culture texts.[7] The killer's descriptions tend to focus on their normalcy and intelligence, which hides the *unheimlich* or evil desires within, like the safe-seeming police officer in *The Body Finder*. Repeatedly, killers thwart their pursuers, and it is up to the teen detectives to unmask them, using special skills they are working to master. In the final moments of *Imposter*, Tessa confronts the killer: "He crouched in front of me, bringing his face close, far too close. So close that I saw the cold calculation in his eyes. I wished there had been madness there; that would have been easier to deal with" (Winnacker 234). While his fog-based murders may have been highly uncanny, what most horrifies Tessa is the calculating intelligence behind his actions, a misreading of the terrifying nature of the serial killer. It's the conjunction of "madness" and intelligence that allows these killers to uncannily exist in plain sight. Similarly, in *A Madness So Discreet*, Grace "glanced up and locked her eyes with his [and] for the barest of moments she could see [the killer's] intelligence, no less quick than her own" (Johnson 298). Grace's intelligence directly mirrors the killer's, anticipating the cold canniness Grace shortly uses to murder him.

Some killers are paranormal themselves, which mirrors the investigator's abnormal abilities. The killers are, however, canny first and paranormal second. When victim Ruta Bates encounters the demonic killer from *The Diviners*, he charms her, first and foremost. He compliments her looks and claims there is "something quite special" about her (63). She finds herself thinking, "The stranger—no, he wasn't a stranger at all, was he? He was Mr. Hobbes. Such a nice man. Such a smart man—classy too. Mr. Hobbes thought she was special" (64). The killer knows what his victims need to hear: they are pretty, he can make them rich, he can make them immortal (63, 170, 503). He manipulates their desires with his charm before unleashing the monster within. Similarly, Rory describes the ghost killer in *The Name of the Star* as "disarmingly normal" (325). It is an interesting turn of phrase, as it indicates how normalcy unarms us. The serial killer's special power, whether human or otherwise, is to hide in plain sight. The teenage investigators have used their powers to avoid being disarmed, using their uncanny abilities to see beyond a canny façade. Ultimately, they do not merely unmask a killer but put a definitive stop to the deaths.

Uncanny Justice as Resolution

The nature of most detective or investigatory entertainment is to reassure viewers or readers that there are competent experts keeping the "bad guys" from getting away with it. Murder narratives reify a comfortable belief in the American criminal justice system and tidy packaging of crime as consistently solvable by hard work and science.[8] Jane Latman, of the Investigation Discovery network, views it as a "cathartic journey" that "in the end makes you feel somehow safer. It's counterintuitive, but when the handcuffs are on, justice is served and the perpetrator is behind bars and you see these real people getting on with their lives you kind of feel like 'okay I can go to bed and I'm not going to check my door ten times'" (qtd. Conger). However, in this subgenre, it is the exception to the rule that we ever see handcuffs on or perpetrators behind bars. The resolution is generally an extrajudicial killing at the hands of the protagonist or a close colleague. Maturity thus aligns with the ability to defeat the killers at any cost.

This subgenre does not promote law abiding as an element of mature adulthood, as the extrajudicial killings illustrate. This is due to the lack of guilt any individual character feels, even when helping to kill a family member, as Cassie does in *The Naturals*. The teens never express guilt for the extrajudicial killings that happen in the texts, which is one element that makes them uncanny. It is not merely that they use abnormal abilities to catch these killers but also that they never feel a moment's remorse at ending a life. It also promotes the idea that working outside the law is acceptable, particularly if you are white, middle-class, and heterosexual. Some extrajudicial killings are justified by self-defense, particularly in *The Body Finder*, *The Naturals*, and *Imposter*, which is not unusual. In crime fiction the protagonist will often take justice into his or her own hands. The distinction between Patricia Cornwell's Kay Scarpetta and, say, the resolution in *Conjured* as discussed below is the justification of self-defense. Scarpetta and her colleagues *must* kill the "bad guy" to survive in *Postmortem*, *The Body Farm*, and *From Potter's Field*.[9] In these cases readers feel that perhaps the justice system has been circumvented, but for necessary reasons.

In the paranormal-teen subgenre, teens instead can literally get away with murder as they mature. In *A Madness So Discreet*, Grace, with her uncanny ability to see what others miss at a crime scene, uses her skills to bring a form of justice to those who have wronged her. After she and the doctor successfully profile a serial killer, she sets out to murder him. Grace does not do this in a moment of self-defense, unlike Tessa in *Imposter*. Instead, she deliberately decides to track down and murder the man who has been killing young women in her small Ohio town. Later, she remembers how "Beaton's face in the moonlight had not affected her, the dark spray against the untouched snow had not given her pause, and the hot, coppery scent of flowing blood had not brought her to gag" (McGinnis 317). Readers may feel satisfaction at his death, but the uncanny justice continues after Beaton's murder. Grace frames her father for the murders Beaton committed, convincing her friend Elizabeth to lie on the witness stand. Certainly, her father is guilty of sexual abuse. Yet Grace cannily manipulates the situation to her advantage, ensuring that her cancer-ridden father will be confined to a mental institution, one where she knows a cancer-eating madman waits in the dark. Grace has actively, and with a great deal of self-possession, subverted the justice system in her need for revenge.

The resolution to *Envy* is even more troubling. The protagonists, twin psychics in a small Washington town, set out to discover what happened to their neighbor. Was it murder? Was it suicide? Will there be more murders? As it turns out, no. It was a tragic accident, which, for some reason, requires two teen psychics to solve. There is a subplot involving the toddler twins attempting to save a woman from a serial killer, but that is a mere footnote to the hunt for answers regarding their neighbor's death. One would think the novel would end without any additional deaths, since no murder was ultimately committed. However, a nosy reporter has been trying to uncover the twins' secret. Instead of convincing her to keep quiet, or brushing off psychic alphabet-soup reading as ridiculous, the girls watch as a family friend runs the reporter off a cliff with her car (281). The twins feel only relief at this homicide, and the chapter ends with the claim, "*It had to be done*," a direct refutation of the guilt that leads to lawfulness (282, original italics). To maintain their identity as normal teenagers, an innocent woman had to die, a deeply unjust resolution.

When placed in a paranormal setting, the challenges to justice remain similar. Rory ends *The Name of the Star* able to dispel spirits, making her an unwitting ghost executioner. She has the potential to wipe out any lost soul, no matter how innocent. The book promises a new paranormal ability that she must master in the coming sequels.[10] Similarly, at the end of Ritter's *Jackaby* series, Abigail has inherited all of Jackaby's paranormal powers and is now the detective keeping her town safe from otherworldly threats. In *Conjured*,

Eve finally regains her memories and testifies against the Magician. However, after he is sentenced to life without parole, Eve watches her shapeshifting colleague turn into a snake; the snake "reared back and sank her fangs into his neck" upon which his "eyes bulged and then bled, red tears streaking his purple veined cheeks" before he dies (Durst 347). The handcuffs *were* on, the Magician behind bars, and the characters assured he was no longer a threat. Yet one of Eve's paranormal teen colleagues found the resolution unacceptable. The human guards and courtroom attendants can do nothing to stop her need to take justice into her own hands, and Eve watches the death play out. The subversion of the criminal justice system leaves readers in an uncomfortable position. While we are accustomed to characters becoming mature or self-possessed by the end of a YA novel, what do we make of a resolution that claims becoming a murderer oneself is the natural result of training and maturation? The teenagers have merely taken the place of the uncanny serial killers, now cannily able to use their skills to hunt down others.

Conclusion

This subgenre's appeal comes in many forms. Detective fiction is exciting; serial killers are a reliable evil that clearly must be stopped, and the paranormal twists keep readers unsettled and engaged. While at first it seems a surprising subgenre, considering the nostalgic popularity of Nancy Drew, YA literature's ongoing engagement with the paranormal, and the proliferation of death as a source of lessons, it begins to make more sense. As Amber Gray points out in her article "Fathoms Below," after the success of the *Twilight* series, publishers were anxious to find new representations of paranormal characters. While Gray focuses on mermaids in her piece, a similar desire is represented in the variety of paranormal abilities in this chapter. Reflecting Tribunella's melancholia as maturation, characters face repeated horrors that help them gain some qualities of mature adulthood: they are more serious, knowledgeable, experienced, and hardworking, and remain heteronormatively gendered at the end of the books. Yet it is their lack of responsibility or law-abiding nature even as they mature that is troubling.

The books are not merely straightforward tales of justice, as the complicated resolutions show. The uncanny abilities the teenagers use disrupt our expectations for maturation in a YA novel. The self-possession the characters gain is one that allows them to manipulate and kill. Returning to Abate's definition of necropedagogy, which asks characters to "grapple with questions of trauma, mourning" and "moral claims about progress, the universal human, and the ordering of time itself" (224), it is worth reflecting on how this subgenre upends some of these elements. Loss is figured differently in this subgenre, as what the characters lose is a sense of normalcy and safety in the world around them. Instead of accurate claims about progress and the universal human, the subgenre raises more questions than answers. The characters progress as killers, serial killers are decidedly outside what readers would like to think of as a universal human, and time itself is sometimes challenged in the form of ghosts or Leopard People. What these characters lose is normalcy itself as they embrace paranormal powers. The necropedagogy in this subgenre focuses on moral claims about progress, to be sure. The process of maturation and training is essential to the teenager's success, and at these novels' ends the serial killers are all dispatched, one way or another. Yet it is an uncanny resolution, as the characters move on to their next journey (and often next books) able to use their paranormal abilities to comfortably kill other killers.

Notes

1. I've focused explicitly on novels here, purposefully leaving out superhero comics.

2. All the primary uncanny protagonists are female. *The Diviners*, *Graceling*, and *Akata Witch* feature paranormal male characters, but they are not the focus of the narrative.

3. See articles by Gray, Coste, and Day elsewhere in this collection.

4. When dealing with a series, I use the first book as the exemplar.

5. There are several additional books I would deem "subgenre adjacent," including Barry Lyga's *I Hunt Killers* series, Holly Black's *Curseworkers* series, Brittany Cavallaro's Charlotte Holmes series, and Tsugumi Ohba and Takeshi Obata's *Death Note* manga. They contain either serial killers or uncanny teens, but they do not directly overlap. Lyga's protagonist is a fairly normal teen with terrible memories of his serial killer father, Black's main character has uncanny abilities but primarily interacts with mob contract killers, Charlotte Holmes's deductions are always explained (unlike Nancy Drew's hunches), and Ohba and Obata feature an uncanny teen killer and an adult detective.

6. Abate discusses the ongoing use of psychics by real-world police forces and federal crime-fighting organizations, from the 1890s through the present (124–29). With this in mind, the paranormal investigative branches of government agencies seen in these four books seem slightly less outrageous.

7. The other reliable evil figure in American popular culture was, until recently, the Nazi. Both were seen as uncomplicated monsters, so "other" as to warrant a stamp of villainous approval. Of course, in the wake of Charlottesville and President Trump's comments, "some very fine people" were marching in the streets carrying Nazi symbols, we need to rethink the assumption that Nazis are seen as universally bad (Gray).

8. See Rachel Dean-Ruzicka, "Vengance, Healing, and Justice: Post 9–11 Culture through the Lens of *CSI*," *Quarterly Review of Film and Video* 26, 2009, 118–30.

9. Similar examples crop up in Sue Grafton's *A Is for Alibi*, Thomas Harris's *The Silence of the Lambs*, and others.

10. Rory does end up using her power as a terminus to hunt more paranormal serial killers in subsequent books, but the resolution is currently incomplete after the first three in the series.

Works Cited

Abate, Michelle Ann. *Bloody Murder: The Homicide Tradition in Children's Literature*. Johns Hopkins UP, 2013.

Barnes, Jennifer Lynn. *The Naturals*. Disney-Hyperion, 2013.

Bonn, Scott. "5 Myths About Serial Killers and Why They Persist [Excerpt]." *Scientific American*. Springer Nature America, Inc. 24 Oct. 2014. Accessed 24 June 2019.

Bray, Libba. *The Diviners*. Little, Brown, 2012.

Cashore, Kristin. *Graceling*. HMH Books for Young Readers, 2009.

Conger, Cristen. "Why Are Women So Bloodthirsty for True Crime?" *Stuff Mom Never Told You. How Stuff Works*, 18 Oct. 2013. Accessed 19 May 2017.

Derting, Kimberly. *The Body Finder*. Harper, 2010.

Durst, Sarah Beth. *Conjured*. Bloomsbury Children's, 2013.

Edelman, Lee. *No Future: Queer Theory and the Death Drive*. Duke UP, 2004.

Freud, Sigmund. *The Uncanny*. Translated by David McLintock. Penguin Books, 2003.

Gray, Rosie. "Trump Defends White-Nationalist Protestors: 'Some Very Nice People on Both Sides.'" *Atlantic*, 15 Aug. 2017. Accessed 11 Dec. 2017.

Hathaway, Jill. *Slide*. Balzer + Bray, 2010.

Jackson, Anna. "Uncanny Hauntings, Canny Children." *The Gothic in Children's Literature: Haunting the Borders*, edited by Anna Jackson, Karen Coates, and Roderick McGillis, Routledge, 2007. pp. 157–76.

Johnson, Maureen. *The Name of the Star*. Putnam Juvenile, 2011.

Lane, Robert. *Murder in America, a History*. Ohio State UP, 1997.

McGinnis, Mindy. *A Madness So Discreet*. Harper Collins, 2015.

Murley, Jean. *The Rise of True Crime: Twentieth Century Murder and American Popular Culture*. Praeger, 2008.

Okorafor, Nnedi. *Akata Witch*. Viking, 2011.

Olsen, Gregg. *Envy*. Splinter, 2011.

Pellegrini, Ann. "What Do Children Learn at School? Necropedagogy and the Future of the Dead Child." *Social Text*, vol. 26, no. 24, 2008, pp. 97–105.

Ritter, William. *Jackaby*. Algonquin Young Readers, 2015.

Sheldon, Rebekah. *The Child to Come: Life after the Human Catastrophe*. Minnesota UP, 2016.

Tribunella, Eric. *Melancholia and Maturation: The Use of Trauma in American Children's Literature*. U of Tennessee P, 2014.

Trites, Roberta Seelinger. *Disturbing the Universe: Power and Repression in Adolescent Literature*. U of Iowa P, 1998.

Winnacker, Susanne. *Imposter*. Razorbill, 2013.

Further Reading

Barnes, Jennifer Lynn. *All In*. Harper Collins, 2015.

Barnes, Jennifer Lynn *Killer Instinct*. Hyperion, 2015.

Black, Holly. *The White Cat.* Simon & Schuster, 2010.

Bray, Libba. *Before the Devil Breaks You: A Diviner's Novel.* Little, Brown, 2017.

Bray, Libba *Lair of Dreams.* Little, Brown, 2015.

Cashore, Kristin. *Bitterblue.* Speak, 2017.

Cashore, Kristin. *Fire.* Speak, 2017.

Cavallaro, Brittany. *A Study in Charlotte: A Charlotte Holmes Novel.* Katherine Tegen, 2017.

Derting, Kimberly. *Dead Silence.* Harper, 2014.

Derting, Kimberly. *Desires of the Dead.* Harper, 2012.

Derting, Kimberly. *The Last Echo.* Harper, 2013.

Hathaway, Jill. *Imposter.* Harper Collins, 2013.

Johnson, Maureen. *The Madness Underneath.* G. P. Putnam's Sons, 2013.

Johnson, Maureen. *The Shadow Cabinet.* Speak, 2016.

Lyga, Barry. *I Hunt Killers.* Little, Brown, 2014.

Ohba, Tsugumi, and Obata Takeshi. *Death Note.* Viz Media, 2006.

Okorafor, Nnedi. *Akata Warrior.* Speak, 2018.

Older, Daniel Jose. *Shadowshaper.* Arthur A Levine Books, 2015.

Ritter, William. *Beastly Bones: A Jackaby Novel.* Algonquin Young Readers, 2016.

Ritter, William. *The Dire King: A Jackaby Novel.* Algonquin Young Readers, 2017.

Ritter, William. *Ghostly Echoes—a Jackaby Novel.* Algonquin, 2017.

Winnacker, Susanne. *Defector: A Variants Novel.* Razorbill, 2014.

Fathoms Below: An In-Depth Examination of the Mermaid in Young Adult Literature, 2010–2015

Amber Gray

The figure of the mermaid has a complicated history, alternately monstrous and innocent, tormented and tormenting. Until comparatively recently, the mermaid was often evoked in literature within the context of folk and fairy tales. However, in response to the rise of young adult paranormal romance in the mid-2000s, more than thirty young adult (YA) novels with mermaids as central characters (many of which belonged to multivolume series) were published between 2010 and 2015. This chapter will examine the figure of the mermaid and the protagonist's position between worlds in mermaid-themed YA novels, particularly in relation to the theme of bodily transformation and identity. Mermaids, as depicted in YA novels, are and continue to be compelling characters to young adult readers because they illustrate the possibility of identity and the body as characteristics potentially capable of transformation, providing a point of identification for readers wrestling with how to begin an independent life and how to create and shape their own identities as they prepare to enter their own adulthoods.

A Brief History of the Mermaid

Before discussing the types of mermaids that appear in YA fiction, it is important to discuss the ways in which depictions of mermaids throughout folklore and fiction have changed through time. The contemporary concept of a mermaid, a creature that appears human from the waist up and has the tail of a fish from the waist down, grew from a mélange of myths and legends from different eras. The mermaid's earliest known predecessor is the siren, a creature originating in Greek mythology that lived on a rocky island and used her sweet singing voice to entrance sailors into wrecking their ships on the rocks (White 184). Some early mermaid legends borrow heavily from siren myths, featuring mermaids with beautiful voices singing sailors to their deaths.

Tales of mermaids varied widely across cultures; sometimes they were sinister and sirenlike, while at other times they were more beneficent creatures who could provide humans with prosperity, good luck, or even a newly human (or human-appearing) bride (Warner 396). Mermaids were predominantly water-dwelling creatures, with the possibility of their living on land rarely discussed.

Hans Christian Andersen changed that in 1837, when he first published his story "The Little Mermaid" (Warner 396); he may have been inspired in part by the 1811 novel *Undine*, which featured a water sprite marrying a knight in an attempt to gain an immortal soul (Holbek 221). Unlike sirens, Andersen's mermaid (she is never named) is a kindhearted mermaid princess who saves the life of a human prince and wishes to become human so she can win an immortal soul and the prince's love (Fraser 247). Mortensen argues that Andersen's mermaid can be considered "a siren in reverse" because she is seduced by the appeal of joining human life on land rather than seducing humans to join her in her watery home (451). Indeed, this is the first significant fictitious depiction of a mermaid being positioned as able to choose her identity both physically and culturally. She must decide whether her preferred body is human or mermaid, just as she must decide between a long life in the sea, which will end with her becoming seafoam, or a shorter life on land, which holds the promise of an afterlife. "The Little Mermaid" was translated and published internationally, and it became successful and popular enough for its depiction of a mermaid caught between two worlds and two possible lives to have a strong and lasting impact on the depiction of mermaids in fiction.

Even in works presenting mermaids as unsympathetic, villainous, or ambiguous characters, Andersen's influence could be found. In 1901 H. G. Wells published a work of serial fiction called *The Sea Lady* (published as a novel in 1902), which focuses on a mermaid coming to shore to seduce and drown a human, in the vein of the siren legend. Like Andersen's mermaid, she has the ability to move between the land and the sea, although unlike Andersen's mermaid, she cannot change her tailed body by coming to land. Her identity is fixed; her only interest in humans is to seduce and destroy them.

The mermaids of 1911's *Peter and Wendy* are less influenced by Andersen's; they live in a lagoon and have no interest in any humans other than Peter Pan. Mermaids make the transition to land again in both the novel *Peabody's Mermaid* (1946) and the play *Miranda* (1948), in which the male protagonists accidentally encounter beautiful mermaids while fishing and take them home. As in *The Sea Lady*, these mermaids cannot shift their bodies into more human appearances; Peabody's mermaid, never named, must remain in some amount of water and is kept in a bathtub, while Miranda can live on land but needs a wheelchair for mobility purposes. Neither is, as Andersen's mermaid is, a transitional or transitioning figure; although they are visiting the human world, they express no desire to stay there and no interest in becoming human. They identify fully and unquestioningly as mermaids,[1] and both eventually return to their watery homes, leaving humans and humanity behind.

The mermaid-centered films *Splash* (1984), *The Little Mermaid* (1989), and *Aquamarine* (2006), however, all provide instances of the mermaid as capable of physical transformation and of moving between worlds. (In the case of *The Little Mermaid*, this is unsurprising, as the animated film is loosely based on Andersen's story.) Heroines Madison, Ariel, and Aquamarine all want to find love on land, and all three take human form and live in the human world to do so. Madison and Ariel both meet their love interests by saving them from drowning, as Andersen's mermaid does, before following them to land. Aquamarine, however, is searching for true love on land to escape from an undersea arranged marriage, and the true love she finds is the nonsexual, nonromantic love of her female best friends Hailey and Claire (Fraser 259; Williams 199).[2] Like Andersen's mermaid, Madison, Ariel, and Aquamarine ultimately must choose between their two worlds and their two bodies; Madison and Aquamarine return to the sea and to mermaid form, while Ariel remains human and lives on land.

Mermaids became major players in YA fiction after the 2005–2008 success of the four-book *Twilight* series, which features humans, vampires, and werewolves and has led to both increased awareness and increased popularity of paranormal young adult stories as a genre (Crawford 4). Publishers and literary agents searched for books about supernatural or mythical creatures, including zombies, ghosts, witches, and dark faeries, both to take advantage of current trends and to try to start new trends within paranormal fiction (Freitas 23–24). In light of this search, mermaids were reevaluated and reimagined as the central characters of paranormal young adult novels, creating an intersection between trends in young adult storytelling and mermaid mythology in which the mermaid as a figure of potentially fluid identity could gain deeper resonance.

The Sea and the Land

Young adults and protagonists of YA mermaid fiction share what Waller calls an "in-between-ness" or liminality, a sense of being between worlds (6). Young adults are positioned between childhood and adulthood, as are mermaid and human characters in young adult mermaid stories. Mermaid and human characters are also in-between through their positions between the human world and the mermaid world. In order for liminality to exist, the two worlds being bridged need to be largely separate, with a limited ability to move between them. This separation between worlds is part of what makes liminality so difficult; people caught in between feel they do not have an identity that exists fully in either world. A young adult is not considered an adult, for instance, but is not a child either.

Similarly, the mermaid world and the human world are often portrayed as being significantly separate. In many of the young adult books and book series involving mermaids, the human world is largely unaware of the mermaid world, though the mermaid world knows about the existence of the human world. Although most humans in these books are unaware of the existence of mermaids, many of these books include human characters who know about or who learn about mermaids, most often because they have a deep familial or emotional tie to a mermaid. In *Real Mermaids Don't Wear Toe Rings*, *Tempest Rising*, *The Mermaid's Mirror*, and *The Vicious Deep*, the humans who know about the mermaid world are the human parents of mermaid or part-mermaid children; in *Lies Beneath*, *Wrecked*, and *Sea Change*, the significant others of mermaid main characters discover the existence or possible existence of mermaids. Identity is central to these stories not just because main characters must grapple with their own identities, but because the relationships of these characters, familial or romantic, are directly responsible for the human main characters learning about the mermaid world in the first place. Their identities and the choices they make lead to their discovery of this secret.

Identity also plays a role in the subset of mermaid young adult books in which the human world and the mermaid world are aware of each other but have chosen to remain separate. In these books, mermaids and humans regard each other as entirely discrete groups, even if, as in *Above World*, mermaids are genetically and technologically modified humans. In these stories the identity group of which one is a member is vitally important; neither humans nor mermaids trust members of the other group, and crossing between worlds is viewed with extreme suspicion. Fluidity of identity may be possible but is heavily frowned upon; one is expected to stay with the group one originally belongs to. Main characters in these stories tend to rebel against these social strictures and either cross from world to world or choose an identity that makes life in both worlds possible. This subset of texts suggests the difficulty and pain of choosing and maintaining a fluid identity in societies that have rules or cultural norms meant to prevent such identities from existing, a point initially raised by Spencer's and Hurley's work about the complexity and importance of trans people's readings of and identification with "The Little Mermaid." Since Andersen, stories featuring mermaids have dealt with questions about who people choose to be and where they belong, evoking both the complicated nature and decision-making process of identity (as Spencer and Hurley point out) and the possibility of someone with a complex and multifaceted identity finding places to fit in. These narratives portray young adults approaching their own adulthoods and discovering new worlds they could be part of, all while trying to realize fully their own complicated identities and to find their own places to belong, both inside and outside their existing families and original homes.

Having an identity that stretches between the human and mermaid worlds means that human and mermaid protagonists often become entangled in political problems unique to mermaid culture. These problems often stem from one or more mermaids either attempting to gain or to maintain a position of political power and leadership. Human characters newly introduced to the mermaid world may be caught in these struggles as potential candidates for political leadership themselves or as someone personally connected to the sitting government. In both cases, however, identity and politics are interrelated; characters' connections to the mermaid world involve them in mermaid political struggles, and mermaid political struggles can be influenced by who the characters are and what actions they choose to take. One example of this is the character of Tristan in *The Vicious Deep* trilogy; he discovers he is a half-mermaid prince, and enters the competition to become Sea King. Although at first he wants the position, he sees over the course of the competition what terrible effects the struggle for power can have, and the damage it can cause. Tristan wins the title of Sea King but yields it to his friend and fellow competitor Kurt. Without his mermaid heritage, Tristan would not have been involved in undersea political machinations in the first place, but being involved in these machinations also shows him what kind of person he wants to be, allowing him to make choices in line with that identity. To readers, such stories make clear that a person's identity can have political elements and ramifications, but also that politics can have an influence, for good or ill, on the identity a person claims or chooses to claim.

Political problems are not the only influences on main characters' identities and choices. Identity can also be influenced by the romantic or familial love that brought characters into contact with both the mermaid and human worlds to begin with. Stories that focus on romantic love often posit potential relationships in which one member is human (or human-seeming) and the other is a mermaid, creating a reason for one or both characters to want to bridge worlds or to choose a more fluid identity. One example of this occurs in *Of Poseidon*, in which Emma discovers she is half-mermaid and wants to be able to change between human and mermaid form so she can be with the boy she loves no matter which world he lives in. Other stories focus on both familial and romantic love as a possible influence on identity—for instance, Lena of *The Mermaid's Mirror* journeys to the mermaid world to reunite with her mother but falls in love while living there. The presence of both her mother's family and her boyfriend in the mermaid world keeps Lena interested in living underwater to the point that she considers becoming a mermaid permanently. There are also stories in which main characters leave the world they know for family reasons alone, often to save or to rescue one or more family members. Most of these stories include an initial tension between the main character's romantic commitments and familial commitments, although the reason for this tension varies from story to story. These texts imply that both romantic relationships and familial relationships are deeply important to young adults, but that the novelty and intensity of romantic relationships can potentially challenge or bring conflict to existing familial relationships. In most cases, this conflict is resolved by redefining family to include the main character's significant other, either implicitly (Lily's father in *Just for Fins* gives Lily's boyfriend Quince the ability to shift between human and mermaid form so he can share her life in both worlds) or explicitly (Emma and Galen marry in *Of Neptune*).[3] *Just for Fins* illustrates one way this redefinition can happen—by granting fluidity of identity to the originally human (or human-seeming) protagonist.

Notably, the fluidity of identity that occurs among the main characters in YA mermaid fiction is rarely granted to the adult characters. In stories featuring one land parent and one sea parent, for instance, the mother is always a mermaid and is often limited to living in one of the two worlds for part or all of the narrative (usually the mermaid world, although the mermaid mother in *The Vicious Deep* lives in the human world). Similarly, the human fathers are limited to living in the human world. While the protagonist may move from the land to the sea and back again in these stories, their parents may not be able to do the same, suggesting an eventual solidification of identity over time and in connection with adulthood.

This ability of protagonists in young adult mermaid fiction to move between the human and mermaid worlds is often facilitated by the possibility of physical transformation. While many of the adults in these stories do not have or have lost the ability to change forms, the young adults can shift between their human and mermaid bodies, a metamorphosis echoing the physical changes that are part of adolescence.

Transformation and Identity

Waller suggests that "[t]here is a clear correspondence" between the puberty-induced physical transformations of adolescence and the metamorphoses that occur in paranormal young adult literature, pointing out that bodily changes faced by adolescents are transmuted through fiction into "fantastic transformation into a body that is materially, and particularly physically, 'other'" (Waller 44). In young adult mermaid fiction, the ability to transform from a mermaid to a human, or vice versa, is tied into the concept of identity and can be seen as a metaphor for the transformation involved in moving through adolescence and into adulthood. (This metaphor is made particularly explicit in *Real Mermaids Don't Wear Toe Rings*, in which Jade transforms into a mermaid for the first time on the day her first menstrual period begins.)

However, as with the transition to adulthood, the transformation from human to mermaid is not always straightforward or easily managed. In some YA mermaid stories, perhaps as a nod to Andersen, changing form is associated with acute physical or emotional pain, or a transformation that is supposed to be easy to undertake may be unpredictable or uncontrollable. Sometimes the transformation can occur only once or in one direction, making a change back to one's original body impossible. These potential elements of transformation find parallels in the bodily changes of adolescence; young adults experience through puberty what it is like to have their bodies change with little to no ability to control those changes. Medically induced bodily transformation occurs in mermaid fiction as well. In *The Twice Lost*, a newly discovered medical advance lets Luce decide whether she wants to undo her transformation into a mermaid or to remain as she is, with the understanding that this choice will be final. She has to choose one body or the other, one identity or the other—but not both, again indicating an ultimate solidity of identity that comes with adulthood after the choices of young adulthood.

The *Above World* series takes a different view of medically induced bodily transformation by separating the relatively fixed nature of the body post-transformation from the more mutable nature of identity. Aluna must decide with finality whether she wants a mermaid body or a human body, and at the end of *Above World*, the first book, she chooses a mermaid body. However, once Aluna has chosen her preferred body type, she is not prevented from living either on land or underwater; in fact, a substantial portion of the series involves Aluna's friends creating adaptive technology for her that will allow her to ride a horse and engage in other activities on land with the tailed body she has chosen to have. Her future is not determined by her physicality, and her identity is not determined by what her body looks like or is able to do, pointing to an ability to counterbalance bodily form with the identity fluidity necessary to continue moving between worlds.

Other mermaid stories forgo the need for a final choice entirely, allowing their main characters to keep the ability to transform physically and to claim both land and sea as part of their identities. For instance, Lily in *Forgive My Fins* can move between land and sea at will, with her body shifting depending on where she is. Though at several points in the series it appears that Lily will have to give up her ability to become a mermaid physically, she never does, and her human boyfriend Quince is eventually given the ability to shapeshift as well. Stories of this sort present a more mutable form of bodies and of identity, in which one final stable form is never reached, and in which growth and change are near-constants. This textual focus indicates that, in fact, a stable form of identity may not exist at all—that identity and bodies may be constantly in transition—and thus that flexible methods of dealing with ongoing changes are not just available but deeply valuable.

By dealing with issues of transformation and identity in a fictional context, young adult mermaid stories highlight different ways in which these issues could potentially be addressed and considered in a young adult's life. Identity may be considered the result of a series of choices, where the endpoint is the final, fixed identity a person has chosen, or it may be understood as something more fluid, in which a person may belong to more than one category at the same time and may be able to move between different identities in different environments. Similarly, physical transformation may be perceived as something permanent and irrevocable, as a bodily change separate from identity, or as an ongoing process that has no well-defined endpoint. These different ways of regarding identity and physicality present readers with different potential methods of making choices and perceiving their own identities as they move from adolescence to adulthood and decide what type of adult they want to be.

Conclusion

Mermaid young adult books are an intriguing amalgamation of elements of mermaid legend and lore and themes relevant to young adult readers. Such disparate legendary and fairy-tale elements as mermaids' ability to come to land, mermaid-human romances, and the pain mermaids can suffer upon taking human form make appearances in one or more of these stories. At the same time, mermaid stories address issues and challenges pertinent to young adult readers, such as identity, transformation, and dealing with the liminality of being a young adult progressing into adulthood and the adult world. Although these stories all contain mermaids, each story's methods of dealing with the issues and challenges mentioned in this chapter vary, providing the young adult reader with many potential ways that identity, bodily changes, one's own choices, or the transition to adulthood might be perceived and traversed. Not all identities are fixed and immutable. Not all bodily changes are permanent, and some are negotiable.

These stories also, through the filter of fiction and fantasy, deal with romantic relationships and the impact those relationships can have on one's identity. Various elements of love stories in young adult literature have been criticized, but at their core, stories about romantic love address questions about what romantic love is, how romantic love looks and feels to someone involved in it, and how to navigate a romantic relationship, including when to end it. Much has been written and will yet be written about whether or not young adult literature has helpful or harmful answers to these questions, but those conversations do not alter the importance and relevance of these questions to young adult readers, who are learning about and exploring what their own romantic lives might look like in their real lives and through the fiction they consume.

Familial love and relationships are an equally significant aspect of mermaid stories. At the same time that the young adult protagonists of these stories are struggling to discover who they are and what they want in life, they are renegotiating their roles in their own families. Sometimes this renegotiation involves discovering that their families are different than they thought, or that there are family secrets that have been kept from them; sometimes it involves the geographic and/or emotional separation of different members of a family, with the young adult caught in the middle. It may even involve the loss of a family member through death or distance. Mermaid stories provide a fictional lens through which to examine one's position in one's own family as well as familial changes and challenges; the separate existences of the human and mermaid worlds can symbolize the distance between childhood and adulthood, and the difficulty, but also the possibility, of finding a way to keep connections to both.

The existence of mermaids and magic in young adult fiction provides an opportunity to look at issues of identity, choice, and transformation that contemporary young adults face in different contexts and from different perspectives, and the ways in which these books speak to or deal with the potential mutability of identity is crucial not just in understanding the books themselves but also in understanding their readers. For young adult readers, like the protagonists of mermaid young adult stories, have the ability to choose the worlds they want to live in when they read, and the worlds they choose tell us who they are.

Notes

1. Both Spencer and Hurley have interesting things to say about the connection between identity in Andersen's and Disney's "The Little Mermaid" and trans identity. Spencer argues that both iterations of "The Little Mermaid" lend themselves to trans readings, and Hurley argues that the reported cultural connection between trans children and "The Little Mermaid" needs to be investigated more deeply and discussed in all its complexity. "The Little Mermaid" lends itself to questions of identity and self-identification in ways that these stories, which feature mermaids who never examine their own identities, do not.

2. Alice Hoffman's 2001 novel *Aquamarine*, on which the 2006 film is loosely based, gives Aquamarine neither the bodily transformation nor the life on land she experiences in the film. The novel's Aquamarine is deposited in a swimming pool by a storm, befriending Hailey and Claire and falling in love with teenage boy Raymond before becoming so sickened by living in the chlorinated water that she must return to the ocean.

3. In a few instances, the tensions cannot be resolved, and the main characters either choose or are left with their family as their relationships with their potential significant others end, that aspect of their identity ended or lost. Lena in *The Mermaid's Mirror* deserves special notice here. She has both a land boyfriend and a sea boyfriend in the course of her story. At the end of the story, rather than choosing between them when she chooses to return to land to live, she is so shattered by her undersea experiences that she ends her relationships with both of them.

Works Cited

Banks, Anna. *Of Neptune*. Feiwel and Friends, 2014.
Banks, Anna. *Of Poseidon*. Feiwel and Friends, 2012.
Barrie, J. M. *Peter and Wendy*. Charles Scribner's Sons, 1911.
Blackmore, Peter. *Miranda: A Comedy in Three Acts*. W. H. Baker, 1948.
Brown, Anne Greenwood. *Lies Beneath*. Random House, 2012.
Boudreau, Helene. *Real Mermaids Don't Wear Toe Rings*. Sourcebooks, 2010.
Childs, Tera Lynn. *Fins Are Forever*. Katherine Tegen Books, 2011.
Childs, Tera Lynn. *Forgive My Fins*. Katherine Tegen Books, 2010.
Childs, Tera Lynn. *Just for Fins*. Katherine Tegen Books, 2013.
Cordova, Zoraida. *The Savage Blue*. Sourcebooks, 2013.
Cordova, Zoraida. *The Vast and Brutal Sea*. Sourcebooks, 2014.
Cordova, Zoraida. *The Vicious Deep*. Sourcebooks, 2012.
Crawford, Joseph. *The Twilight of the Gothic? Vampire Fiction and the Rise of the Paranormal Romance*. U of Wales P, 2014.
Davies, Anna. *Wrecked*. Simon and Schuster, 2012.
Deebs, Tracy. *Tempest Rising*. Walker 2011.

Fraser, Lucy. "Reading and Retelling Girls across Cultures: Mermaid Tales in Japanese and English." *Japan Forum*, vol. 26, no. 2, 2014, pp. 246–64.

Freitas, Donna. "The Next Dead Thing." *Publishers Weekly*, vol. 255, no. 46, 2008, pp. 23–24.

Friedman, Aimee. *Sea Change*. Scholastic, 2009.

Hoffman, Alice. *Aquamarine*. Scholastic, 2001.

Holbek, Bengt. "Hans Christian Andersen's Use of Folktales." *Merveilles & Contes*, vol. 4, no. 2, 1990, pp. 220–32.

Hurley, Nat. "The Little Transgender Mermaid: A Shape-Shifting Tale." *Seriality and Texts for Young People: The Compulsion to Repeat*, edited by Mavis Reimer, Nyala Ali, Deanna England, and Melanie Dennis Unrau, Palgrave Macmillan, 2014, pp. 258–80.

Jones, Guy Pearce, and Constance Bridges Jones. *Peabody's Mermaid*. Random House, 1946.

Madigan, L. K. *The Mermaid's Mirror*. Houghton Mifflin Harcourt, 2010.

Mortensen, Finn Hauberg. "The Little Mermaid: Icon and Disneyfication." *Scandinavian Studies*, vol. 80, no. 4, 2008, pp. 437–54.

Porter, Sarah. *The Twice Lost*. Houghton Mifflin Harcourt, 2013.

Reese, Jenn. *Above World*. Candlewick Press, 2012.

Reese, Jenn. *Horizon*. Candlewick Press, 2014.

Reese, Jenn. *Mirage*. Candlewick Press, 2013.

Spencer, Leland G. "Performing Transgender Identity in *The Little Mermaid*: From Andersen to Disney." *Communication Studies*, vol. 65, no. 1, 2014, pp. 112–27.

Waller, Alison. *Constructing Adolescence in Fantastic Realism*. Routledge, 2009.

Warner, Marina. *From the Beast to the Blonde: On Fairy Tales and Their Tellers*. Farrar, Straus and Giroux, 1995.

Wells, H. G. *The Sea Lady*. D. Appleton, 1902.

White, Susan. "Split Skins: Female Agency and Bodily Mutilation in The Little Mermaid." *Film Theory Goes to the Movies*, edited by Jim Collins, Hilary Radner, and Ava Preacher Collins, Routledge, 1993, pp. 182–95.

Williams, Christy. "Mermaid Tales on Screen: Splash, The Little Mermaid, and Aquamarine." *Beyond Adaptation: Essays on Radical Transformations of Original Works*, edited by Phyllis Frus and Christy Williams, McFarland, 2010, pp. 194–206.

Further Reading

Banks, Anna. *Of Neptune*. Feiwel and Friends, 2014.

Banks, Anna. *Of Poseidon*. Feiwel and Friends, 2012.

Banks, Anna. *Of Triton*. Feiwel and Friends, 2013.

Brown, Anne Greenwood. *Deep Betrayal*. Delacorte Press, 2013.

Brown, Anne Greenwood. *Lies Beneath*. Random House, 2012.

Brown, Anne Greenwood. *Promise Bound*. Delacorte Press, 2014.

Boudreau, Helene. *Real Mermaids Don't Hold Their Breath*. Sourcebooks, 2012.

Boudreau, Helene. *Real Mermaids Don't Need High Heels*. Sourcebooks, 2013.

Boudreau, Helene. *Real Mermaids Don't Sell Sea Shells*. Sourcebooks, 2014.

Boudreau, Helene. *Real Mermaids Don't Wear Toe Rings*. Sourcebooks, 2010.

Childs, Tera Lynn. *Fins Are Forever*. Katherine Tegen Books, 2011.

Childs, Tera Lynn. *Forgive My Fins*. Katherine Tegen Books, 2010.

Childs, Tera Lynn. *Just for Fins*. Katherine Tegen Books, 2013.

Cordova, Zoraida. *The Savage Blue*. Sourcebooks, 2013.

Cordova, Zoraida. *The Vast and Brutal Sea*. Sourcebooks, 2014.

Cordova, Zoraida. *The Vicious Deep*. Sourcebooks, 2012.

Davies, Anna. *Wrecked*. Simon and Schuster, 2012.

Deebs, Tracy. *Tempest Revealed*. Walker, 2013.

Deebs, Tracy. *Tempest Rising*. Walker, 2011.

Deebs, Tracy. *Tempest Unleashed*. Walker, 2012.

Dolamore, Jaclyn. *Between the Sea and Sky*. Bloomsbury USA, 2011.

Donnelly, Jennifer. *Deep Blue*. Disney/Hyperion, 2015.

Friedman, Aimee. *Sea Change*. Scholastic, 2009.

Madigan, L. K. *The Mermaid's Mirror*. Houghton Mifflin Harcourt, 2010.

Nielson, Sheila A. *Forbidden Sea*. Scholastic, 2010.

Nielson, Sheila A. *Shadow in the Sea*. Sheila A. Nielson, 2015.

Pearce, Jackson. *Fathomless*. Little, Brown, 2012.

Porter, Sarah. *Lost Voices*. Houghton Mifflin Harcourt, 2011.

Porter, Sarah. *The Twice Lost*. Houghton Mifflin Harcourt, 2013.

Porter, Sarah. *Waking Storms*. Houghton Mifflin Harcourt, 2012.

Reese, Jenn. *Above World*. Candlewick Press, 2012.

Reese, Jenn. *Horizon*. Candlewick Press, 2014.

Reese, Jenn. *Mirage*. Candlewick Press, 2013.

5

Who Are These Books *Really* For?
Police-Violence YA, Black Youth Activism,
and the Implied White Audience

Kaylee Jangula Mootz

Angie Thomas's first novel, *The Hate U Give* (2017), fits perfectly the descriptor "blockbuster." *The Hate U Give* (hereafter, *THUG*) debuted as number one on the *New York Times* Young Adult top sellers list on February 28, 2017 (Alter). In the first month, *THUG* had more than 100,000 copies in print. *THUG* represents the crest in a wave of Black Lives Matter–inspired activist literature for teens, with more still coming. Through an investigation into the genre of police-violence YA, I have identified several significant conventions: embracing Black identity; confrontation of white privilege; attention to police brutality and structural racism; the impetus to speak out; and active remembering. The genre also shares many similarities with street lit[1]—a genre defined by the politics, poetics, and culture of hip-hop (Cooper 55)—and hip-hop literary aesthetics,[2] though police-violence YA is targeted to a younger (and perhaps wider/whiter) audience. To illustrate the genre's conventions, I have chosen to compare and contrast four texts: Angie Thomas's *THUG*; Jason Reynolds and Brendan Kiely's *All American Boys* (2015); Nic Stone's *Dear Martin* (2017); and Tony Medina's *I Am Alfonso Jones* (2017). Each text offers a pointed look at police violence against Black youth and its aftermath. The genre is not defined by a specific form or narrative style; rather, it is defined by the shared subject matter and emphasis on racial justice. Police-violence YA texts offer recognition to Black teen readers by tapping into their personal experiences of racism and violence and educate white teen readers about racism faced by their peers. The different approaches to blackness and whiteness by these texts will be investigated at length later in this essay but ultimately these differences point to the texts' perception that white teens do not understand their Black peers' experiences and moreover do not understand their place in discussions of race and violence. While attempting to fill these gaps in understanding, these texts offer characters who confront racism and speak out, either in individual interactions or in large-scale protests, thereby modeling social justice activism for both Black teen readers and their would-be allies, urging them to rise up in revolution themselves.

Despite the many positive aspects of the genre, I have identified another problematic trend: a pandering to a white teen audience. While this trend could be explained by many factors, including expectations of mainstream publishers, it is concerning that texts about Black youth activism often seem to be roadmaps for understanding whiteness during times of racial tension, rather than inspirational reflections of radical Black youth. Nevertheless, I argue that all four texts have something productive to offer in conversations about racial violence. Multiple narratives aimed at dismantling white supremacy and systemic racism by foregrounding powerful depictions of Black youth and explicit discussions about confronting white privilege are necessary to begin upsetting racial hierarchies. This genre signifies a vibrant brushstroke in the portrait of antiracist literature for teens and therefore warrants extended study.

Contextualizing Black Lives Matter, Children's Literature, and Police Violence Texts

The Obama era, while filled with many triumphs for the nation, was plagued by an epidemic of racialized police violence. In response, the *Washington Post* launched an interactive database tracking all police shooting fatalities in the nation ("995"). After compiling all of the data and controlling for population variables, the *Washington Post* concluded that Black Americans were 2.5 times as likely to be shot and killed by police as white people (Lowery). Furthermore, the *Post* concluded that unarmed Black Americans are five times as likely as unarmed white Americans to be shot and killed by the police. However, politicians and much of the general public pointed to President Obama, the nation's first Black president, as evidence that the US had become postracial and "color-blind." Many Americans were, and still are, invested in understanding police violence against Black and brown people as deserved, believing that Black criminality was to blame for violence against Black victims (Taylor 27).

After the acquittal of George Zimmerman for the murder of Trayvon Martin in 2013, a particularly devastating blow to the nation's people of color and their allies, #BlackLivesMatter became the rallying cry for those seeking justice against police violence. What started as a Twitter hashtag, created by Black women activists Patrice Cullors, Alicia Garza, and Opal Tometi, soon grew to be a national movement.[3] Russell Rickford, in his analytical profile of the movement, has dubbed Black Lives Matter (hereafter, BLM) a movement that recognizes the shortcomings of traditional avenues for achieving justice and that has "wholeheartedly embraced the arena of the street" (36). They are not afraid to be loud, in the way (often blocking highways or shopping malls with walls of bodies), and proudly Black. Rickford pointedly writes of their approach, "As exponents of Black Lives Matter are keenly aware, rituals of propriety will not dignify dark skin that society as a whole detests and degrades" (36). It is unclear if their unapologetically Black activist stance has helped or hurt them in the face of opposition. Police spokespeople and apologists, according to Rickford, have been behind most of the backlash against BLM, encouraging their demonization and characterization as a hate group (40). BLM represents not only the defining social justice movement of the Obama era,[4] but also an extension of the long history of political activism in the African American community, which has continually been met with suspicion, contention, and derision.[5]

BLM is certainly not the first or only social movement to be reflected in literature for children. In fact, dozens of children's books have already been published about the 2016 election and the subsequent Women's March on Washington. But long before the new millennium and rapid-fire publishing technology, children were being included in social movements via children's literature. To put it more bluntly, literature for Black children has always been political.[6]

In addition to the influence of political history on children's publishing, scholars, librarians, and parents have been pushing for more-diverse representations (including race, gender, disability, class, and sexuality) in books for children. For decades, scholars have criticized the "all-white world"[7] of children's publishing, which overwhelmingly preferences white authors, protagonists, and casts of characters.[8] This prioritization of white child readers over readers of color has been the subject of critical discussion in scholarly and nonscholarly circles for many years, but only recently have publishers begun to respond. Most often attributed to the #weneeddiversebooks movement,[9] publishers have been, slowly, complying with the demand for books by and about people of color.

Authors of color have also publicly responded to the continued dearth of books for children of color. Walter Dean Myers has written extensively about being an African American author for children and teens when there are so few texts for and about Black youth. In 2014 Myers wrote to the *New York Times* asking, "Where are the people of color in children's books?" and discussing what he perceives to be his contribution in countering this lack. Myers writes, in encountering texts like his, that young Black readers "have been struck by the recognition of themselves in the story, a validation of their existence as human beings, an acknowledgement of their value by someone who understands who they are." Because the world offers so little affirmation to youth of color from low socioeconomic backgrounds, Myers creates each book with this goal in mind: "to make [youth of color] human in the eyes of the readers and, especially, in their own eyes" ("Where"). Curiously, even Myers, writing explicitly for Black youth, assumes in this passage that "readers" means white readers. Furthermore, Myers's assumption that white readers must be instructed about people of color signifies the larger problem of white readers continuing to be preferenced, even in books for Black youth. However, Myers's instruction of white readers, and his writing against the narrative of Black youth as always already criminal by depicting authentic, multidimensional characters of color, is a political act. Redeeming readers of color by reflecting their humanity in spite of narratives that would rather see them degraded is a form of activism. Texts from Myers and authors like him contribute to the children's and young adult literature landscape by attempting to fill the pervasive lack of antiracist texts that has continued in children's publishing for decades despite numerous calls from scholars, teachers, and communities for affirming representations of youth of color.

Similarly, police-violence YA is explicitly political in its discussions of racial and police violence in the US and ruminates at length on what it means to be a Black teen when facing institutional and interpersonal racism. The police-violence YA novel is a new and rapidly expanding subgenre to the field of young adult literature. The four texts I have chosen are representative though not exhaustive and will likely be only the tip of the iceberg for this genre. Several police-violence YA texts were released in 2018, including Jay Coles's *Tyler Johnson Was Here*, Mark Oshiro's *Anger Is a Gift*, and a film adaptation of *THUG*.[10] However, it is unclear if the genre's rapid proliferation and popularity can withstand the political chaos of the post-Obama era. It is equally difficult to deduce whether the genre's popularity is due to the texts' personal relevance for Black readers or to the novelty for white readers of nicely packaged Black characters and plots pointed at investigating whiteness. The question then becomes, as my title suggests, who are police-violence YA texts really for?

Do these Black-authored YA texts about Black victims of violence uplift and empower Black readers? Or do they foreclose Black experience in order to educate white readers about whiteness?

Plot Overviews

THUG is narrated by Starr Carter, who witnesses her childhood friend Khalil, who is Black, shot by a white police officer. As the novel progresses, Starr must come to terms with her identity as a young Black girl from "the ghetto" and learn to speak out against the racial injustices she and her community face.

All American Boys is a novel told in alternating chapters with two narrators: Rashad, a smart and creative Black teen who is assaulted by police officer Paul Galluzzo, and Quinn, a white teen who witnesses Rashad's assault. As Rashad recovers from his assault and decides whether he will march in the protest with his friends, Quinn must confront his own racism and decide if he will speak out against what he has seen. Interestingly, it is Quinn who goes through the most drastic change in the text and who spends the most time meditating on the question of racism in American culture.

Dear Martin follows main character Justyce in his senior year of high school at a mostly white private boarding school. Justyce and his best friend Manny learn to confront the racism they experience at school, only to have Manny shot for playing loud music. After Manny's death Justyce nearly gives up on his quest to be "like Martin" (Luther King Jr.), but comes to understand that the fight to achieve civil rights is not over and that he must continue moving forward the best he can.

I Am Alfonso Jones is a graphic novel that uses nonlinear time to tell the story of Alfonso Jones, a Black teen killed by police for holding a coat hanger, which the officer claimed was a gun. Alfonso finds himself riding the Ghost Train, accompanied by other victims of police violence called The Ancestors. Alfonso learns he must ride the train until there is justice for his death and for the deaths of the other ancestors. Unfortunately, justice never arrives and the train never meets its terminus.

Contemplating Black Identity vs. White Privilege

A powerful element of the police-violence YA genre is the way it embraces blackness. Like street lit, police-violence YA is imbued with Black cultural references and "street knowledge" of Black history, politics, pop culture, and slang.[11] In each of the novels (with the exception of *Dear Martin*), the Black teen characters are proud of their blackness, are experts in their own culture, and are not afraid to "educate" the other characters and the readers about what it means to be Black today. For example, Starr references repeatedly Black Jesus, the Black Panthers, and other activists. Similarly, the students in *I Am Alfonso Jones* are very invested in Black history, culture, art, and literature. However, this embrace of blackness is not without difficulty; the Black teens must repeatedly navigate the tensions between unapologetic blackness, characterized as belonging to the younger generation, and respectability politics, characterized as belonging to their parents' generation. The unfortunate reality, each narrative seems to suggest, is that regardless of on which side of the tension the Black teens exist, neither will protect them from danger. The most illustrative example comes from Rashad's father directly following his attack. He demands, "Were your pants sagging?" and continues to insinuate that Rashad's clothing and demeanor provoked the attack from Officer Galluzzo (Reynolds and Kiely 49, 50). Rashad's father is characterized as part of an old-school Black respectability politics, whereas his brother Spoony is characterized as unapologetically Black, with dreadlocks, oversized clothing, and a "gritty" nineties hip-hop style (51). Rashad must decide whose side of Black politics he will align with, or if he will create his own.

Alternatively, the weakest example of embracing blackness is offered by *Dear Martin*. *Dear Martin* offers a surface-level, and perhaps uneven, picture of blackness. Justyce and Manny, the two principal Black characters, seem unfamiliar with Black history or culture beyond a baseline understanding of MLK Jr. Unlike the Black teens from other texts, they rarely defend their blackness, engage in cultural criticism, or consider the implications of their appearance or affect, even after Justyce is wrongly cuffed and detained by police. Readers have criticized Stone on this issue, as well as the author's characterization of Black girls, a subject which I will return to later.

Concomitantly, while the genre considers the struggle of navigating blackness in dangerous times, the genre also expends significant energy on narratives of confrontation with whiteness and white privilege. In *All American Boys*, Quinn spends much of the narrative confronting his whiteness and privilege. One of Quinn's basketball teammates, English, who is a friend of Rashad's, condemns Quinn's willingness to act as if Rashad's assault does not concern him—"White boy like you can just walk away whenever you want. [. . .] like this shit don't even exist" (Reynolds and Kiely 176). English's indictment is a turning point for Quinn as he begins to realize the privilege he is afforded by his white skin (180). Quinn thinks through his privilege, laying bare for the reader what it means to be white when Black youth are being assaulted and murdered—"They were probably afraid, too. Afraid of people like Paul. Afraid of cops in general. Hell, they were probably afraid of people like me. I didn't blame them. I'd be afraid too. [. . .] But I didn't have to be because my shield was that I was white" (180). Quinn models for white readers what purposeful reflection on whiteness and privilege looks like without being patronizing. Quinn recognizes that his whiteness has shaped his experience of the world, a realization that is important for white readers to come to terms with as well. Quinn's understanding of himself continues to grow as he is repeatedly forced to confront his racism and privilege, illustrating that overcoming socialized racism is a process that continues throughout one's lifetime.

Characters in *Dear Martin* are also asked to confront their whiteness and racial biases. However, these characters are not nearly as receptive as Quinn to critique. In fact, they react with hostility. Rather than discuss each moment of racial bias, I have chosen to consider the white character Sarah-Jane, who educates those who perpetuate stereotypes and racist rhetorics. When main antagonist Jared, a rich white classmate, announces he believes that racism no longer exists, all races are equal, and that America is "color blind," Sarah-Jane confronts him—"I know you'd prefer to ignore this stuff because you *benefit* from it. [. . .] You and Manny, who are equal in pretty much every way but race, could commit the same crime, but it's almost guaranteed that he would receive a harsher punishment than you" (Stone 23, 28). Sarah-Jane's continual arguments with Jared over his racism, in which she offers extensive factual information (as if heavily researched), refute all of the classic arguments used as evidence for racial equality. By educating Jared, Sarah-Jane is also educating the white reader and dispelling racist myths disseminated by white supremacy. Like Reynolds and Kiely's choice of Quinn to voice white introspection, Stone uses Sarah-Jane to instruct white audiences about their privilege. These similar tactics in *Dear Martin* and *All American Boys* point to the genre's recruiting of white teen readers to the side of active antiracism. These troubling moments of preferencing white character development over Black experience may be due to the belief that it is easier for a white reader to accept racial confrontation from a likable white character than from a character of color. While there is also an intent to educate white readers in *THUG* and *Alfonso Jones*, these moments of instruction are voiced by Black characters. Both strategies represent the genre's attention to dismantling white supremacy. However, when comparing each pair, *All American Boys* and *Dear Martin*'s strategy forecloses the possibility of Black youth speaking for themselves about the ways their peers' white privilege affects their experience in the world.

Thug Life: Confronting Structural Racism

One of the most significant similarities that police-violence YA shares with street lit/hip-hop texts is its confrontation of structural racism.[12] Street-lit texts are defined by a hip-hop aesthetic, which Brittney Cooper describes as "a generational confrontation with economic lack, privation, and the reality of civil rights era and Black Power era dreams deferred" (56). Police-violence YA, like street lit, enacts hip-hop "truth telling" by exposing "the breaks" (unfortunate circumstances) that shape the characters' lives, like racialized poverty, abuse, violence, and targeting by police (61). Each text in this study is invested in the truth telling of structural racism and exposing how it defines the lives of Black youth.

The largest, looming presence of structural racism in these texts is the police. All four of these texts have a discussion of "the rules" for interacting with police while Black (Thomas 20; Reynolds and Kiely 50; Medina 131; Stone 8). Each text phrases "the rules" differently, but all essentially communicate that Black people need to protect themselves by being completely obedient, submissive, and silent when confronted by the police. Unfortunately, each text proves time and again that "the rules" do not actually protect Black youth from violence at the hands of the police. Each text mourns the loss of Black youth, men, and women, and each text offers a victim who was brutalized or killed for nothing or next to nothing (e.g., a loud radio or a broken taillight). Furthermore, each text investigates the ways that victims are blamed for their own deaths and discredited by the media. The violence against these victims is explicitly denounced by the main characters, and any voices attempting defamation are disregarded as mal-intentioned. However, the genre does not only focus on the extreme events of police violence, arguing that attention is needed for all of the stratified layers of racial oppression. To paraphrase English from *All American Boys*, Black teens should not have to die for white people to care about systemic racism (Brendan and Kiely 175).

THUG's title is inspired by a Tupac Shakur[13] song, "Thug Life," which is an acronym for "The Hate U Give Little Infants Fucks Everybody." Readers learn this early in the text from Khalil on the night he is shot, and the idea of "thug life" repeats throughout the text. Starr's father, Maverick, breaks down the logic of THUG for Starr and helps her to understand its meaning (Thomas 168). The "U," Maverick explains, is the people in power, and the "Little Infants" are not simply children, but all the oppressed. Maverick tells Starr that those in power work to keep the oppressed down via lack of opportunities, jobs, and quality education, and via drugs and alcohol being funneled into poor neighborhoods of color. This oppression limits their choices and often results in their criminalization (169). Maverick tells Starr, "That's the hate they're giving us, baby, a system designed against us. That's Thug Life" (170). The text in this moment refutes the narrative that being a thug is a free choice, but rather a constrained choice designed by systemic racism. This is a powerful moment in the text: likable, funny, intelligent Starr recognizes that if her circumstances had been different she might have chosen thug life, by dealing drugs or being part of a gang—the same choices that supposedly made Khalil responsible for his own death. Thomas forces readers to consider their own circumstances and question if they, like Starr, may have made the same constrained choices too. By asking them to consider their own privilege (or burdens) and the wider structures of racism that dictate life experiences for so many people, white readers (and potentially middle- and upper-class Black readers) must investigate their racial and class assumptions and decide what it is that they will do about it.

Like *THUG*, *I Am Alfonso Jones* considers the layers of structural racism that lead to the deaths of Alfonso and the Ancestors. A particularly striking example is the observations made by several characters denouncing how the white gaze consumes blackness for entertainment but denies Black personhood. When speaking out against Alfonso's death, his grandfather makes this speech:

> In America, if you are black, you can run on a football field, a baseball field, a track field, and a basketball court but God forbid you should run from the police. Your blood'll run from your flesh and your breath will run out of time. When an unarmed citizen—a child—is shot and killed in a rush to judgment, none of us are safe. (Medina 47)

This same narrative repeats later when Alfonso's classmates are grieving his death. A student comments: "We're only good enough to entertain them with singing and dancing—and sports!" (98). These two indictments, of white people's consumption of Black culture via singing and dancing, and Black athleticism through sports, and the concomitant disregard for Black lives as anything other than entertainment is particularly resonant at this contemporary moment, especially in light of the #TakeAKnee movement.[14] Medina points to racism behind the desires to consume Black people while silencing them. What was once, perhaps, viewed positively as a recognition of Black talent or a way out of poverty is now exposed as just another way that white culture consumes and then disposes of Black lives. These moments validate Black youths' laments over their continued devaluation despite their collective talents and intellects. Alternatively, this will be a radical concept for white readers to confront. Asking them to investigate the ways that they are directly complicit in these racist structures is radical and will produce discomfort, but Medina is unapologetic in his purpose—to expose the ways that American culture continues to oppress, disenfranchise, and dispose of Black people. His express confrontations with racism are meant to deconstruct racism through a Black lens and potentially inspire his readership to speak out against racial injustice.

A Call to Activism: But Who Gets to Speak Out?

It is not surprising that, considering BLM's influence on the genre, activism, protest, and speaking out are central parts of police-violence YA. In fact, *THUG*, *All American Boys*, and *I Am Alfonso Jones* follow the same plot pattern: police violence early in the text; grief and struggle over how, when, and if to speak out; rising action culminating in mass protest; and resolution reflecting on the continued fight for racial justice. However, when comparing the four texts, it is necessary to ask: if police-violence YA as a genre encourages protest and activism, *who* is called to speak out? A disappointing commonality between *Dear Martin* and *All American Boys* is the silencing of Black women and girls. In fact, *Dear Martin* received a scathing review from well-known children's author Zetta Elliott for this very issue. Elliott is disturbed by "novels by Black authors about police violence against Black boys where *White girls* take center stage" and elucidates the ways that the narrative denigrates and silences Black girls, including Manny's insistence that Black girls are intimidating and the perpetual favoring of the voice of Sarah-Jane over any Black female character ("No More"). Elliott has a similar critique for *All American Boys*, noting that the only Black girl character with any voice in the text is Berry, Spoony's girlfriend, who helps organize the protest ("Nobody's"). Though Berry certainly had potential to be an instrumental character—an educated law student, savvy, kind, and an activist—she appears only briefly to visit Rashad in the hospital, and briefly at the protest where she calls names of victims into a bullhorn. This commonality gestures toward the continued devaluation of Black girlhood not only by the publishing market, which understands white girls as a target market, but also by the Black antiviolence movement itself. Other similar examples such as the creation of #SayHerName to address women victims who seem to be forgotten by BLM and the criticism of President Obama for the exclusion of Black women and girls in his "My Brother's Keeper" policy suggest that the continued focus on Black men and boys to the detriment of Black women and girls still needs to be addressed despite calls from decades of Black women activists.

In opposition to *Dear Martin* and *All American Boys*, *I Am Alfonso Jones* focuses a substantial portion of the narrative on Alfonso's mother—her grief, the ways that she has been targeted by institutional violence, and her place in the protest—and Alfonso's friend Danetta, who witnessed his murder. *Alfonso Jones* also features a Black young woman activist who helps to organize the rally and performs a spoken word poem in Alfonso's honor. The narrative of *Alfonso Jones* recognizes the importance of women to racial justice activism and highlights the interconnected community of Black activists, including considering the roles of historical activists, the Ancestors, multiple generations in Alfonso's family, and several non-Black ally characters.

Similarly, *THUG*'s narrative emphasizes Starr's place in her community as a powerful voice for justice. Starr speaks out in many ways, some small and private and others grand and public. But the most powerful moment when Starr speaks out is after the jury decides not to indict Officer 115 on any charges regarding Khalil. Starr feels the rage burning within her and *must* act. She joins the others in her community who are rioting, saying, "My anger is theirs, and theirs is mine" (393). Starr recognizes in this moment that Khalil's death and the perpetual threat of police violence affected everyone in her community, and she feels that she must participate in the communal uprising. During the riot, Starr climbs onto a car and publically recognizes Khalil by shouting into a bullhorn, "'His life mattered. Khalil lived!'" (412). Starr's efforts at proclaiming Khalil's humanity and worth culminate in this moment of shouting to the crowd, the police, and the TV news media. In this moment she speaks for Khalil, for herself, for her community, and for all Black youth. Starr's position as a formidable voice for protest recognizes the worth and power of Black girls and seems to ask Black girl readers to speak out as well.

Alternatively, Rashad's journey toward speaking out is significantly down-played in comparison to both Starr's development and the evolution of Quinn. Rashad spends most of the narrative reluctant to join the protest happening in his name (Reynolds and Kiely 199). Ultimately, it is Mrs. Fitzgerald, a kindly Black gift-shop worker, who convinces Rashad that he should walk in the march—"And it's perfectly okay for you to be afraid but remember whether you protest or not, you'll still be scared. Might as well let your voice be heard" (245). Mrs. Fitzgerald's story of regret over not marching during the civil rights movement inspires Rashad, and he forces himself to confront his experience of violence by watching the video of his attack on the news. Mrs. Fitzgerald's influence over Rashad points to the importance of intragenerational solidarity in opposing racism and encourages Black youth to understand their historical significance to the continued struggle for civil rights. Ultimately, though, this positive reinforcement of Black youth activism is eclipsed by Quinn's development into a white ally.

Quinn's ruminations over whether he should protest are given significantly more narration than Rashad's. As Quinn comes to terms with his whiteness and his complicity in systems of oppression, he realizes that if he wants anything to change, he has to speak out (Reynolds and Kiely 184). Before he makes the final decision to protest, Quinn thinks—"Nothing was going to change unless we did something about it. *We!* White people! We had to stand up and say something about it too, because otherwise it was just like what one of these posters in the crowd outside school said: OUR SILENCE IS ANOTHER KIND OF VIOLENCE" (292). This is a direct call to white teen readers. Quinn speaks directly to them and calls for their action. Reynolds and Kiely use Quinn to model white introspection, transformation, and allyship, and to explicitly ask white readers to support their Black peers when they speak out against racism.

Each of these four texts offers revolutionary teen characters, white and of color, who speak out against racism and police violence. The genre implicitly, through the struggles and triumphs of the characters, and explicitly, through directive language like "we" and "us," asks teen readers to use their voices to better the world. These books, like many past and present books for Black youth, are attempting to create radicalized young people in hopes that they will continue the struggle for racial justice. As Katharine Capshaw writes, that contemporary civil rights texts "ask children [and teens] to see themselves as an extension of black history's commitment to social change" (72). By asking readers to see themselves as an extension of history, police-violence YA recognizes that, despite views to the contrary, civil rights, racial equality, and racial justice have not been achieved.

Eve Tuck and K. Wayne Yang, in their special issue introduction on "What Justice Wants," define justice as "a political interval 'between the no longer and the not yet' [. . .] desired, deferred, haunting, always past and promised but never delivered. It is a set of political possibilities for limited relief, for continual resistance, *until*" (9). Like Tuck and Yang, police-violence YA texts reify for readers that the fight for justice is not finished in the same way that civil rights is not finished. The struggle for social justice is continual and these texts recognize the need for continued resistance. They demand that readers rise up and fight for change, while also recognizing that there is no clear end in sight. Starr concludes her narrative by thinking, "Yet I think it'll change one day. How? I don't know. When? I definitely don't know. Why? Because there will always be someone ready to fight. Maybe it's my turn. [. . .] I'll never give up. / I'll never be quiet. / I promise." (Thomas 443–444). Similarly, the last stanza of the last page of *All American Boys* features Rashad's proclamation—"For all the people who came before / us, fighting this fight, I was here, / Screaming at the top of my lungs. / Rashad Butler. / Present" (Reynolds and Kiely 310). Alfonso also recognizes the continual struggle for justice, even in the afterlife as he rides the ghost train—"Armed with my trumpet—and my Ancestors, I do my part in the struggle for peace and justice" (Medina 160). Each of these texts recognizes that justice and change is not immediate, but that speaking out and acting on their knowledge and experiences is necessary. It is the characters' responsibility, and the readers' implied responsibility, to continue the struggle.

Remembering and Recognition: Reflecting on the Genre

Despite the pandering to white readers exhibited by the genre, I argue that this genre does significant political work. Like hip-hop literature, police-violence YA demands recognition for violence against Black youth by the police. William Jelani Cobb describes the essence of street lit, "At the core of hip hop's being, its rationale for existence, is this refusal to exist as unseen and unseeable" (109). In the same way, police-violence YA forces white readers to *see*—to see the truth of police violence, the truth of white privilege, the truth of structural racism—and to recognize and acknowledge the personhood of those affected by racial injustice.

Also of political worth is the ways that police-violence YA remembers victims of police violence. Tuck and Yang write "Justice re-members, refuses to forget, refuses erasure and historical forgetting" (9). In this way police-violence YA enacts justice; by telling stories that the dominant powers would prefer to forget, this genre actively remembers racial violence at the hands of the state. Further, in the act of reading, each teen reader re-experiences the truth of race-relations and racial violence in their lives. More specifically, *THUG*, *All American Boys*, and *I Am Alfonso Jones* save the names and stories of real-world victims who face silencing. On *THUG*'s second to last page, Starr lists the names of victims of police violence, gesturing to her place in the national story of violence and forcing their names to be recalled and remembered (Thomas 443). In *All American Boys*, Berry calls into the bullhorn at the die-in for Rashad—Sean Bell, Oscar Grant, Reika Boyd, Ramarley Graham, Aiyana Jones, Freddie Gray, Michael Brown, Tamir Rice, Eric Garner, Tarika Wilson— all followed with the shout of "Absent again today!" from the crowd (Reynolds and Kiely 308). The last page of *I Am Alfonso Jones* is drawn as a wall of placards with the names, ages, dates, and locations of police-caused deaths (Medina 161). The act of remembering those who have died in this way is an act of justice and activism in the face of structural racism.

These aspects, demanding recognition and remembrance for victims of police violence, in conjunction with the genre's conventions of embracing blackness, confronting white privilege and structural racism, and the impetus to speak out, make police-violence YA a supremely important genre within the realm of anti-racist children's literature. Regardless of whether the texts in this genre act, as Rudine Sims Bishop formulates, as mirrors for Black readers looking for activist role models or windows for white readers to understand their place in unjust racial hierarchies, perhaps we can think of police-violence YA texts as maps. Christopher Myers argues that "[Children and teens] see books less as mirrors and more as maps. They are indeed searching for their place in the world, but they are also deciding where they want to go. They create, through the stories they're given, an atlas of their world, of their relationships to others, of their possible destinations." Myers's formulation is especially poignant when considering police-violence YA. I argue that police-violence YA offers readers a map for how to deal with BLM-era racial injustice, by modeling how to confront racism they experience, how to recognize and accept their privilege, and how to stand up and speak out against racism and racial violence in their world. Then, it is our job as parents, scholars, and educators to demand as many maps as possible and support the police-violence YA titles beyond just the one blockbuster title.

Notes

1. Street lit is sometimes also called ghetto lit, urban fiction, or lit hop. I generally refer to the genre as street lit or hip-hop literature.

2. For an extended study of hip-hop aesthetics, see William Jelani Cobb's *To the Break of Dawn* (2007), and for a shorter application of hip-hop aesthetics to a work of street lit, see Brittney Cooper's "'Maybe I'll Be a Poet, Rapper' . . ."

3. For a more extended history and meditation on the Black Lives Matter movement and the context from which it springs, see *Policing the Planet: Why the Policing Crisis Led to Black Lives Matter* (2016), edited by Jordan T. Camp and Christina Heatherton, and *From #Black-LivesMatter to Black Liberation* by Keeanga-Yamahtta Taylor.

4. Though still active, BLM's activist presence has fallen out of public attention since the 2016 election. Because of the constant onslaught of political crises and the media oversaturation of stories about the forty-fifth presidential administration's hijinks, reporting and public discussion of BLM and police-violence victims seem to have become an afterthought. More visible, at least at the time of this writing (spring/summer 2018), are the numerous public callouts via Facebook and Twitter of white people calling the police on Black people when nothing criminal is occurring. These callouts are not BLM affiliated but do rely on assumed general knowledge that calling the police on Black people puts their lives in immediate danger.

5. The BLM movement has inspired several offshoot activist cries and political action, including the #SayHerName movement, drawing attention to the gender disparity in BLM proper's activism, and the #TakeAKnee movement protests in the NFL. Both Say Her Name and Take A Knee were also met with the same derision directed at BLM.

6. For more information about the political work being done in literature for Black children, see: Michelle Martin's *Brown Gold: Milestones of African-American Children's Picture Books, 1845–2002* (2012); Katharine Capshaw's *Children's Literature of the Harlem Renaissance* (2004), or *Civil Rights Childhood: Picturing Liberation in African American Photobooks* (2015);

Robin Bernstein's *Racial Innocence* (2011); and Anna Mae Duane's *Suffering Childhood in Early America: Violence, Race, and the Making of the Child Victim* (2010).

7. I borrow the phrasing "All White World" from Nancy Larrick's "All-White World of Children's Books," written in 1965—often cited as one of the first articles to question the oversaturation of white children, characters, authors, and assumed readers.

8. Since 1985 the Cooperative Children's Book Center (CCBC) has been tracking the number of books published each year written by authors of color, written for children of color, and written about children of color. Their findings are striking. And though there has been some improvement in the number of minorities being represented in children's publishing, the number of white-authored texts for and about white children still drastically outweighs any other category.

9. In its current form We Need Diverse Books is a nonprofit that advocates for expanded diversity in children's publishing (you can find their website at diversebooks.org). However, this movement began as a Twitter hashtag, #weneeddiversebooks, and a Tumblr site of the same tag. Brief articles about the movement have been published by NBC news, the *Author's Guild*, and *Publishers Weekly*.

10. The film adaptation of *THUG* was generally met with positive reviews, but it is important to note that Patrisse Cullors (one of the founders of BLM) and Melina Abdullah write in the *Los Angeles Sentinel* that the film *THUG* is not a BLM film, because it re-creates narratives of Black pathology rather than directing its attention at institutionalized racism.

11. This definition of street knowledge is paraphrased from Brittney Cooper in her description of hip-hop aesthetics (56).

12. Marah Gubar also argues that a defining element of *THUG* is its articulation of structural racism. She argues that Thomas's goal in creating *THUG* was to direct the reader away from "the personal and the particular" of police violence, and to instead educate them on how structural racism affects the lives of Black youth in America. Gubar's argument is also relevant to each of the other three texts that I have chosen to compare.

13. It is interesting to me that the cultural references that Thomas preferences in *THUG* are from several decades before Starr's cultural moment, for example, Tupac Shakur, possibly the king of the golden age of hip-hop, but most popular in the late 1980s through the 1990s, and Will Smith's *Fresh Prince of Bel-Air* instead of, say, Nicki Minaj, Beyoncé, or Kendrick Lamar. Unfortunately, I do not have time to unpack these choices in this article.

14. #TakeAKnee began as a response to Colin Kaepernick's refusal to stand for the National Anthem during football games in protest against police violence. Kaepernick was extremely clear about his motivations for kneeling or sitting while his teammates stood. Ultimately, Kaepernick was let go by the 49ers and not picked up in the following year's draft, sending the message that political activism would not be tolerated on the football field. In response, the majority of players and even several coaches knelt during the national anthem in protest, which garnered extremely negative attention from white fans, conservatives, and the White House.

Works Cited

"995 shot dead by police in 2015." *Washington Post*, Dec. 2015.

Abdullah, Melina, and Patrisse Khan-Cullors. "Why 'The Hate U Give' Is Not a Black Lives Matter Movie." *Los Angeles Sentinel* 18 Oct. 2018.

Alter, Alexandra. "New Crop of Young Adult Novels Explores Race and Police Brutality." *New York Times*, 19 Mar. 2017.

Bernstein, Robin. *Racial Innocence: Performing American Childhood from Slavery to Civil Rights*. New York UP, 2011.

Bishop, Rudine Sims. "Mirrors, Windows, and Sliding Glass Doors." *Perspectives*, vol. 6, no. 3, 1990, pp. ix–xi.

Bonilla-Silva, Eduardo. *Racism without Racists: Color-Blind Racism and the Persistence of Racial Inequality in the United States*. Rowman and Littlefield, 2003.

Capshaw, Katharine. *Children's Literature of the Harlem Renaissance*. Indiana UP, 2004.

Capshaw, Katharine. *Civil Rights Childhood: Picturing Liberation in African American Photobooks*. U of Minnesota P, 2014.

Cobb, William Jelani. *To the Break of Dawn: A Freestyle on the Hip Hop Aesthetic*. New York UP, 2007.

Cooper, Brittney. "'Maybe I'll Be a Poet, Rapper': Hip-Hop Feminism and Literary Aesthetics in *Push*." *African American Review*, vol. 46, no. 1, Special Issue: Hip Hop and the Literary, 2013, pp. 55–69.

Duane, Anna Mae. *Suffering Childhood in Early America: Violence, Race, and the Making of the Child Victim*. U of Georgia P, 2010.

Durham, Aisha, Brittney C. Cooper, and Susana M. Morris. "The Stage Hip-Hop Feminism Built: A New Directions Essay." *Signs: Journal of Women in Culture and Society*, vol. 38, no. 3, 2013, pp. 721–37.

Elliott, Zetta. "Nobody's Cheerleader." *ZettaElliott.com*, 19 Jan. 2016, http://www.zettaelliott .com/nobodys-cheerleader/.

Elliott, Zetta. "No More 'Becky Books.'" *ZettaElliott.com*, 25 Apr. 2018, http://www.zettaelliott .com/no-more-becky-books/.

Gubar, Marah. "Empathy Is Not Enough." *Public Books*, 19 July 2017.

Larrick, Nancy. "The All-White World of Children's Books." *Journal of African Children's and Youth Literature*, vol. 3, 1965, pp. 1–10.

Lowery, Wesley. "Aren't More White People than Black People Killed by Police? Yes, but No." *Washington Post*, 11 July 2016.

Martin, Michelle. *Brown Gold: Milestones of African American Children's Picture Books, 1845–2002*. Routledge, 2012.

Medina, Tony. *I Am Alfonso Jones*. Tu Books, 2017.

Myers, Christopher. "The Apartheid of Children's Literature." *New York Times*, 15 Mar. 2014.

Myers, Walter Dean. "Where Are the People of Color in Children's Books?" *New York Times*, 15 Mar. 2014.

Pough, Gwendolyn D. "What It Do, Shorty? Women, Hip-Hop, and a Feminist Agenda." *Black Women, Gender + Families*, vol. 1, no. 2, 2007, pp. 78–99.

Reynolds, Jason, and Brendan Kiely. *All American Boys*. Atheneum, 2017.

Rickford, Russell. "Black Lives Matter: Toward a Modern Practice of Mass Struggle." *New Labor Forum*, vol. 25, no. 1, 2016, pp. 34–42.

Stone, Nic. *Dear Martin*. Crown Books, 2017.

Taylor, Keeanga-Yamahtta. *From #BlackLivesMatter to Black Liberation*. Haymarket Books, 2016.

Thomas, Angie. *The Hate U Give*. Balzer + Bray, 2017.

Tuck, Eve, and K. Wayne Yang. "What Justice Wants." (Editor's Introduction). *Critical Ethnic Studies*, vol. 2, no. 2, 2016, pp. 1–15, 2018.

Further Reading

Coles, Jay. *Tyler Johnson Was Here*. Little, Brown, 2018.

Magoon, Kekla. *How It Went Down*. Square Fish, 2015.

Medina, Tony. *I Am Alfonso Jones*. Tu Books, 2017.

Oshiro, Mark. *Anger Is a Gift*. Little, Brown, 2018.

Reynolds, Jason, and Brendan Kiely. *All American Boys*. Atheneum, 2017.

Rhodes, Jewell Parker. *Ghost Boys*. Little, Brown, 2018.

Stone, Nic. *Dear Martin*. Crown Books, 2017.

Thomas, Angie. *The Hate U Give*. Balzer + Bray, 2017.

6

New Directions for Old Roads:
Rewriting the Young Adult Road Trip Story

Jason Vanfosson

From *Easy Rider* (1969) to *Road Trip* (2000), highway journeys have developed into a widely recognized motif in American cinema. Since the late 1990s, this motif has increasingly focused on young adults and frequently originates in books written for children and teens. After the success of the film *The Fault in Our Stars*, John Green's road book *Paper Towns* was adapted for the big screen in 2015. Likewise, Jeff Kinney's successful *Wimpy Kid* franchise adapted the road narrative found in the ninth installment of the series, *The Long Haul*. Significantly, both films failed to match or exceed their predecessors in box office sales or critical reception, despite the popularity of the books among young readers. *Paper Towns* currently has lifetime box-office sales of $32 million, a $92 million decrease from the lifetime box-office sales of *The Fault in Our Stars* ("Fault" and "Paper"). Likewise, *Diary of a Wimpy Kid: The Long Haul* has garnered only $20 million in box-office sales, a $44 million decrease from the first and most successful film in the *Wimpy Kid* franchise ("Diary"). These numbers stand in contrast to the sales and critical reception of the books on which these films are based. *Paper Towns* debuted at number five on the *New York Times* best-seller list, while *Diary of a Wimpy Kid: The Long Haul* became an immediate bestseller, and, as president and CEO of ABRAMS noted, "more than 1 million copies sold in the first seven days" (qtd. in Cader). This contrast in critical and economic success between the road trip films and the books that inspired them suggests a difference in how the road narrative functions in films and books for teens and young readers.

While many contemporary audiences may immediately think of teenage films featuring road trips, books offer a more varied and storied history of teenagers on the road that moves beyond a dominant narrative established in the larger canon of highway literature. The road trip narrative is often viewed as a requisite coming-of-age experience for young North American, white, heterosexual males who have the resources available to go on the road for leisure and self-actualization. Many young adult authors such as John Green (*An Abundance of Katherines*, 2006) and Barbara Shoup (*Looking for Jack Kerouac*, 2014) have replicated for YA readers the conventions of the American road trip that were codified by such classics as Jack Kerouac's *On the Road* (1957) and John Steinbeck's *Travels with Charley* (1962). More recent trends in the YA road story, however, reveal an influx of travelers who identify as female, Indigenous persons, persons of color, LGBTQIA+, and people with disabilities. These contemporary young adult road narratives rewrite the story of the road to include more diverse representations that reveal the challenges of traveling in a country that stigmatizes marginalized identities within the larger, dominant culture. Basic features of road travel, such as refueling a vehicle, using the restroom, or finding a place to spend the night, become contentious spaces for marginalized groups and expose the inherent privileges of mobility associated with the American road story.

Critics have struggled to define the American road narrative in a way that represents the array of texts that occupy this category, yet these definitions must be considered to understand how YA road stories contribute to the canon of highway books and children's literature. Ronald Primeau first defines the genre in his 1997 book *Romance of the Road: The Literature of the American Highway* by explaining:

> American road narratives are fiction and nonfiction books by Americans who travel by car throughout the country either on a quest or simply to get away. The most common narrative structure follows the sequence of a journey from preparation to departure, routing, decisions about goals and modes of transport, the arrival, return and reentry, and finally, the recording or reconstructing of events in the telling of the story. (1)

Recent road trip scholars have challenged and furthered earlier definitions of the road narrative, such as Primeau's, because of the notable exclusion of road stories that feature non-automobile travel, such as by bus, motorcycle, or foot.

In her study *The Road Story and the Rebel: Moving through Film, Fiction, and Television* (2006), Katie Mills explains:

> Our aim here will not be to define the road genre, articulate a canon, or stay within the disciplinary borders of any academic department, but to trouble all of these concepts—not for the sake of rebellion, but simply because the contemporary road story, as a uniquely postwar and postmodern genre, requires new approaches before its social significance can be fully appreciated. (7)

Mills's resistance to definition, canonicity, and disciplinarity provides an open space for including non-automobile and marginalized road narratives that do not easily fit within the traditional framework initially setup by Primeau. For the practical purposes of a consistent and focused study, this essay employs the definition of the American road narrative that features a journey of substantial distance in the United States on a defined road by a motorized vehicle. I agree with Mills and concede that the canon of American road narratives needs to be more inclusive. Therefore, I challenge the same restrictions that inform this analysis to engage new methodologies that help situate and explain the significance and trends of the road narrative in contemporary YA fiction.

Initial YA road novels repurpose the road story that American road writers such as Jack Kerouac and Robert Pirsig (*Zen and the Art of Motorcycle Maintenance*, 1974) establish in their road writings. Primeau notes that adult road fiction typically "presented a white male's world oriented toward success, fast movement, and little concern for women or multicultural experience" (108). The adult canon of the road narrative emphasizes and celebrates white, heterosexual, cisgender masculinities that embark on road trips to either understand that identity or understand the United States. The focus of road books showcasing white, male protagonists has not been because of a lack of books available that feature counternarratives. Texts such as Oscar Zeta Acosta's *The Autobiography of a Brown Buffalo* (1972), Erika Lopez's *Flaming Iguanas: An Illustrated, All-Girl Road Novel Thing* (1997), and Jade Chang's *The Wangs vs. the World* (2016) offer critiques of the dominant road story through the perspective of marginalized groups on the road. Stories of women on the road also abound, particularly in YA fiction, yet these texts remain marginalized in the canon of road literature despite their copublication alongside male stories of the road. Women's road trips provide yet another perspective that writers use to challenge the dominant narrative of the road.

The first forays into road stories specifically published for teenage audiences presented this dominant narrative. For example, Gary Paulsen's *The Car* (1993) follows Terry Anders, a fourteen-year-old boy whose parents abandon him, leading him to build the Blakely Bearcat car kit that his father left behind and to teach himself how to drive. Terry takes to the road from Ohio to Oregon, where he encounters two Vietnam veterans, a madam, a commune with oppressive rules for women, and a high-stakes poker game.

The reviews for Paulsen's novel provide the most insight into how this text, one of the earliest contemporary YA road novels, reproduces the adult road narrative for a teenage reader. The *Kirkus Review* opens its thoughts on the novel by suggesting, "Paulsen's latest comes close to a *classic teenage male fantasy* of fleeing from home to seek independence and self" (emphasis mine). This one-sentence review of the text identifies several of the tropes that mark the prevailing American road narrative by identifying it as a male-centric story focused on fleeing the domestic space of the home for the independence associated with the open road. Additionally, it cites the desire to find some abstract concept of the "self" as one of the substantial motivating forces in Paulsen's text, which is a characteristic trope of the American road genre. The *Publishers Weekly* review likewise situates the text in this tradition of the classic American road tale. The review begins, "Fourteen-year-old Terry Anders is a 1990s Huck Finn, with parents as neglectful as 'Pap.' Like Huck he escapes, not on a raft but by constructing a kit car. He takes his red Blakely Bearcat out to the highway and points it west, intending to leave his home in Cleveland for Oregon." Road scholars often cite Mark Twain's *The Adventures of Huckleberry Finn* (1884) as one of the earliest examples of an American road trip.[1] This review in *Publishers Weekly*, then, aligns one of the first YA road novels with the tradition of the American road story and establishes that preliminary attempts to rewrite the road story for teens repurposed many of the structures, themes, and motifs that define the genre for adult audiences in quintessential road texts.

While Paulsen's novel helped bring the conventions of the road narrative to young adult audiences, the YA road trip novel did not begin to flourish until the mid-2000s. Then several road trip books were published in succession. In 2005 Alex Sanchez published the third installment of his Rainbow trilogy, *Rainbow Road*, in which three gay teens embark on a cross-country road trip before parting ways for college. The next year, after success with *Looking for Alaska*, John Green published *An Abundance of Katherines* (2006). That same year, HMH Books for Young Readers reissued Gary Paulsen's *The Car* with a redesigned and updated cover. This time period proved to be a turning point for YA road stories, as writers began to understand the possibility of the genre for teenage audiences. Not only were more books published, celebrated authors, such as Green, wrote multiple road trip books. Two years after his first road trip story about a child prodigy, Green published *Paper Towns*, which featured a road trip from Florida to New York to find a runaway girl.

The increase in YA road trip fiction, however, also maintained the dominant narrative of the road story beyond Paulsen's early text. In many of the novels published in the mid-2000s, the protagonist remained a white, heterosexual, middle-class, cisgender male. While there are certainly exceptions, including the Hispanic and gay-identified characters in Sanchez's *Rainbow Road*, the books that received the most attention have re-created a narrative of privilege on the road. Barbara Shoup's 2014 teenage road story, *Looking for Jack Keraouc*, offers a particularly interesting example, because the storyline focuses on two boys who, inspired by *On the Road*, embark on a road trip in 1964 to find Kerouac in St. Petersburg, Florida. Not only does this text directly allude to Kerouac and make several parallels to the way the main characters, Paul and Duke, mirror Kerouac's Sal and Dean, but this text also engages the dominant road narrative through the disregard of minority and female characters on the road and focuses on two white, male characters.

Several authors have since repurposed this narrative to confront the concept of the open road and the entitlements associated with it. Mills considers how writers of adult road stories perform similar work when she explains, "Storytellers use the road genre to recycle certain tropes in order to highlight the differences in identity between a new type of protagonist and its predecessors, or to exploit the similarities" (6). For example, Sanchez's *Rainbow Road* considers how gay characters must negotiate varying levels of outness on the road when traveling through homophobic areas of the country. Allan Wolf's *Zane's Trace* (2007) portrays a triracial teen who must understand his Indigenous heritage within the context of his current road trip. In Jonathan Friesen's *Jerk, California* (2008), a teen with Tourette syndrome travels across the country to reconnect with his family and past, but he must navigate other people's perceptions of his disability while traveling. Brian Meehl's *You Don't Know about Me* (2011) and Brett Hartman's *Cadillac Chronicles* (2012) challenge racial mobility on the road when a white teenager accompanies a Black adult on a trip. Kristin Elizabeth Clark's *Jess, Chunk, and the Road Trip to Infinity* (2016) challenges cisgender privileges on the road when a transwoman must negotiate safe places to go to the restroom and motel policies that require government-issued identification. These examples are varied and provide a specific point of subversion, yet each one offers insight into the myth of the open road in US culture by questioning who has access to and mobility on the road. Significantly, the barriers that these marginalized protagonists must overcome to travel on US highways reveal that systemic structures operate to limit the movement and mobility of people who do not fit into the dominant American road story. More recent YA road trip fiction further interrogates the privileges associated with the open road by offering more intersectional approaches to road mobilities. Randy Ribay's *An Infinite Number of Parallel Universes* (2015) and Chris Colfer's *Stranger than Fanfiction* (2017) provide road stories in which a group of four friends from varying marginalized groups hit the road and must factor their own identities while considering the other identities on the trip.

These texts indicate a trend in YA road trip fiction that moves away from the dominant narrative of the American road story by representing road travelers who are overlooked or marginalized by the broader culture that celebrates the fantasy of the open road. Mills explains this point when she notes, "People at the margins of society who find their freedom curtailed because of gender, class, income, race, or sexual orientation have *always* found ways to 'get around,' despite the barriers or prohibitions imposed upon them" (emphasis original, 13). In short, groups that have systemically been oppressed or stigmatized, such as people of color, LGBTQIA+ people, and working-class people, learn how to function and to move in and through society by maneuvering or avoiding the same systems of privilege from which they are excluded—even if those systems cannot be completely eschewed.

These representations of marginalized groups on the road subvert and challenge the established patterns, motifs, structures, and ideologies that have come to define the American road story. While there are several ways in which these texts challenge the dominant narrative of the road, one important method emphasizes the motives for hitting the road. Marginalized characters in YA road books frequently hit the road for reasons that go beyond leisure or self-discovery to include finding missing family members, escaping inadequate home situations, or fulfilling elaborate suicide plans. In her 2015 book *American Road Narratives: Reimagining Mobilities in Literature and Film*, Ann Brigham succinctly identifies the dominant road story as a "story about men on the move" that "maps a male protagonist's search for something currently elusive—his country, himself, vital knowledge—during a time of unsettling social and historical change" (53). Brigham's explication of the typical motives found in road stories featuring white, affluent men provides further insight into the ways YA novels with diverse protagonists develop another viewpoint that decentralizes the privileges and motives of the open road narrative since many of YA road stories focus on the *need* to move on the road for a number of reasons.

The road story commonly gets categorized as a masculine story that prominently features male-identified travelers on the road. Brigham's synthesis above of prevailing road narrative theories as "the story about men on the move" points to the way road trips in practice, as well as in scholarship, have been biased toward masculine representations. In *Driving Visions: Exploring the Road Movie*, David Laderman, who analyzes cinematic interpretations of the road story, explains, "Whether in traditional exaltation of machismo, or as an exploration of masculine identity crisis, the bulk of the road movie genre seems to presuppose a focus on masculinity. This presupposition often bears patriarchal baggage, which both the feminist and gay road movies of the 1990s explicitly challenge" (21). Films have debunked the masculine space of the road, and the same can be said about the road story in literature and young adult fiction. An overwhelming number of texts that feature men on the road have received critical attention, but texts representing the female road trip experience have had less critical attention given to them, even though these novels were published alongside their male counterparts. Deborah Paes de Barros's *Fast Cars and Bad Girls: Nomadic Subjects and Women's Road Stories* (2004) and Deborah Clarke's *Driving Women: Fiction and Automobile Culture in Twentieth-Century America* (2007) offer two significant analyses of women's road stories that recover these previously overlooked stories. In women's road novels written for adult audiences, some of the same genre-challenging techniques used in YA road fiction manifests, such as different motives for embarking on a road trip or different narrative structures that reconfigure single, linear narratives.[2]

YA road novels with female protagonists abound, though these texts do not receive the same acclaim as their male-centered counterparts. Several of these female-focused road novels feature women on the road alone, such as David Arnold's *Mosquitoland* (2015), or on the road with a small group of female friends, such as Hilary Weisman Graham's *Reunited* (2012). These texts offer insight into how female protagonists rewrite the narrative that the road is a masculine space. In *Moving Lives: Twentieth Century Women's Travel Writing* (2001), Sidonie Smith aptly notes the difference of boys and girls hitting the road when she observes, "To climb into the driver's seat, for a young boy, has been to get an identity as manly and desirable. To get into an auto[mobile], for a young girl, has often been to get into trouble" (186). Cultural expectations that code the road as a masculine space indicate that women who hit the road, whether alone or in groups, are already engaging in acts of rebellion.

Road texts that feature *both* male and female teenagers on the road provide another template of the road story, such as Morgan Maston's *Amy and Roger's Epic Detour* (2010) and Bill Konigsberg's *The Porcupine of Truth* (2015). Konigsberg's novel provides a particularly clear view of how writers challenge the dominant road narrative when working with male and female main characters on the road. *The Porcupine of Truth* features the story of Carson Smith and his friend Aisha on their trip from Billings, Montana, to San Francisco, California. The two discover that Carson has a mysterious family history, which leads them to follow clues on the road to Carson's grandfather in California.

Meanwhile, Aisha struggles with her family since her father kicked her out of the house because she came out as lesbian to her parents. The majority of the novel focuses on Carson, yet the reader gets many glances into Aisha's troubles as a Black, lesbian girl living in a rural place that is not accepting of LGBTQIA+ populations. The novel takes a turn toward the end of the trip when Aisha exclaims, "I'm not your sidekick. [. . .] All this trip, it's like, Carson's stuff. We're in my car, but this is Carson's journey. To find your grandfather. Did it ever occur to you, even once, that I might be doing this for me too?" (279). Not only does this passage confront the ways Carson has selfishly used Aisha for his journey, but Aisha's statement indicates the ways women characters have been commonly overlooked in favor of male-centric road narratives. Konigsberg's novel calls for a corrective to include road stories of diverse protagonists, particularly women of color, while simultaneously perpetuating the dominant road story by focusing on Carson's character.

E. Lockhart, Sarah Mlynowski, and Lauren Myracle's *How to Be Bad* (2008) provides one narrative in which three authors tell three alternating viewpoints of the road story for teen readers. The polyvocal narrative structure and coauthored text shifts away from the monovocal and single-author narratives that are standard in many road trip novels. Nonetheless, the text itself provides further insight into privileges commonly associated with the road. In this novel, Vicks and Jesse work at a local Waffle House. Vicks's boyfriend has gone to college in Miami and has not been in contact with her for two weeks, so the two decide to embark on a road trip from Niceville, Florida, to Miami. Unfortunately, their Waffle House wages and lack of a car expose the ways their working-class status limits their ability to hit the road. However, Mel, an affluent newcomer from Canada who is desperate to make friends, agrees to finance their trip, as long as she can come along. The women then borrow-without-asking Jesse's mother's station wagon. This collaboration among the three teens, as well as the three writers, also shows a shift away from the traditional narrative of self-reliance and independence on the road that becomes characteristic of mainstream road texts.

Queer representations of the road story in YA books challenge the dominant narrative through spatial concerns of geography and movement throughout different areas of the country. Alex Sanchez's *Rainbow Road* provides one example of the ways geography influences the road narrative to reveal special concerns for queer travelers. This book follows the story of Jason Carrillo, Kyle Meeks, and Nelson Glassman in the summer after they graduate from high school. Jason, the jock of the group, who is also dating Kyle, gets invited to speak to an LGBT high school in Los Angeles. Unfortunately, the invitation comes during the only week Jason and Kyle can steal away for a solo camping trip before Kyle leaves to start college at Princeton University. Kyle's friend Nelson suggests that the three embark on a cross-country road trip to round out their summer before parting ways. After making the necessary arrangements, Nelson offers up his car and the three set off for a trip from D.C. to L.A. The book follows their weeklong trek across the country and the various experiences the boys have as they come of age and prepare for their futures.

In this text the car becomes an avatar of identity for the passengers. Where the automobile can afford a certain amount of anonymity on the road for marginalized characters in other novels, in *Rainbow Road* the car serves as an extension of that identity because of the presence of a rainbow bumper sticker. As Jason loads his bags into Nelson's car, he tells Nelson, "You'd better take that flag off. [. . .] We're going through redneck country, you know?" (41). Ironically, Jason is being celebrated on this road trip for coming out as an athlete who is a member of the LGBTQIA+ community, yet he is eager to deny that identity visually on the car. This passage shows how Jason ascribes the vernacular "redneck country" as a code for rural places that are frequently seen as unwelcoming of LGBTQIA+ people. Nonetheless, when Jason confronts him, Nelson merely shrugs and says, "I'm not taking it off" (41).

The rainbow bumper sticker serves to mark the car as a queer vehicle of identity. Not long into the trip, the boys run out of gas while searching for a gas station on a side road. When a pickup truck pulls behind them, the boys are all scared about why someone is stopping. Then, Nelson asks, "What if they're rednecks? Or zombies?" The truck begins beeping at the boys, to which Jason explains, their honking is likely "because of [Nelson's] stupid rainbow flag" (66). Jason leaves the car to talk to the pickup truck occupants, who saw the flag and stopped because they thought the boys, like themselves, are headed to the inclusive Radical Faerie sanctuary. In this instance the vehicle functions as a site of queerness that saves the boys, an outcome that calls into question the stereotypical view of rural spaces as being solely the province of homophobia in the road narrative.

Other road novels, like Kristin Elizabeth Clark's *Jess, Chunk, and the Road Trip to Infinity* (2016), further complicate assumptions of gender and rural spaces that have been intertwined with the American road. This novel indicates many of the recurring tropes that trans travelers contend with on the road. In Clark's road story, a transgender teenage girl, Jess, travels across the United States to attend her estranged father's marriage to her mother's former best friend. Set during Jess's summer between high school and college, the road trip serves as her transition into a future of adulthood and an outwardly female gender presentation. Jess even maps her gender transition onto the country when she explains, "I imagine a gender clothing continuum for myself, stretching from San Jose (male: baggy sweatshirts and guy's jeans) to Chicago (female: the Muzzy dress and ballet flats)" (78). While gender comprises more than clothing, this provides one way for Clark to represent Jess's transition while on the road. Clark further reveals the cisgender privileges of the road by constructing a narrative around the fear and brutality that trans bodies face when traveling through places that are perceived as dangerous for LGBTQIA+ travelers.

Throughout her road trip, Jess experiences numerous moments of fear and anxiety connected to her gender identity. Jess must question her decision to use a public restroom or not each time she stops at a rest area or gas station. She explains her methods, noting, "Wherever possible, I avoid using public restrooms. It feels wrong to use the men's because I'm really not a guy, but at this stage of my transition I worry about using the women's and getting called out for looking too masculine. So should I be true to myself, or play it safe?" (65). This decision of which bathroom to use becomes an issue of safety for Jess that cisgender travelers do not need to consider in the same ways while on the road. In another instance, Jess's anxiety escalates when she and Chunk check into a motel and the clerk asks for identification from both. In narrating the experience, Jess depicts the motel clerk as "giv[ing] it the TSA treatment," an allusion to increased body and gender policing enforced at a systemic level and justified by "policy," as the motel clerk notes (71). These moments of anxiety and fear of being revealed as trans point to the possible discrimination or danger that trans bodies face on the road, thereby demonstrating the ways trans people do not have the same mobility on the road as cisgender travelers. Brigham, in analyzing the film *Transamerica*, explains, "Gender mobility becomes both a sign of the heterogeneity of the national body and the recuperation of heteronormativity as the trans body maps the imperative to discern the male/female, familiar/strange, us/them" (211). Much of the trans road story, then, focuses on passing in different locations, particularly rural locations, to reinforce the binaries that determine societal expectations, while simultaneously exposing the privileges inherent with these same binaries. In Jess's case, she tries to reinforce the binaries by conforming to an abstract ideal of femininity that allows her to pass as female. Nonetheless, she challenges these same binaries in moments when she must decide which bathroom to use and determines that the men's restroom is "play[ing] it safe" (65).

One significant area in the YA road narrative that has seen minimal publication and almost no critical attention features racial and ethnic minorities as main characters. For example, there are no protagonists who are Black or Hispanic that embark on the road in YA literature.[3] Black road stories, particularly, provide an opportunity to challenge the dominant road narrative given recent trends in YA publishing that address the police brutality that many Black drivers face. For example, as Kaylee Jangula Mootz notes in her essay in this collection, Angie Thomas's *The Hate U Give* (2017) and Nic Stone's *Dear Martin* (2017) both feature Black bodies suffering police brutality in the contexts of an automobile, but not on a road trip. Similarly, from 2010 to 2017 only one YA road story has been published that features an Indigenous protagonist, Allan Wolf's *Zane's Trace* (2007). This lack of publishing Native road stories mirrors the larger adult road canon that has limited representations of Native travelers.[4] Nonetheless, Indigenous representations appear in several road trip stories in which the traveling protagonist encounters Native people as part of his or her road trip experience.

The Indigenous road trip story remains underdeveloped in the body of road literature as a result of a larger tendency to erase Native cultures and representations. Writing within the framework of critical Indigenous literacies, Debbie Reese, who is tribally enrolled at Nambé Pueblo, notes, "Our status as sovereign nations whose people were—and are—Indigenous to this continent are erased" (389). The tendency toward erasure, then, helps account for the lack of Indigenous road stories. Nonetheless, the two road stories featuring an Indigenous protagonist are necessary to consider when examining the trends and developing the canon of YA road fiction because of the way space and time function differently in these narratives. Where the dominant narrative of the road plots trips on linear notions of time and space, Native road stories necessarily include temporal journeys that merge the past and the present in ways that frequently call attention to narratives of colonization that have marked the history of Native people in the United States.

The Indigenous road trip in YA fiction weaves personal history with national and Native history. In Wolf's *Zane's Trace*, Zane Guesswind, a triracial teenager, goes on a road trip to kill himself in Zanesville, Ohio, at his mother's gravesite with a gun filled with historical and familial significance. Zane's racial tensions focus on reconciling his whiteness, blackness, and Wyandot heritage.[5] Spectral presences of his ancestors fill Zane's trip from Baltimore to Ohio that construct a journey not unlike the traditional vision quests, in which the ghosts help him to understand his purpose, move him to manhood, and, ultimately, prevent him from ending his life.

On Zane's road trip, his ancestors travel *through* time to speak to him at contemporary places such as a fast-food drive-through. In other instances, Zane himself travels through time to historical moments that are significant to his Wyandot heritage, such as the Siege of Fort Henry. While seemingly inconspicuous, this motif challenges the Euro-American road narrative that frequently posits the road as a linear, temporal journey from one starting place to another. Brigham explains this critique when she notes, "The story of connecting past and present needs to be routed through the story of colonialism, and that story is a spatial one. In these [American Indian] texts, the protagonists' movements critique a mainstream Euro-American ideology in which mobility represents progress as a forward movement that erases the past" (151). Not only does Zane's road trip challenge the narrative of the road through merging the past and present, but his goal to kill himself using a historical gun eliminates the forward movement that marks the road journey in the canon of American road literature.

The texts discussed in this essay focus on a small section of YA road fiction that, in some way, challenges the dominant narrative of the literary road trip. One important consideration is how these books fit into the recent movements for diversity in children's and young adult literature, including the We Need Diverse Books (WNDB) and #OwnVoices campaigns. These books, and others, provide an opportunity to feature diversity on the road, and therefore perspectives that actively challenge the popular ideas of the American road trip in literature. These texts promote the mission of WNDB "to address the lack of diverse, non-majority narrative in children's literature . . . [and] the ideal that embracing diversity will lead to acceptance, empathy, and ultimately equality" through their portrayals of marginalized young people on the road ("Media"). Still, there remain opportunities for scholars to continue critiquing these texts and the narratives of the road in children's and young adult literature in ways that encourage authentic representation of diverse experiences and voices. Furthermore, many of the road narratives discussed in this essay remain written by authors who do not self-identify as the group that they portray in their fiction. The #OwnVoices movement celebrates texts in which "the protagonist and author share a marginalized identity" and provides an opportunity to promote authors who share some of the same experiences and perspectives of their characters. While I am not suggesting that this is a prerequisite to challenging this dominant narrative, I am suggesting that this is a future trend in upcoming road fiction because it will reveal more nuanced readings of the road that further expose the myth of the open road. These books have the unique opportunity to show the ways individuals who remain marginalized by the larger culture have limited mobility; they therefore provide insight into effecting change in societal structures that seek to keep these same groups restricted in their mobility on the road. Nonetheless, the books mentioned and analyzed in this essay provide a starting point to the ways the road is not open to everyone in the United States.

Notes

1. In his foundational study on highway literature, Ronald Primeau notes, "The American road tradition includes as well a heritage of river journeys, foremost of which is Huck Finn's escape from civilization, his sometimes free-spirited float down the river on a raft, and his encounters with a variety of characters who advance the rebellious American quest motif" (20). See also Aaron Latham's "Visions of Cody," in which Latham explains how Twain's text inspired Kerouac and the many ways *On the Road* becomes a mid-century *Huck Finn*.

2. See specifically Erika Lopez's 1997 hybrid novel, *Flaming Iguanas: An Illustrated All-Girl Road Novel Thing*.

3. Middle-grade road trip fiction, however, includes more representation of racial and ethnic minorities. See specifically Christopher Paul Curtis's *The Watsons Go to Birmingham—1963* (1995) and Tanita S. Davis's *Mare's War* (2009).

4. William Least Heat-Moon's *Blue Highways: A Journey into America* (1982) stands as one of the only books that centers on an Indigenous person on the road. In film, the Native road experience is limited to *The Powwow Highway* (1979) and *Smoke Signals* (1998), which is based on Sherman Alexie's short story "This Is What it Means to Say Phoenix, Arizona."

5. Wolf's *Zane's Trace* received favorable reviews upon publication. Significantly, none of these reviews were written by Indigenous, or more specifically Wyandot, reviewers. Wolf's verse novel, however, presents several problematic Native representsions, such as depicting the Native character as a savage figure and a magical doctor capable of raising the dead. Karen Coats is one of the only reviewers to mention the Wyandot representation, which she describes as a "vengeful Wyandot Indian" (193).

Works Cited

Acosta, Oscar Zeta. *Autobiography of a Brown Buffalo*. Vintage, 1989.

Arnold, David. *Mosquitoland*. Viking, 2015.

Brigham, Ann. *American Road Narratives: Reimagining Mobility in Literature and Film*. U of Virginia P, 2015.

Cader, Michael. "Corporate: Opening Sales of Over 1 Million for Wimpy Kid, and PRH Launches Audio App." *Publishers Lunch*, 13 Nov. 2014, https://lunch.publishersmarketplace .com/2014/11/corporate-opening-sales-1-million-wimpy-kid-prh-launches-audio-app/. Accessed 12 Dec. 2017.

Chang, Jade. *The Wangs vs. the World*. Houghton Mifflin Harcourt, 2016.

Clark, Kristin Elizabeth. *Jess, Chunk, and the Road Trip to Infinity*. Farrar, Straus, and Giroux, 2016.

Clarke, Deborah. *Driving Women: Fiction and Automobile Culture in Twentieth-Century America*. Johns Hopkins University Press, 2007.

Coats, Karen. Review of *Zane's Trace*, by Allan Wolf. *Bulletin of the Center for Children's Books*, vol. 61, no. 4, 2007, pp. 193–94.

Colfer, Chris. *Stranger than Fanfiction*. Little, Brown Books for Young Readers, 2017.

Diary of a Wimpy Kid. Box Office Mojo, IMDb.com, http://www.boxofficemojo.com/movies /?id=diaryofawimpykid.htm. Accessed 12 Dec. 2017.

The Fault in Our Stars. Box Office Mojo, IMDb.com, www.boxofficemojo.com/movies /?id=faultinourstars.htm. Accessed 12 Dec. 2017.

Friesen, Jonathan. *Jerk, California*. Puffin, 2008.

Graham, Hilary Weisman. *Reunited*. Simon and Schuster, 2013.

Green, John. *An Abundance of Katherines*. Speak, 2006.

Green, John. *Paper Towns*. Speak, 2008.

Hartman, Brett. *The Cadillac Chronicles*. Cinco Puntos Press, 2012.

Kerouac, Jack. *On the Road*. Penguin, 2003.

Kirkus Review. Review of *The Car*, by Gary Paulsen, 1 Apr. 1994, https://www.kirkusreviews
.com/book-reviews/gary-paulsen/the-car/. Accessed 15 Dec. 2017.

Konigsberg, Bill. *The Porcupine of Truth*. Arthur A. Levine Books, 2015.

Laderman, David. *Driving Visions: Exploring the Road Movie*. U of Texas P, 2002.

Latham, Aaron. "Visions of Cody." *New York Times*, 28 Jan. 1973, http://www.nytimes.com
/books/97/09/07/home/kerouac-cody.html.

Lockhart, E., et al. *How to Be Bad*. HarperTeen, 2008.

Lopez, Erika. *Flaming Iguanas: An Illustrated All-Girl Road Novel Thing*. Simon and Schuster, 1997.

Maston, Morgan. *Amy and Roger's Epic Detour*. Simon and Schuster, 2011.

"Media Kit." We Need Diverse Books, We Need Diverse Books, https://diversebooks.org/media
-kit/. Accessed 2 Jan. 2018.

Meehl, Brian. *You Don't Know about Me*. Ember, 2011.

Mills, Katie. *The Road Story and the Rebel: Moving through Film, Fiction, and Television*.
Southern Illinois U P, 2006.

Paes de Barros, Deborah. *Fast Cars and Bad Girls: Nomadic Subjects and Women's Road Stories*.
Peter Lang, 2004.

Paper Towns. Box Office Mojo, IMDb.com, www.boxofficemojo.com/movies/?id=papertowns
.htm. Accessed 12 Dec. 2017.

Paulsen, Gary. *The Car*. 1993. HMH Books for Young Readers, 2006.

Pirsig, Robert. *Zen and the Art of Motorcycle Maintenance*. 1976. HarperTorch, 2006.

Primeau, Ronald. *Romance of the Road: Literature of the American Road*. Bowling Green State
University Popular Press, 1996.

Publishers Weekly. Review of The Car, by Gary Paulsen, 2 Feb. 1994, https://www.publishersweekly
.com/978-0-15-292878-0. Accessed 15 Dec. 2017.

Reese, Debbie. "Critical Indigenous Literacies: Selecting and Using Children's Books about
Indigenous Peoples." *Language Arts*, vol. 95, no. 6, 2018, pp. 389–93. http://www.ncte.org
/library/NCTEFiles/Resources/Journals/LA/0956-jul2018/LA0956Jul18Language.pdf?_ga
=2.87145880.1617763930.1533935274–1211330858.1533935274.

Ribay, Randy. *An Infinite Number of Parallel Universes*. Simon Pulse, 2015.

Sanchez, Alex. *Rainbow Road*. Simon and Schuster, 2005.

Self, Jeffery. *Drag Teen*. Push, 2016.

Shoup, Barbara. *Looking for Jack Kerouac*. Lacewing, 2014.

Smith, Sidonie. *Moving Lives: 20th Century Women's Travel Writing*. U of Minnesota P, 2001.

Steinbeck, John. *Travels with Charley: In Search of America*. Penguin, 2002.

Wolf, Allan. *Zane's Trace*. 2007. Candlewick, 2010.

Further Reading

Alsaid, Adi. *Let's Get Lost*. Harlequin Teen, 2014.

Andrews, Jesse. *The Haters*. Amulet, 2016.

Bray, Libba. *Going Bovine*. Ember, 2009.

Flores-Scott, Patrick. *American Road Trip*. Henry Holt, 2018.

Hoole, Elissa Janine. *Kiss the Morning Star*. Skyscrape, 2012.

Karim, Sheba. *Mariam Sharma Hits the Road*. Harper Teen, 2018.

Kokie, E. M. *Personal Effects*. Candlewick, 2012.

Moriarty, Laura. *American Heart*. HarperTeen, 2018.

Spieller, Lauren. *Your Destination Is on the Left*. Simon and Schuster, 2018.

7

New Heroines in Old Skins: Fairy Tale Revisions in Young Adult Dystopian Literature

Jill Coste

Young adult (YA) dystopias and YA fairy tale retellings have each bloomed in the young adult publishing market over the first fifteen years of the twenty-first century, resulting in numerous hybrid novels. Marissa Meyer's popular Lunar Chronicles series, for example, envisions a cyborg Cinderella fighting for liberty alongside modern interpretations of Little Red Riding Hood, Rapunzel, and Snow White; Anna Sheehan's *A Long, Long Sleep* situates Sleeping Beauty in a futuristic hypercapitalist society; Stacey Jay's *Of Beast and Beauty* envisions a privileged domed community competing with desert-dwelling "beasts" for scarce resources. Even dystopian stories that are not overt retellings have evocations of the tropes that accompany fairy tales. Bluebeard's halls of horror appear in Lauren DeStefano's *Wither*, while a variation of "The Swan Maiden" complicates Julianna Baggott's *Pure*. With their twin efforts to examine societal standards, serve as cautionary tales, and highlight a hero or heroine setting out to overcome villainy, fairy tale retellings and dystopian novels are a natural pairing.

Fairy-tale dystopias fall into roughly three categories: more dystopia than retelling (Karen Healey's *When We Wake*; Bethany Wiggins's *Stung*), more retelling than dystopia (Jackson Pearce's *Sisters Red* and *Sweetly*), or a balance between the two (Jay's *Of Beast and Beauty*; Sheehan's *A Long, Long Sleep*; Meyer's Lunar Chronicles). One could argue that many of the fairy tale retellings that remain fixed in a fantasy realm also fall under the dystopian category—these tales often feature an authoritarian royal rule the protagonist fights to overthrow (Rhiannon Thomas's *A Wicked Thing*; Stacey Jay's *Princess of Thorns*). But the texts that provide the most compelling social commentary are those evoking elements of our own world. These retellings acknowledge the complexity of social structures and the personal struggles that can complicate a happy ending, inviting readers to consider their own agency through familiar heroines' journeys. With heroines who not only confront their own individual issues but also face systemic injustices that affect their societies' well-being, dystopian fairy tales transcend the hero's journey and stress the importance of social awareness and the ongoing efforts required to enact social change. Especially primed for this kind of narrative is the Sleeping Beauty tale, which I will use in this chapter as representative of the themes and issues that run through YA fairy-tale dystopias. With its heroine who literally wakes up to a different society and must establish her agency within it, the Sleeping Beauty revision represents the adolescent experience of "waking up" to the power structures that govern our lives.

Fairy tales, an indelible part of our cultural memory, have long been tweaked, twisted, fractured, and revised to suit myriad needs. These tales pull on folkloric history while positioning themselves in a unique cultural moment, and recently that cultural moment is one rife with dystopias both fictional and real. As Maria Tatar explains, fairy tales "are constantly altered, adapted, transformed, and tailored to fit new cultural contexts. They [are] . . . always doing new cultural work, mapping out different developmental paths, assimilating new anxieties and desires" (*Secrets* 11). Cristina Bacchilega notes that postmodern tales "reactivate the wonder tale's 'magic' or mythopoeic qualities by providing new readings of it, thereby generating unexploited or forgotten possibilities from its repetition" (22). The unexploited possibilities in the YA dystopian fairy tale are not new ideas, but rather the merging of ideas familiar to both the dystopia and the fairy tale. Both genres have tropes of subversion in common, like the strong heroine who bucks gendered tradition and the scrappy nobody who helps to start a revolution, but they also raise thorny questions about individual versus collective agency and the nature of social change, asking readers to consider their own roles in societal structures. Dystopian fairy tales especially engage with ideas of embodiment, romance and its troubled relationship with rape culture, and social activism. These tales take feminist concerns and lay them against a stark backdrop of dystopian oppression, highlighting their significance. Furthermore, these narratives call upon a long history of feminist fairy tale subversion and underscore the way YA literature has shifted to provide more empowering narratives for girls, narratives that pose complex scenarios regarding agency and awareness.

Fairy-tale dystopias have arisen out of a rich history of revision and marketability, reflecting cultural interest in powerful female characters and possible utopian futures. In modern Anglophone literature, feminist writers have increasingly harnessed fairy tales in order to critique patriarchal power. The 1970s and 1980s saw a rush of feminist fairy tale revisions and a flood of scholarship on the oppressive patriarchal narratives inherent in canonical fairy tales. The YA retellings that appeared in this same time frame do similar work as the adult revisions, featuring young women who appear to make their own decisions, taking on the role of hero usually reserved for male characters. In her 1997 work *Waking Sleeping Beauty*, Roberta Trites says of feminist writers of children's literature:

> In rewriting folktales to advance feminist ideologies and to identify female subjectivity, feminist writers are both protesting the powerlessness of women inherent in our culture's old folkways and giving voice to a new set of values: a set that allows for the princess to have power, a set that allows Sleeping Beauty to wake up not to a destiny that immerses her in her husband's life but to a destiny that is self-defined. (45)

Put simply, feminist revisions have long featured young women choosing their own paths. Over the twenty years since Trites's analysis, fairy tale revisions have continued to offer strong heroines forging their own way, but contemporary revisions are not immune to falling back into traditional patterns. That is, fairy tale retellings still tend to repeat familiar journeys: young girl teaches others that beauty is not as valuable as integrity; young girl learns to say no to domineering prince and forge an unconventional path; young girl rescues boy instead, but her ultimate pairing with said boy reproduces a heteronormative scenario.

When merged with the dystopia, though, the fairy tale reaches more overtly into the realm of social justice and political critique, extending the tale of feminist empowerment from the individual to the collective. The dystopian YA fairy tale becomes a new kind of feminist revision, one that moves beyond questions of individual feminist agency and instead addresses the role of young women in a volatile society. That is not to say, though, that these novels leave behind questions of agency altogether. Indeed, as S. R. Toliver notes in her essay in this collection, dystopian YA has offered new lines of feminist agency through its spate of tough female protagonists. Fairy tale retellings have followed suit, offering a variety of strong, Katniss-like heroines[1] who deal with many of the themes Toliver outlines in her chapter.

Furthermore, twenty-first-century dystopian fairy tales are often complex and gritty, drawing on the darker side of literary fairy tales.[2] Indeed, contemporary fairy tale retellings reach back through that literary history; the literary fairy tale has always featured protagonists who "devise ways of opposing [danger], avenging themselves on the perpetrators, and of turning the status quo upside down" (Warner, *Once* 80). Amy Montz notes that fairy tales have an inherently dystopian bent, as they feature heroines who defy authority. The Cinderella tale, Montz claims, is one that "encourages young girls to resist totalitarian structures . . . and that demonstrates that while you may not have absolute power yourself, you can encourage those who do to defeat the unfair absolute authority of others" (114). While Cinderella does not overthrow the system, her story speaks to a larger truth about dystopias and fairy tales: they fit well together because each already has a history of characters resisting authority in some way. This engagement with historical iterations of a story features in the dystopia as well. Balaka Basu, Katherine Broad, and Carrie Hintz note that the YA dystopia requires us to ask "whether this genre as a whole charts new territory, remains rooted in old conventional forms, or reflects a combination of both past and future" (9). The YA dystopia, of course, cannot help but draw from its literary ancestors, just as the fairy tale cannot. The fairy-tale dystopia, then, calls upon a history of revision and a spate of assumptions and associations about both genres.

The Sleeping Beauty story evinces this connection to history. With its own focus on a princess who goes to sleep in the past and wakes up decades later, the Sleeping Beauty tale forces a consideration of how past actions resonate long into the future. Furthermore, Sleeping Beauty retellings are poised to provide a new iteration of heroine, calling as they do on the historically placid and passive sleeper. They also raise questions of collective agency, as the dystopian world to which the sleepers wake demands action for social change. By placing an already disoriented heroine in an even-more disorienting dystopic future, these Sleeping Beauty revisions emphasize for young readers the importance of being awake and aware in their own increasingly technological world.

Fairy tale retellings are already primed to engage active readers. With their familiar beats and characters, fairy tale elements anchor the reader in something known. According to Shirley Brice Heath and Jennifer Lynn Wolf, young readers view fairy tales as avenues for rereading and restructuring, and the more familiar the tale, the more satisfying the experience. They offer the example of teen reader Willow, who "enjoys encountering the new: new motivations, new personality components, new kinds of magic, new tests and trials" (152). Willow "reads forward into the novel looking for the places where the new story 'surprises' her" (152). Regarding her reading of a Sleeping Beauty retelling,

Cameron Dokey's *Beauty Sleep*, Willow likes that "she can see the seeds of independent, defiant thinking" on the part of the princess (153). Willow is an example of a reader who is already familiar with fairy tales, who knows that in the classic literary tale, the heroine is rarely outright defiant. She looks for subversion in her fairy tale retellings, and YA indeed delivers, showing that "it is possible to transform fate into agency; adolescence has a dark and powerful relationship with magic; and . . . good things can happen when teenagers rebel against their parents" (153).

That rebellion has broader implications in the dystopia, where teens push against totalitarian governments. Our familiar fairy-tale heroines must grapple with wide-ranging concerns. And as they grapple, so do readers. Jack Zipes notes that subversive fairy tale retellings have a liberating potential, "bring[ing] undesirable social relations into question and forc[ing] readers to question themselves" (188). When a dystopian scenario takes the place of the fantasy realm featured in the classic fairy tale, readers must especially question what they consider to be the status quo. And if, as Heath and Wolf assert, readers identify with characters and scenarios, they cannot help but consider the ways that these new heroes and heroines quest to bring about a better world. Thus, the fairy-tale dystopia provides not hope for the future in a broad sense, but hope for individual power in a practical sense. The troubling questions a dystopia raises about the nature of humanity overshadow the traditional fairy-tale happy ending, offering a more complicated resolution that opens up the narrative for further exploration.

The Sleeping Beauty tale is one that invites examination of a more complicated resolution. Certainly, the tale about a young woman who wakes up to a prince's kiss and lives happily ever after is primed for feminist revision. While numerous retellings subvert stereotypes of submissive princesses, instead offering tough-girl teenagers who fight against patriarchal oppression, the subverted Sleeping Beauty tale is especially powerful because its heroine is ostensibly the most passive princess of all. But in a dystopian fairy tale, Sleeping Beauty no longer sleeps through her life—she sleeps through major societal change, which she must then learn to navigate and, in some cases, manipulate. Furthermore, the Sleeping Beauty story is particularly suited to dystopian revision, precisely because of that extended sleep. Long employed as a sci-fi trope for intergalactic travel, the extended sleep has also appeared in historical utopias. Notably, in Edward Bellamy's 1888 *Looking Backward*, the male protagonist goes into a hypnotized sleep and wakes up 112 years later, in the year 2000, to a civilized utopian society. William Morris's 1892 *News from Nowhere*, a response to Bellamy's text, also features a protagonist who wakes to a future utopia. The texts serve as critiques of the capitalist industrialist practices of nineteenth-century America and England, respectively, with each focusing on a different socialist vision for the utopian future. These texts offer a fairy-tale-esque dream—that society's contemporary pains will ultimately be assuaged, either through progress or revolution, and that a sleeper can escape the dystopian present and wake to a better life. Thus, a dystopian Sleeping Beauty retelling with an empowered heroine draws on a history of both feminist revision and utopian sleepers. However, the fairy-tale dystopia, unlike Bellamy's and Morris's work, does not envision such an idealized future. In skipping over a hundred years, Sleeping Beauties wake to the same kind of societal concerns that existed in their time (or worse). These tales highlight the cyclical nature of history and the importance of making change now, drawing on the didactic and revolutionary nature of both fairy tales and dystopias.

Culturally, we are fascinated by Sleeping Beauty. Tatar notes, "We not only want to talk to her but also talk about her and make sense of her story" ("Sleeping Beauty" 156). Indeed, in the literary fairy tale itself, Sleeping Beauty is an object of intense interest, both before she sleeps and after she wakes up. Contemporary revisions pick up this thread of fascination, featuring heroines who become subjects of overwhelming media scrutiny and romantic overtures. Often, all this fascination leads to personal growth and even political revolution—the heroines learn their own worth, and others follow their lead. In the Sleeping Beauty revisions I examine here, the heroines inspire a devotion that helps them subvert the status quo and resist tyranny. Anna Sheehan's *A Long, Long Sleep*, Karen Healey's *When We Wake*, and Bethany Wiggins's *Stung* offer different spins on the dystopian Sleeping Beauty, but they all address the themes of embodiment, romance, and political activism that color fairy-tale dystopias.

Sheehan's novel features Rose, a sixteen-year-old who awakens in the twenty-third century after being in stasis for sixty-two years. Sheehan's novel envisions the fallout from the very long sleep, harshly depicting not only the emotional aftershocks of such a huge change, but also the physical effects of atrophy. Rose is sickly and haunted, with long gaps in her memory and inhabiting a disconcerting position as a young woman who belongs nowhere. She comes to understand her own troubled past, where her gaslighting parents regularly put her in stasis as a way to control her. Healey's work also employs science fiction and technology as the reason for its heroine Tegan's hundred-year-sleep. Placed in cryo-suspension after being accidentally shot, Tegan wakes up to a world that seems to have changed for the better. In her home country of Australia, everyone adheres cheerfully to environmental regulations; gay marriage is not only legal, but utterly normal; women's rights are unquestioned. But Tegan discovers that her country has not actually managed to fix the problems of the past, and those problems have, of course, given rise to new ones.

Wiggins's *Stung* is more derivative of the standard postapocalyptic dystopia: in a future United States, scientific manipulation of honeybees has resulted in a virulent flu, the vaccine for which goes awry and turns young people into "beasts," super-strong, unthinking killing machines. Seventeen-year-old Fiona, having been pricked in the past with this vaccine, wakes disoriented and alone, unsure of how long she has slept and unaware of how much the world has changed around her. Fiona herself is marked as a potential "beast," and she must hide from those who would harm her as she comprehends the full extent of her own role in this new world.

All three protagonists wake up after an extended sleep to a disorienting future where those around them view them with fascination and suspicion. Rose and Tegan respectively wake to a seemingly "normal" world, and their disorientation comes from the world's technological advances rather than from the dystopian scenario, which lurks under the surface. Rose and Tegan's respective narratives take them to the mundane world of high school, where the standard teen gossip is heightened because of their unusual situations. They are worthy objects of interest because they actually *are* different. They were in stasis—essentially dead—and now they are alive. Fiona, on the other hand, wakes up to a nightmare: her childhood home and neighborhood are decrepit with decay; her brother has transformed into a feral monster; and the only place she is somewhat safe is in the sewers beneath her city, provided she cuts her hair and hides her curves. In the dangerous dystopian landscape of *Stung*, Fiona's body marks her as a target, evoking the kind of objectification that feminist revisions aim to critique.

Embodiment in Sleeping Beauty retellings speaks to the time that has passed, and it also exemplifies the way that the fairy-tale dystopia uses embodiment to signify a character's growth, self-acceptance, and empowerment. Rose is very slender and weak after coming out of suspended animation, so skinny as to be unrecognizable to herself. Tegan, while not atrophied the way Rose is, is hairless and marked with scars, evidence of doctors' manipulation of her body. For Rose and Tegan, their physical state is not a choice, but rather evidence of something that was done to them against their will. Fiona's body, on the other hand, signifies the passage of time because she has gone through puberty during her hibernation. Fiona's long sleep only spanned four years, but it was enough to make Fiona feel at odds with her own body. She frequently fixates on her breasts and hips, the latter of which she calls "wide" (69) and "too big" (76). Thus, embodiment in these tales echoes the disorientation the characters feel in their unfamiliar future societies.

In these retellings, though, embodiment also represents empowerment or lack thereof. Sara K. Day notes the cultural discomfort with adolescent female bodies, which have "long been the site of contradictory cultural expectations and demands" (75). The tension that arises from a body in the liminal space between childhood and womanhood results in the societal perception of young women as "creatures whose sexuality must be controlled by implicit or explicit rules and regulations" (Day 75). As Day points out, fairy tales offer a didactic message that girls must depend on princes for their happy endings, but dystopias offer a futuristic remove and "attempt to reframe that danger [of female sexuality] as empowerment for their young protagonists" (75).

Embodied empowerment in these Sleeping Beauty retellings is less about sexual awakening and more a reflection of the teens' progress and abilities. In all three of these novels, the respective heroine wakes up and immediately takes stock of her body and its sensations to orient herself—Fiona notes her weak legs (2), Rose her blurred vision (3), Tegan her blinking eyelids (13). Furthermore, each one wakes up to a physical change that makes her feel momentarily powerless and thus gives her something to work toward. Feeling comfortable and strong in their bodies again is an essential journey for these heroines, and the more comfortable they get, the stronger they become. Additionally, their bodies signify their abilities and weaknesses. Tegan's embodiment is the most immediately empowering: as someone who used to do freerunning—a more accessible version of parkour—in her past life, she puts her skills to use moments after waking up, jumping off the roof of the hospital in an attempt to escape the scientists who revived her. Moreover, her petite stature belies her rebellious nature and is a direct send-up of fairy-tale heroines. She has "pale skin that looks like it might tear in a strong wind and big, dark, innocent eyes" (258), a kind of physicality that prompts her handlers to dress her in a costume reminiscent of Snow White for her first big television interview, in which she is meant to spout propaganda praising the government program that revived her. Dressed as Snow White, manipulated to look as powerless as possible, Tegan goes directly against her superiors' orders and shouts for the audience to look at all the destructive elements of their dystopian world.

Rose's embodiment also reflects the way others underestimate her. Though she is truly fatigued and emaciated from being in stasis for so many years, her weakened body signifies the docility that was forced upon her by her abusive parents. Thus, Rose's delicateness is not the quality of a fairy-tale heroine, but rather the effect of years of abuse. Seeing herself as "haunted" (178) and "a phantom" (251) speaks to the way her past affects her present, revealing the Sleeping Beauty tale as one that requires a reckoning with the trauma that led to the long sleep, not an easy awakening to a new future. Ultimately, Rose has a moment of subversion similar to Tegan's, where another character tells Rose "you're scaring *me* . . . I've never seen you be anything but passive" (339, emphasis original), again highlighting the way that a nonthreatening body conceals a reservoir of strength.

Subverting the passive Sleeping Beauty body makes readers consider what lies underneath beauty. Issues of embodiment and romance are especially primed for feminist critique, considering how thoroughly fairy tales perpetuate the idea that young women are objects of the male gaze. Contemporary dystopian fiction, with its efforts to advance feminist heroines, mitigates some of these issues, but it has its own fraught relationship with embodiment and perpetuation of heteronormative ideals. *A Long, Long Sleep* and *When We Wake* manage to make embodiment about the heroine's progress to power, but *Stung* focuses so much on Fiona's puberty that it becomes another exercise in objectification. Even more unfortunately, this objectification leads to a warped romance.

While the romance is often a hallmark of YA and of the fairy tale, the dystopia complicates it. Love blooms against a backdrop of struggle, thus taking on less importance than fighting for survival and social justice. *Stung*, however, focuses excessively on the bodily change of its slumbering heroine, fitting in with Tatar's notion that Sleeping Beauty is "*the* story that captures, with a single stroke, the notion of woman on display, to be looked at as erotic spectacle" ("Sleeping Beauty" 143). In Fiona's dystopian world, men outnumber the women seven to one, and "women are hunted" if they're outside of the walled city where the privileged live (Wiggins 81). Unfortunately, this lazy narrative device ensures a female heroine has to have a male companion to keep her safe. While this does draw upon Sleeping Beauty's literary forebears, evoking the rape that colors early versions of the tale,[3] it also perpetuates female disempowerment.

The disempowering focus on embodiment in *Stung* also carries into the character's romance with her "protector," revealing how romance can undermine feminist agency in these texts. Wiggins falls into the trap of many dystopian authors: in their efforts to offer a heroine who has some agency and awareness, they end up regressing into damaging patriarchal patterns, often by saddling the strong heroine with a male savior, with whom she will have an inevitable romance. Basu, Broad, and Hintz point to the problem of romance in dystopias, noting that "romance is historically a conservative genre and . . . often serves to affirm traditional norms, advancing the primacy of heterosexual couples while associating such relationships with growing up and finding a place in the world" (8). When romance is paired with a heroine's identity development, it often stymies that heroine's growth. Moreover, as in *Stung*'s case, romance can perpetuate rape culture. The narrative places Fiona in the awful situation of having to hide her body because men simply can't control themselves in her dystopian world. Furthermore, her protector-cum-love-interest policies her clothing choices, and, when she dons a dress, tells her, "You're not safe from me . . . [W]hen I look at you, especially when you're dressed like this, I can't think straight" (179). Fiona actually *apologizes* and changes into something else. This exchange is disturbing in its glaring representation of rape culture and victim blaming. Not only can the boy not control himself, but the girl *blames herself* for the boy's lack of self-control. In this exchange, it's only natural that a "beautiful woman" is unsafe around a "man." Indeed, a book like this espouses the message that "boys will be boys" and applies it to Prince Charming himself.

A Long, Long Sleep and *When We Wake*, however, handle romance differently. In retelling Sleeping Beauty, authors have to wrestle with the trope of being awakened by a kiss. A nonconsensual sexual encounter is the foundation of the story. *A Long, Long Sleep* and *When We Wake* manage to upend the fairy-tale romance in order to empower the heroines. Of the three heroines, Rose is the only one who is actually awakened by a kiss. *A Long, Long Sleep* sidesteps the issue of a prince "rescuing" a princess, though, in a few ways. Bren, the young man who awakens Rose, actually does so by performing mouth-to-mouth resuscitation on her, and he awakens her not to a happy ending, but to a painful existence where everyone she knows is dead. Bren also rejects Rose's affection, effectively shutting down the possibility for romance. This narrative turn forces Rose to focus on herself, understand her past and her parents' abuse, and seize her own agency. Furthermore, Bren has a connection to Rose's past that is the key to her fully understanding what her parents did to her—his grandfather is Rose's first love, who reveals to Rose that it was illegal for her parents to put her in stasis. *When We Wake* also decenters the romance plot. While Tegan does have a love interest, in this case the romance helps Tegan personally comprehend the problems that exist in her future. Her potential boyfriend, Abdi, hails from Somalia on a "Talented Alien" scholarship, the only way that this future Australia allows people from Third World countries to access their resources. Through observing how others treat Abdi and learning about his history, Tegan comprehends the extent to which her home country selfishly hoards its resources and promotes propaganda that paints immigrants as undesirable. Thus, romance in both *A Long, Long Sleep* and *When We Wake* propels the heroines to action. While it's not ideal that Rose's understanding of her past abuse hinges on a love interest—the heterosexual romance still holds significance for this reason—or that Tegan's growth and understanding as a privileged white person depends on a person of color's marginalization, it is beneficial for a Sleeping Beauty story to minimize heterosexual romance as the ultimate awakening for a young woman.

The awakening for these Sleeping Beauties is, instead, one of political agency. Even Fiona of *Stung*, whose regressive romance diminishes her agency, makes an effort to challenge the dystopian structures that restrict her environment. All three of these Sleeping Beauty retellings subvert the compliant sleeper heroine into a resilient teenager whose dawning awareness of her surroundings pushes her into rebellion. Again, these are not passive heroines—these are young women who learn that the systems in place are worthy of dismantling. Furthermore, as each protagonist becomes more aware of her new environment, she learns of her own generation's impact on society. While Rose considers her wealthy family's involvement in a corrupt global empire, Tegan questions how her country's scientific advancements now strangle foreign policy. Fiona learns that her own wealth and privilege meant she got the vaccine that resulted in her country's current perilous situation. By forcing the characters to confront their own involvement in the negative aspects of their culture, these narratives pose complex questions about privilege.

Thus, the Sleeping Beauty retelling draws on the tale's history of royalty and privilege to critique the very privilege these characters have. Tegan and Rose grapple with those questions by exploring their sense of morality. While Tegan spent the teen years of her past following her more fervent friends to rallies for energy regulation and refugee rights, she doesn't fully understand the importance of speaking up and assembling until she is faced with her future country's devastating reality. Rose's journey from passive sleeper to powerful heiress of her parents' company awakens her to the pitfalls of capitalist greed and environmental degradation. Upset that their future societies are still troubled by the same issues from the past, both Rose and Tegan take responsibility for their behavior and exhort their communities to do the same.

Again, *Stung* falls short of offering a truly powerful feminist heroine, partly because Fiona's dystopian world, so overtly violent toward women, requires that she hide herself to survive. Ultimately, she ends up as "the chosen one" due to the vaccine she received and provides hope for the future. However, she never gets to be the mouthpiece of this hope; her love interest is the one who shares this news to the world while she lies recovering in a hospital after a brutal encounter with teenage "beasts." *Stung*, while not outright billed as a Sleeping Beauty retelling, hews the most closely to the fairy tale of passivity and waiting for a prince to do the rescuing.

Tegan and Rose, however, tell their own stories and make efforts to bring about social change. Tegan learns to embrace activism for the collective good. After her outburst on air when dressed as the nonthreatening Snow White, she goes on the run and ultimately records a seditious exposé of government corruption. Her activism is directly connected to her role as a sleeper who wakes: she learns that the government project that revived her, while purporting to be about saving soldiers, is actually a front for taking the lives of refugees and using those refugees as slave labor on future space colonies. Increasingly aware of her country's intense nationalism thanks to her relationship with Abdi, Tegan uses her fame to implore the public to make a change for good and share their resources with those who need them, not exploit refugees for their own far-off salvation.

Like Tegan, Rose also bonds with an outsider whose experiences make her reconsider her own. As the heiress of UniCorp, a powerful multiplanetary corporation, Rose herself holds very little power. As an employee who helps her adjust to her new life points out, "UniCorp owns you, at least until you come of age" (9). Rose learns, however, that she owns others, namely, her class-mate, Otto, an alien-human hybrid created in a lab from DNA found on one of Jupiter's moons. Immediately, Rose knows that it's wrong, and she vows to assign Otto's rights to himself as soon as she comes of age. Rose's impetus to fix the problem even when she doesn't know the politics speaks to the sense of hope embedded in the young adult dystopia—there's an optimism in youth to, essentially, do the right thing.

Otto is Rose's most immediate reminder of her parents' nasty legacy, and she resolves to protect him. She cannot do that, though, until she faces her own traumatic past and disassociates herself from the parents who abused her. Her psychological progress equals activist growth, as she ultimately rejects the memory of her parents, and, with that, the monarchical legacy they created. While the book ends with Rose taking the helm of UniCorp—so, in a sense, perpetuating the capitalist ruling class—she does so with an awareness of the company's flaws and a desire for change.

Conclusion

YA dystopias and fairy tale retellings have a symbiotic relationship: dystopian settings amplify the theme of feminist empowerment that threads through contemporary fairy tale retellings, while trends of government oppression, debilitating plague, and ominous scientific advancement complicate historically straightforward fairy-tale narratives. While the wide swath of recent retellings reveals a clear trend in YA fiction, it also unearths a new perspective on the fairy-tale heroine. By entwining a familiar fairy-tale narrative with dystopian details, these contemporary authors (usually) proffer complex and powerful twenty-first-century heroines.

This new perspective is especially powerful for the Sleeping Beauty tale, thanks to the character's history of passivity. But there's more to that passivity than flat characterization and an ideal slate for subversion. Sleeping Beauty is also fascinating as a tale of neglect. Other characters neglect the humanity of Sleeping Beauty; she is something to be protected and worried over, not a person who gets any say in her own destiny. Successful contemporary versions redress this neglect and focus on the heroine's agency. In *A Long, Long Sleep*, Rose must come to terms with parental neglect and learn how to manage her inheritance, while in *When We Wake*, Tegan learns of wide-scale corporate neglect, and she aims to correct it. *Stung*, on the other hand, remains trapped in neglect—Fiona never strikes out on her own or attempts to undermine the oppressive policies of her new society.

The YA fairy-tale dystopia asks readers not to neglect their own positions in society. Indeed, the metaphor of "waking up" in a Sleeping Beauty narrative extends to any type of YA fairy-tale dystopia in which a heroine learns not only about her own individual agency, but also the power of resistance. As Marina Warner notes, the phrase "They lived happily ever after" "consoles us, but gives scant help compared to 'Listen, this is how it was before, but things could change—and they might'" (*Beast* xxi). Progress is slow and dystopias are alarming, but fairy tales that explore social change offer some hope.

Notes

1. See, for example, Freya in Sarah J. Maas's *A Court of Thorns and Roses* or Yeva in Meagan Spooner's *Hunted*.

2. I refer to the "literary fairy tale" as those written/collected and disseminated by major names such as Jeanne-Marie Leprince de Beaumont, Charles Perrault, Hans Christian Andersen, and the Grimms. Certainly, this definition doesn't cover all literary fairy tales, but rather uses canonized ones.

3. In one of the earliest known versions of the tale, Giambattista Basile's "Sun, Moon, Talia," the passive princess suffers a perverted prince, who rapes her while she sleeps. Charles Perrault's version, "The Sleeping Beauty in the Wood," borrows from this tale, taking it further by having the princess fall in love with her rapist after she wakes up.

Works Cited

Bacchilega, Cristina. *Postmodern Fairy Tales: Gender and Narrative Strategies*. U of Pennsylvania P, 1999.

Basu, Balaka, Katherine R. Broad, and Carrie Hintz. "Introduction." *Contemporary Dystopian Fiction for Young Adults: Brave New Teenagers*, edited by Balaka Basu, Katherine R. Broad, and Carrie Hintz, Routledge, 2013, pp. 1–18.

Day, Sara K. "Docile Bodies, Dangerous Bodies: Sexual Awakening and Social Resistance in Young Adult Dystopian Novels." *Female Rebellion in Young Adult Dystopian Fiction*, edited by Sara K. Day, Miranda A. Green-Barteet, and Amy L. Montz, Ashgate, 2014, pp. 75–92.

Healey, Karen. *When We Wake*. Little, Brown, 2014.

Heath, Shirley Brice, and Jennifer Lynn Wolf. "Brain and Behaviour: The Coherence of Teenage Responses to Young Adult Literature." *Contemporary Adolescent Literature and Culture: The Emergent Adult*, edited by Mary Hilton and Maria Nikolajeva, Ashgate, 2012, pp. 139–54.

Montz, Amy L. "Rebels in Dresses: Distractions of Competitive Girlhood in Young Adult Dystopian Fiction." *Female Rebellion in Young Adult Dystopian Fiction*, edited by Sara K. Day, Miranda A. Green-Barteet, and Amy L. Montz, Ashgate, 2014, pp. 107–22.

Sheehan, Anna. *A Long, Long Sleep.* Candlewick, 2013.

Tatar, Maria. *Secrets beyond the Door.* Princeton UP, 2004.

Tatar, Maria. "Show and Tell: Sleeping Beauty as Verbal Icon and Seductive Story." *Marvels & Tales*, vol. 28, no. 1, 2014, pp. 142–58.

Trites, Roberta Seelinger. *Waking Sleeping Beauty.* U of Iowa P, 1997.

Warner, Marina. *From the Beast to the Blonde.* Noonday Press, 1994.

Warner, Marina. *Once Upon a Time: A Short History of Fairy Tale.* Oxford UP, 2014.

Wiggins, Bethany. *Stung.* Walker Children's, 2013.

Zipes, Jack. *Fairy Tales and the Art of Subversion.* 2nd ed., Routledge, 2006.

Further Reading

Baggott, Julianna. *Pure.* Grand Central, 2012.

Block, Francesa Lia. *Love in the Time of Global Warming.* Henry Holt, 2013.

Bow, Erin. *The Scorpion Rules.* Margaret K. McElderry Books, 2015.

DeStefano, Lauren. *Wither.* Simon and Schuster, 2011.

Jay, Stacey. *Of Beast and Beauty.* Delacorte Press, 2013.

Jay, Stacey. *Princess of Thorns.* Delacorte Press, 2014.

Maas, Sarah J. *A Court of Thorns and Roses.* Bloomsbury USA Children's, 2013.

Maas, Sarah J. *Throne of Glass.* Bloomsbury USA Children's, 2012.

Meyer, Marissa. *Cinder.* Feiwel-Macmillan, 2012.

Meyer, Marissa. *Cress.* Feiwel-Macmillan, 2014.

Meyer, Marissa. *Scarlet.* Feiwel-Macmillan, 2013.

Meyer, Marissa. *Winter.* Feiwel-Macmillan, 2015.

Pearce, Jackson. *Sisters Red.* Little, Brown, 2010.

Pearce, Jackson. *Sweetly.* Little, Brown, 2011.

Prineas, Sarah. *Rose and Thorn.* HarperTeen, 2016.

Spooner, Meagan. *Hunted.* HarperTeen, 2017.

Thomas, Rhiannon. *A Wicked Thing.* HarperTeen, 2015.

8

Manufacturing Manhood: Young Adult Fiction and Masculinity(ies) in the Twenty-First Century

Tom Jesse and Heidi Jones

"Everybody told me to be a man. Nobody told me how."
LAURIE HALSE ANDERSON, *Twisted*

In the years since the "Great Recession" of 2007–2009, working-age males in America, Great Britain, and many other English-speaking countries have reported feeling increasingly marginalized in contemporary society. The exact causes of this twenty-first-century "crisis of masculinity" are difficult to pin down, but recent reports in popular news outlets have blamed everything from decreasing participation in the workforce (Gallagher), to lingering resentment over the loss of demographic and economic dominance since World War II (Jones), to outdated understandings of manliness that run counter to many modern cultural norms (Telegraph Men). Whatever the root cause(s) might be, Jack Myers argues that the end result is "a 'Lean Out' generation of young, discouraged and angry men [who feel] abandoned by the thousands of years of history that defined what it meant to be a real man." As Gallagher notes, members of this "Lean Out" generation are frequently abandoning the public sphere: as a group, they are less interested in working, less invested in their families, and more likely to devote their free time to individual hobbies than were previous generations. They are also increasingly more likely to take their own lives (Swami, Stanistreet, and Payne). And when these general behavioral changes become crystallized in specific tragedies—like the white nationalist protests in Charlottesville or any one of America's recent mass shootings—it becomes impossible to ignore that there are deep, underlying challenges facing masculinity in the twenty-first century.

As educators committed to critical literacy in our work with current and future English Language Arts (ELA) teachers, we believe that young adult literature can—and *should*—play an immense role in the search for answers to these challenges.[1] Fictional worlds are not merely fictional; they are also spaces where readers try on new ways of thinking and feeling at a safe distance from the pressures of life out in "The Real World."[2] So if the core issue facing men right now is that their role in society "has changed so much and so quickly that expectations and reality can be far apart" (Jones), and if the changes to this role are primarily the result of cultural, political, and economic trends that are unlikely to be reversed anytime soon, then it is imperative that today's teachers provide young men opportunities to reevaluate their expectations of masculinity so that they are better prepared to cope with the realities of the present age. In the ELA classroom, this would mean reading and discussing YA texts within a critical literacy framework that focuses on the ways these texts do or do not challenge the tropes of masculinity traditionally depicted in popular culture.[3]

But—and this is the core issue we address in this chapter—are there texts readily available that enable young readers to actually *do* the difficult work of critical literacy? As Tami Bereska argued in the early 2000s, representations of masculinity in YA literature remained remarkably stable from the 1940s to the 1990s; the unchanging "Boys' World" presented in these texts is almost always "supposed to be a heterosexual world, comprised of active male bodies, where no sissies are permitted entry" (161). More importantly, Bereska noticed little difference between the codes of male behavior in young adult fiction and the characteristics featured in parenting guidebooks and school curricula during the late nineteenth century (168).[4] Rather than change with the times, male characters in the 1990s were still being written according to the rules that their counterparts in the 1890s lived by—and the results of this disconnect can be seen in both the increasing rates of depression, violence, and suicide among young males and the enduring presence of patriarchal tendencies in society as a whole (169).

In the hope of reversing these trends, we wanted to see if authors and publishers are doing a better job presenting readers with varied portraits of what it means to "be a man" in the twenty-first century. We began by select-ing a cross-section of popular and award-winning young adult novels pub-lished over the past decade (2005–2015) that focus on male protagonists from a range of racial, ethnic, and socioeconomic backgrounds, as well as those dealing with physical disability and mental illness (see "Further Reading" for complete list). Our intention was never to create an exhaustive list of texts, but instead to "cast a wide net" and see how contemporary YA authors were presenting masculinity in the years leading up to and directly after the "Great Recession." And while reading our way through a list that includes acclaimed novels written by lesser-known authors and lesser-known novels written by acclaimed authors, we noticed a clear and consistent pattern of male characters who fail to conform to traditional expectations of masculinity—and who do so in new and exciting ways. This pattern is so consistent, in fact, that we see YA fiction in the twenty-first century as a vital resource for manufacturing understandings of manhood that accommodate a far wider range of gender identities, many of which have traditionally been marginalized in Western culture. Most importantly, these multiple iterations of "new manhood" offer today's students opportunities for reading and learning that extend far beyond the library shelves and classroom walls.

(Re)Thinking Masculinity in Young Adult Literature

Before diving into the texts, some words about how we understand "masculinity" are in order. Our conception of gender draws upon the work of Judith Butler, whose groundbreaking *Gender Trouble* (1990) helped establish the now widely accepted idea that gender is less an innate characteristic of individual bodies than an attempt by those bodies to perform aspects of socially constructed "gender(s)." Yet as Butler points out in her 1993 follow-up to *Gender Trouble*, *Bodies That Matter*, the performance of gender is never "a singular or deliberate 'act,' but, rather, [is] the reiteration and citational practice by which discourse produces the effects that it names" (xii). That is, one cannot simply wake up and "put on" a new gender; instead, successful performance requires a chain of repeated acts that a given society recognizes as representative of certain gender identities.[5] For Butler, these "reiterations" of recognizable acts function as "citations" of the broader social norms that govern current and future performances of these identities. And since any given norm "derives its power through the citations that it compels" (xxii), individuals are under immense pressure to abide by these norms or risk becoming one of those "abject" bodies forced to live on the margins of society (xiii).[6]

For the purposes of our study, the term "masculinity" will be used to refer to the construct of social norms that regulates the performance of "male" identities in the present cultural and historical moment. It is important to remember, however, that the "iterations" Butler theorized are in constant flux as cultural norms evolve over time; the academic fields of boyhood studies and masculinity studies have been working to better understand these changes for more than four decades now. In Michael Kimmel's account, media images have quickly become the primary source for adolescents' grasp of what their "performance [of masculinity] is supposed to look like"—despite the fact that many of these images "misframe masculinity" in potentially dangerous ways (3). Jack Halberstam's *Female Masculinity* (1998) reads media's influence in a more positive light, exploring how representations of "butch" women across Hollywood films, black-and-white photography, and drag shows might be further "exploited to hasten the proliferation of alternate gender regimes" in other parts of our culture (41).[7] Such proliferation, however, is not necessarily a good thing; as Kenneth Kidd has argued, increasing the number of "model masculinities" available to adolescents does little to disrupt the racial, economic, and heterosexual privilege associated with traditional iterations of masculinity (188–89). For Kidd, the more pressing work involves investigating the discourses that surround these traditional iterations in order to understand how they establish (and continually reestablish) the grounds for their own legitimacy (189). This, we would argue, is precisely why YA fiction is such an ideal site for critically examining contemporary iterations of gender: as an explicitly *discursive* and *imaginary* space, it makes possible the work of deconstructing the social norms surrounding masculinity by offering opportunities to explore new conceptions of how things are—and how things could be—for young men in the twenty-first century.[8]

According to Thomas Bean and Karen Moni, recent YA novels have embraced a more Butler-ian view of identity construction, with major characters who represent more fluid notions of what it means to be a young adult. In addition, they contend that this shift in the construction of identity is a direct reflection of recent changes in society, which have made it possible for "teen social actors [to] use action and experience to forge identities in this shifting, unstable landscape" (641). Josephine Young's study of adolescent boys (aged ten to thirteen) demonstrates, however, that navigating this landscape is an immensely difficult task. When boys were asked to read texts from multiple genres and compare how diction changed with gender, they struggled to do so before eventually arriving at an awareness of "how their constructions of masculinity influenced their interpretations of the texts" (6). Young's participants found this work challenging, admitting that they sometimes didn't know what to say. Yet her study reminds us that the work of critical literacy, however difficult it may be, encourages adolescents to "explore and critique hegemonic practices of masculinity" at precisely the moment when they are most susceptible to those practices (13).

While Bean, Moni, and Young discuss using texts in classrooms, other recent work has focused on critical analyses of gender in the texts themselves. Vera Woloshyn, Nancy Taber, and Laura Lane analyze masculinity and femininity in *The Hunger Games* and determine that the three main characters each represent unique iterations of gendered discourse. Whereas Gale represents stereotypical masculinity, Peeta represents "marginalized masculinity," and Katniss is constrained in "heteronormative ways" (1). In a similar study, Helen Harper focuses her attention on masculinities in books about girls because "[i]n Western thought, masculinity and femininity are often organized as binary, a highly polarized binary in which the terms gain meaning only in relation to the other, such that what is feminine is not masculine, what is masculine is not feminine" (509). Taken together, these studies suggest the need for a more nuanced understanding of how masculinity is being performed in contemporary YA texts—one that, ideally, helps educators encourage students to question the traditional binary and stop settling for "a paucity of classifications when it comes to gender" (Halberstam 27).

Four Iterations of Masculinity in Contemporary YA Novels

Almost as soon as we started reading these eleven novels, clear patterns in the ways that authors were challenging conventional masculinity began to emerge. In an abrupt shift from Bereska's findings in the early 2000s, we saw authors consistently using their protagonists and antagonists to explore alternative formations of manhood that, to borrow from Butler's model of performative reiteration, represent new "iterations" of identity that rely on repurposing or revising the norms of traditional masculinity. By (mis)performing these norms in new ways, male characters in these texts participate in what Butler describes as a process of "repetition and displacement," a form of "insubordination that appears to take place within the very terms of the original, and which calls into question" the power of those original norms (18). Some of the "displacements" we discuss below are quite subtle, while others are more dramatic; each, however, contributes to the larger project of manufacturing new possibilities for successfully "being a man" in the twenty-first century. After exploring each of these four iterations in detail, we close our analysis with a brief discussion of how approaching these novels from a critical literacy perspective can help students more effectively evaluate the images of masculinity they receive from popular media.

Iteration #1: The Stereotypical Dude-Bro

While the pejorative term "dude-bro" may lack technical precision, we think it more than makes up for this shortcoming by so perfectly capturing a host of stereotypes surrounding hypermasculinity (often referred to as "toxic masculinity") in post-1980s American culture.[9] The typical dude-bro character in YA fiction is loud, brash, and exceptionally self-confident; he enjoys significant racial and economic privilege; and he displays a tendency to compete over everything from academic and athletic accomplishments to romantic conquests. He steadfastly adheres to "a conventional masculinity that doesn't leave room for much individuality" and is especially hesitant to embrace any "serious deviation from heterosexual male norms" (Filipovic). In these novels, the stereotypical dude-bro performs this rigid adherence to a narrowly defined sense of manliness in two specific ways: (a) he establishes his status as the "alpha male" in any and all social situations, and (b) he shows a near-total lack of self-awareness regarding his own hypermasculine identity. By taking the norms of traditional masculinity to extreme lengths, the dude-bro is at once an *exemplar* of twenty-first-century manhood and a *caricature* of that same identity.

Take, for instance, Wendell Holmes in Francisco X. Stork's *Marcelo in the Real World*. As the Harvard-attending son of a major partner in the law firm founded by Marcelo's father, Wendell treats every other character in the novel as his inferior and shows no concern for the little work he is asked to complete during his summer internship. Instead, his primary focus is taking advantage of Marcelo's Asperger's-like condition in order to lure another employee (Jasmine) onto his yacht for what is suggested would be nonconsensual sex. "Once we're below deck," Wendell informs Marcelo, "it won't matter what she feels about me. I'll take care of her feelings. There are ways to create feelings or change them or make them disappear for a while" (Stork 125). As a stereotypical dude-bro, Wendell views those around him—especially women—as playthings for his personal amusement. And the contrasts between Wendell and Marcelo don't stop there. Wendell lies to and manipulates those around him, while Marcelo can be almost *too* candid in his social interactions. Wendell excels at multiple sports, whereas Marcelo is exceptionally adept at dealing with animals. And while Wendell is never shown to doubt his abilities or question his actions, Stork spends a great majority of the text detailing Marcelo's inner struggle with doubt and uncertainty. These contrasts make it easy for readers to know which male character they are supposed to be rooting for, but the ease with which Wendell escapes negative consequences for his dude-bro actions may leave some wondering if it isn't better (or at least more fun) to put off the responsibilities of manhood and simply enjoy the pleasures of male adolescence indefinitely.

Iteration #2: The Sensitive Thinker

Much like Marcelo, the "sensitive thinker" stands in near-perfect opposition to the stereotypical dude-bro, because he spends a significant portion of the novel contemplating how his actions have affected or might affect those around him.

He may talk freely with friends about fear and self-doubt. He may open up to adult characters (parents, teachers, coaches) regarding at least a portion of the difficulties he is facing. Or he may spend time writing in a journal or thinking out loud so that readers are invited into his complex, nuanced decision-making processes. Whatever his exact behaviors might be, the sensitive thinker eschews boasting about his successes or blaming others for his failures—two hallmarks of hypermasculinity in popular culture—in favor of recognizing and appreciating the role his "supporting cast" plays in his personal journey. And while it is certainly possible for these characters to also embody some of the norms of dominant masculinity, the key difference here is that *these components always remain secondary aspects of the character's social persona.* Other characters may take note of the protagonist's physical strength or socioeconomic status, but as a sensitive thinker, he refuses to see himself in such limiting terms. And while the sensitive thinker's introspection is sometimes read by other characters as a sign of weakness, his ability to remain calm under pressure and exhibit behaviors that are "grown-up, adult, responsible, and reliable" (Kimmel 3) represents a direct challenge to hypermasculine notions of what adolescence looks like.

Quinn from Jason Reynolds and Brendan Kiely's *All American Boys* acts as a foil to the novel's stereotypical dude-bro, Paul. Quinn is forced to think deeply about the altercation he sees between Paul (a white police officer) and Rashad (a Black teenager), because he is not able to make sense of the violence he has witnessed. And since Paul is both a close family friend and someone Quinn looks up to, he is also forced to consider his own whiteness and how that might shape his perception of the power struggle that occurred between Paul and Rashad. Quinn feels powerless to speak up when he hears his peers chant "Rashad is absent today!" at school, which only adds to his inner turmoil. And when Paul confronts him about the altercation in an attempt to get Quinn "on his side," Quinn resists the urge to respond physically and instead tries to think about the incident from Paul's point of view, aligning himself with Paul in both familiarity and in whiteness.

As a sensitive thinker, Quinn thinks things through before taking action and listens to all sides before making a decision. In the process, he shatters the stereotype of the dude-bro by not immediately taking Paul's side simply because he knows him better than Rashad. Instead, he contemplates what he witnesses, considers multiple interpretations of the event, and then makes the choice that is best for him in terms of joining the protest at school. Although Quinn is only a high schooler, he is catapulted into a scenario involving race relations, racial profiling, and police brutality, and the reader gets a front-row seat to watch how he will attempt to resolve such serious and life-altering issues. This type of character is critical for young adults to see, because it demonstrates that masculinity can lie within someone who deliberates before taking action, and that issues like racial profiling and police brutality can be handled with nonviolence.

Iteration #3: The Rebel Outsider

Probably the least-common iteration of alternative masculinity in the novels we studied, the rebel outsider exists on the periphery of mainstream school/social culture and, in response to this marginalization, adopts an outwardly defiant or rebellious persona. The rebel outsider wears his exclusion as a badge of honor that grants him the power to openly question the codes that govern adolescent social life. This power, however, comes at a price: each time he questions the way things are, he makes his peers nervous about their own position in the prevailing order—which they then attempt to resecure by further reinforcing the outsider's marginalized position.[10] For these characters, then, "being a man" is linked to sticking one's neck out for friends and family members, whatever the social costs may be. And while this kind of risk-taking may, on its surface, seem more honorable than the physical aggression of the stereotypical dude-bro or the calculated passivity of the sensitive thinker, the narratives we studied clearly communicate that standing up for those he cares about means sacrificing any chance he might have to be embraced by the mainstream culture. His willing self-sacrifice disrupts the logic of conventional masculinity by suggesting that there is more to being a man than being liked or accepted by large numbers of one's peers. Far more than the dude-bro or the thinker, his presence in the narrative destabilizes the norms surrounding "masculine" behaviors and opens up new ways of performing manliness—both for other characters in the novel and for readers out in "The Real World."

Park in Rainbow Rowell's *Eleanor & Park* evolves into a rebel outsider as his relationship with Eleanor deepens, and he even begins wearing eyeliner as a way of standing up to his father's preconceived notions of what it means to be male. Both Eleanor and Park stand out from the crowd because of the way they look: Eleanor is considered "big," with curly red hair, and Park is one of very few Asian Americans in town. Given the novel's rural Nebraska setting, the two are quickly "othered" in a place where everyone looks the same and seems to accept stereotypical gender roles. In addition to these physical differences, Park and Eleanor's shared passion for unpopular hobbies (comic books, punk music, challenging gender stereotypes) illustrates for readers how questioning the status quo can actually open up possibilities that most young adults are missing out on. The two protagonists don't seem to worry that their peers can't understand them; in fact, they actually seem to *like* the fact that other people don't understand them. Park refuses to bow down to his father's pressures to not wear makeup, and, despite his mother's initial doubts about Eleanor, he never stops being her friend. More importantly, their "gender-bending" behaviors (e.g., Park's eyeliner and Eleanor's baggy, ripped, men's jeans) work to open the construct of masculinity to an even broader range of iterations—a move that helps make the characters in our final section possible.[11]

Iteration #4: The Problematic Other

Somewhat surprisingly, this was the most prevalent iteration of alternative masculinity we encountered in our readings. For our purposes, the term "problematic other" refers to any major character who identifies as male but embodies his male-ness in ways that directly contradict the norms of dominant masculinity. From physical weakness and self-doubt to cooperation and homosexuality, the problematic other performs his gender in all the "wrong" ways. As one of Butler's "abject" bodies, he exists in "those 'unlivable' and 'uninhabitable' zones of social life which are nevertheless densely populated by those who do not enjoy the status of the subject, but whose living under the sign of the 'unlivable' is required to circumscribe the domain of the subject" (xiii). Annette Wannamaker takes Butler's analysis one step further, arguing that when these characters appear in children's literature, they help other characters "perform the necessary rituals of subject formation" by marking the boundary between self and other—between what makes sense according to the norms of dominant masculinity and what must remain forever "unintelligible" (29). These are not characters who challenge masculine norms in quiet, subtle ways or in defiant support of their friends; these are characters who have been denied full subjecthood because their existence exposes the constructedness of traditional masculinity and then reveals the exceptionally fragile nature of that construction.

The two most common reasons for this radical other-ing of male characters are sexual orientation and physical/mental disability. The extent of a given character's abjection, then, depends on how well he can "pass" for a conventionally masculine subject when necessary. In John Green and David Levithan's *Will Grayson, Will Grayson*, the two identically named protagonists pass fairly well but still manage to occupy liminal spaces in their respective schools' social hierarchies. For the first Will Grayson (who happens to be straight), this marginalization is primarily the result of his long-standing friendship with Tiny Cooper, "the world's largest person who is really, really gay, and also the world's gayest person who is really, really large" (Green and Levithan 3). For the second Will Grayson (who happens to be gay), the root cause is far more severe: he suffers from clinical depression and frequent thoughts of suicide that make maintaining social connections a serious challenge. So when, through a series of chance events, Will Grayson #2 and Tiny Cooper meet and fall in love, both protagonists are forced to come to terms with how their connection to Tiny—whose physical size and talent on the football field enable him to embrace his own problematic masculinity—defines them as young men.

What's so unique about their journeys of self-discovery, however, is that neither Will Grayson has to deal with excessive or violent homophobia along the way. Instead of the typical goonlike villain who hurls derogatory slurs, each is battling the inner demons of overanalysis and self-doubt. "[T]iny is being kind," Grayson #2 thinks the first time Tiny comes over to meet his mom, "because he hasn't realized yet who i am, what i am. i will never be kind back. the best i can do is give him reasons to give up" (213). Grayson #1 has his own "self-destruct" experience around this same point in the novel, and it is only through the kindness of those closest to him that he comes to terms with his own masculine identity. In a reversal of the typical young-adult-novel-with-a-gay-protagonist formula, *Will Grayson, Will Grayson* offers readers a world where the problematic other is more problematic to himself than to other characters in the novel.[12] Rather than cutting all social ties, Green and Levithan suggest that the best way to address the crisis of masculinity is to surround ourselves with people who understand us better than we do.

Critical Literacy and Masculinity in the ELA Classroom

As these four iterations suggest, today's young adult authors are increasingly resisting the heteronormative masculinity that was so pervasive in early YA texts. Each of the books we studied features at least one prominent male character who, in his own unique way, challenges long-standing constructions of traditional masculinity. Surprisingly, however, we found ourselves struggling to identify "stereotypical dude-bros"—a form of hypermasculine gender performance that, given its ubiquity in other forms of popular media, we assumed would be prevalent in these novels. The fact that these dude-bros are often absent or exist only as minor characters gives us hope that young adult fiction is becoming more inclusive, more equitable, and more resistant to outdated definitions of what "manhood" means in our world.

These positive trends related to the construction of masculinity(ies) in recent young adult literature should embolden ELA teachers to devote more time to the study of these texts in their classrooms. Working within a framework of critical literacy, teachers can help students adopt an equity lens and investigate how an author's choices shape the dynamic identities of their male characters. In the process, students can also begin to evaluate the relationship between these characters and their own position(s) in society—to move, that is, beyond fictional representations of masculinity and into the realm of everyday gender performance. To promote these kinds of conversations, we recommend the following critical literacy framing questions:

1. What language does the author use when describing characteristics attributed to gender and masculinities?
2. Which character(s) have the power to decide what counts as "masculine" and what doesn't? As readers, how can we tell?
3. How do race and social class intertwine with masculinities to create identities, and who gets to decide which of these constructs are most valued in society?
4. How do the masculinities and gendered identities of the characters change the way I see gender in the world?

We recognize that critical literacy is not a panacea for the underlying issues with contemporary masculinity, but given the exciting work that YA authors are doing to develop alternative versions of manhood, we think it represents an essential starting point for the conversations that we need to be having about the future of men in Western society. These conversations can help students better understand how power is distributed within society while also encouraging them to connect literature to their lives and to the lives of others. Critical literacy also empowers students to recognize that because we do not live in an equitable society, some voices (and genders) matter more than others—but also that change is possible, and perhaps even inevitable.

Given the work that recent YA fiction is doing to manufacture manhood in new ways, we see today's ELA classroom as an ideal place for students to begin challenging the rigid conceptions of masculinity that have been handed down to them. Of course, we think it invaluable that students have experiences reading and discussing these alternative iterations of manliness. But we also think they should be encouraged to question the traditional iterations they see in canonical texts so that they can better understand how the present "crisis of masculinity" was produced. As critical consumers of gender norms, future generations of students should be far better equipped to adapt as more nuanced understandings of what it means to "be a man" continue to emerge over the coming years.

Notes

1. We rely here on Ira Shor's definition of critical literacy: "Critical literacy thus challenges the status quo in an effort to discover alternative paths for self and social development. This kind of literacy—words rethinking worlds, self dissenting in society—connects the political and the personal, the public and the private, the global and the local, the economic and the pedagogical, for rethinking our lives and for promoting justice in place of inequity" (1).

2. Not the television show (sadly), but the fictional construct used by adults everywhere to scare adolescents everywhere into submission. At the time of writing, the authors have yet to confirm that anything approximating "The Real World" actually exists.

3. In their study of the correlation between media consumption and masculinity ideology, Giaccardi et al. list "emotional restrictiveness, self-reliance, aggression, and risk-taking" as core tropes within the now-dominant form of masculinity operating in Western cultures (584). They also include homophobia, competitiveness, and "displays of power over women" as integral to the contemporary system of masculine norms.

4. These eight codes include: particular types and degrees of emotional expression, naturalized aggression, male hang-out groups, hierarchies within those groups, competition, athleticism, adventure, and sound moral character (Bereska 161).

5. Because they are socially constructed and socially maintained, the performative demands of gender land with equal force upon both cisgendered and transgendered bodies. For Butler, "'sex' is an ideal construct which is forcibly materialized through time. It is not a simple fact or static condition of a body, but a process whereby regulatory norms materialize 'sex' and achieve this materialization through a forcible reiteration of those norms" (xii).

6. Butler elaborates further on this link between performativity and exclusion in a later chapter: "The normative force of performativity—its power to establish what qualifies as 'being'—works not only through reiteration, but through exclusion as well. And in the case of bodies, those exclusions haunt signification as its abject borders or as that which is strictly foreclosed: the unlivable, the nonnarrativizable, the traumatic" (140).

7. Although *Female Masculinity* predates Halberstam's work on explicitly transgender issues, the text raises essential questions regarding traditional masculinity's assumption that the "masculine" body is a cisgendered one (rather than a transgendered one). The authors hope that future research will more closely explore how YA texts featuring transgender protagonists construct their own models of masculinity(ies).

8. In *The Modern Age*, Kent Baxter worries that some YA literature is guilty of "essentializing adolescence as volatile and eclipsing its history," thereby perpetuating potentially harmful myths about the "natural" state of teenagers (15). We saw little evidence of this occurring in the texts we examined for this study, but Baxter's words are a much-needed reminder that YA narratives and characters should not be read as representing any universal or inherent aspects of the adolescent experience.

9. See James Hamblin's "Toxic Masculinity and Murder" (*TheAtlantic.com*, 16 Jun. 2016) and Alia E. Dastagir's "Men Pay a Steep Price When It Comes to Masculinity" (*USAToday.com*, 31 Mar. 2017) for more on the impact of toxic masculinity in contemporary culture.

10. This boundary-drawing process of *inclusion via exclusion* in young adult novels closely mirrors Butler's conception of how bodies "matter" in social and political discourse. "[I]t will be as important," she writes, "to think about how and to what end bodies are constructed as is [sic] it will be to think about how and to what end bodies are *not* constructed and, further, to ask after how bodies which fail to materialize provide the necessary 'outside,'

if not the necessary support, for the bodies which, in materializing the norm, qualify as bodies that matter" (xxiv).

11. For Halberstam, the kind of masculinity that Eleanor performs via her attire is ultimately "quite tame," due to her "resolute heterosexuality" (28). Serious gender trouble begins only "when and where female masculinity conjoins with possibly queer identities"—identities not explicitly featured in *Eleanor & Park.*

12. Wickens (2011) laments that authors of contemporary young adult LGBTQ+ fiction often "create antagonists with homophobic attitudes and behaviors" (153) but then "fail to provide any other ways of thinking" that can effectively counter their antagonists' bigotry and hate (156).

Works Cited

Anderson, Laurie Halse. *Twisted.* Viking, 2007.

Baxter, Kent. *The Modern Age: Turn-of-the-Century American Culture and the Invention of Adolescence.* U of Alabama P, 2011.

Bean, Thomas W., and Karen Moni. "Developing Students' Critical Literacy: Exploring Identity Construction in Young Adult Fiction." *Journal of Adolescent & Adult Literacy*, vol. 46, no. 8, 2003, pp. 638–48. *JSTOR*, www.jstor.org/stable/40017169.

Bereska, Tami M. "The Changing Boys' World in the 20th Century: Reality and 'Fiction.'" *Journal of Men's Studies*, vol. 11, no. 2, 2003, pp. 157–74. *SAGE Journals*, doi: doi.org/10.3149/jms.1102.157.

Butler, Judith. *Bodies That Matter: On the Discursive Limits of Sex.* Routledge, 2011.

Filipovic, Jill. "Dude or Dude-Bro: Ten Ways to Tell." *Guardian*, 14 Nov. 2012, www.theguardian.com/commentisfree/2012/nov/14/dude-or-dudebro-ten-ways-to-tell. Accessed 20 May 2017.

Gallagher, Maggie. "The Crisis of Masculinity." *National Review*, 7 Oct. 2016, www.nationalreview.com/article/440849/male-labor-force-participation-rate-drop-about-masculine-identity. Accessed 19 May 2017.

Giaccardi, Soraya, et al. "Media Use and Men's Risk Behaviors: Examining the Role of Masculinity Ideology." *Sex Roles*, vol. 77, no. 9–10, 2017, pp. 581–92. *Springer Link*, doi:10.1007/s11199–017–0754–y.

Green, John, and David Levithan. *Will Grayson, Will Grayson.* Dutton, 2010.

Halberstam, Judith (Jack). *Female Masculinity.* Duke UP, 1998.

Harper, Helen. "Studying Masculinity(ies) in Books about Girls." *Canadian Journal of Education*, vol. 30, no. 2, 2007, pp. 508–30. *JSTOR*, www.jstor.org/stable/20466648.

Jones, Owen. "How to Be a Man: The Quiet Crisis of Masculinity." *New Statesman*, 7 June 2016, www.newstatesman.com/politics/uk/2016/06/how-be-man. Accessed 19 May 2017.

Kidd, Kenneth B. *Making American Boys: Boyology and the Feral Tale.* U of Minnesota P, 2004.

Kimmel, Michael. *Misframing Men.* Rutgers UP, 2010.

Myers, Jack. "Young Men Are Facing a Masculinity Crisis." *TIME*, 26 May 2016, time.com/4339209/masculinity-crisis/. Accessed 19 Jan. 2017.

Reynolds, Jason, and Brendan Kiely. *All American Boys.* Atheneum Books, 2015.

Shor, Ira. "What Is Critical Literacy?" *Journal of Pluralism, Pedagogy and Practice*, vol. 1, no. 4, 1999, www.lesley.edu/journal-pedagogy-pluralism-practice/ ira-shor/critical-literacy/. Accessed 23 Apr. 2017.

Stork, Francis X. *Marcelo in the Real World.* Arthur A. Levine, 2009.

Swami, Viren, Debbi Stanistreet, and Sarah Payne. "Masculinities and Suicide." *Psychologist*, vol. 21, no. 4, 2008, thepsychologist.bps.org.uk/volume-21/edition-4/ masculinities-and-suicide. Accessed 31 May 2017.

Telegraph Men. "'A Crisis of Masculinity': Men are Struggling to Cope with Life." *Telegraph*, 19 Nov. 2014, www.telegraph.co.uk/men/thinking-man/11238596/A-crisis-of-masculinity -men-are-struggling-to-cope-with-life.html. Accessed 19 Jan. 2017.

Wannamaker, Anne. *Boys in Children's Literature and Popular Culture: Masculinity, Abjection, and the Fictional Child*. Routledge, 2008.

Wickens, Corrine M. "Codes, Silences, and Homophobia: Challenging Normative Assumptions about Gender and Sexuality in Contemporary LGBTQ Young Adult Literature." *Children's Literature in Education*, vol. 42, no. 2, 2011, pp. 148–64. *EBSCOhost*, doi:10.1007 /s10583-011-9129-0.

Woloshyn, Vera, Nancy Taber, and Laura Lane. "Discourses of Masculinity and Femininity in *The Hunger Games*: 'Scarred,' 'Bloody,' and 'Stunning.'" *International Journal of Social Science Studies*, vol. 1, no. 1, 2013, pp. 150–60, redfame.com/journal/index.php/ ijsss/article /viewFile/21/52. Accessed 10 Dec. 2016.

Young, Josephine Peyton. "Displaying Practices of Masculinity: Critical Literacy and Social Contexts." *Journal of Adolescent & Adult Literacy*, vol. 45, no. 1, 2001, pp. 4–14. *JSTOR*, www .jstor.org/stable/40007626.

Further Reading

Albertalli, Becky. *Simon vs. the Homo Sapiens Agenda*. Balzer + Bray, 2018.

Anderson, Laurie Halse. *Twisted*. Viking, 2007.

Crutcher, Chris. *The Sledding Hill*. HarperCollins, 2009.

De la Peña, Matt. *Mexican Whiteboy*. Delacorte Press, 2008.

Green, John, and David Levithan. *Will Grayson, Will Grayson*. Dutton, 2010.

Palacio, R. J. *Wonder*. Doubleday, 2012.

Reynolds, Jason, and Brendan Kiely. *All American Boys*. Atheneum Books, 2015.

Rowell, Rainbow. *Eleanor & Park*. St. Martin's Griffin, 2013.

Silvera, Adam. *More Happy than Not*. Simon and Schuster, 2018.

Stork, Francis X. *Marcelo in the Real World*. Arthur A. Levine, 2009.

Yang, Gene Luen, and Lark Pien. *American Born Chinese*. First Second, 2006.

9

Mythopoeic YA: Worlds of Possibility

Leah Phillips

> A feminist project is to find ways in which women can exist in
> relation to women; how women can be in relation to each other.
> It is a project because we are not there yet.
>
> SARA AHMED

First emerging in the early 1980s with the work of Tamora Pierce and Robin McKinley, mythopoeic YA is a speculative,[1] "imaginary world" speculative fiction that brings new worlds into being to actualize new modes of being (see also Wolf). Leigh Bardugo's Grishaverse and Tomi Adeyemi's Orïsha offer excellent, contemporary examples. Both (imaginary) worlds give space to resistance, and themselves resist, in big and small ways, dominant, hegemonic norms and standards. The heroes of the Grishaverse, for example, directly counter conventional heroic markers such as race (the hero is white), class (the hero is of an elevated social position), gender (he is male), and relationships (he and he alone is hero). Adeyemi's Orïsha offers a West African–inspired world countering the predominance of the pseudomedieval and European in fantasy literature (see also Cecire; Fimi), while Zélie, a dark-skinned female-hero, contests the race and gender norms of archetypal heroes. Indeed, mythopoeic YA's imaginary worlds and the female-heroes featured therein offer alternatives to two or more of the archetypal hero's narrow and limiting defining characteristics, as discussed by Margery Hourihan in *Deconstructing the Hero: Literary Theory and Children's Literature*. Briefly, these are race, class and mastery, gender, age, relationships, rationality, and action and violence.

For Hourihan, the heroic markers describe and exist because of the hero story's "conceptual centre" (15). Comprising "a set of binary oppositions: the qualities ascribed to the hero on the one hand and [...] his 'wild' opponents on the other," the conceptual center imposes radical alterity on that which is not hero—monster, body, woman, other—to ensure the hero's "heroicness," while also setting him above and apart from "others."[2] The center of opposition also provides the hero story its impetus to action: the hero (who is male, white, of an elevated social class, youthful and in "good" physical and mental health) must slay the monster (that which he is not). He typically wins marriage to a princess for his efforts, another form of dominance.[3] As a subgenre of YA fantasy drawing on the hero stories of traditional mythic narratives, mythopoeic YA engages and complicates the system of binary opposition at the heart of its source material by occupying spaces between oppositions, by giving space to female authors, and by foregrounding female-heroes (or sheroes),[4] non-Western worlds, and relationships, thereby offering alternative and inclusive models of being-hero.

The figuration "being-X," being-hero for example, is fundamental to *how* mythopoeic YA intervenes in dominant mythic paradigms and, by extension, hegemonic discourse in its relation to those paradigms. Binary oppositions require an unassailable break between oppositional pairs to maintain the appearance of radical difference between those pairs. If, for example, there is no indisputable void between hero and monster, the hero's certain dominance becomes uncertain, because he and the monster might be alike or, potentially, one and the same. The liminal—or that which occupies the space between— disrupts and denies the power of binary opposition. "Being-X" demonstrates liminality by coupling the dynamic "being" (the action of existing and actively occupying a place or position) with, in this case, hero. The hyphen insists upon the correlation of "being" and "X" while also physically occupying the space between terms, thus visually emphasizing their combined meaning.

Coalescing into the subgenre it is recognizable as today in the mid-1980s, mythopoeic YA is an interventionist fiction, cultural work depending on mythopoeic YA's "being-YA." Existing between that which is "for" adults and "for" children, YA is a liminal field. Though it must be noted that YA's liminality—particularly its disruptive potential—is both undertheorized and under-recognized, an issue I explore elsewhere (see *Female Heroes in Young Adult Fantasy Fiction: Reframing Myths of Adolescent Girlhood*). Here, it is sufficient to say that YA's in-between status gives rise to a conceptual center of possibility, not opposition. Through its center of possibility, mythopoeic YA rewrites hegemonic, binary values, encouraging difference and change. Indeed, mythopoeic YA tells new stories, featuring unorthodox heroes (e.g., not the archetypal white, able-bodied, attractive male) set in unconventional imaginary worlds (e.g., not the prototypical Western, pseudomedieval world), while also now taking full advantage of digital opportunities available in the twenty-first century. Mythopoeic YA offers unparalleled avenues for increasing diversity and inclusivity not only through the stories and characters set within its imaginary worlds but also through the boundary-pushing ways in which it affords access to those worlds.

Imaginary World Fiction

Mythopoeic YA is an imaginary world fiction started by women "for" adolescent girls, that is, with adolescent girls in mind. This subgenre of speculative fiction provides windows into (fictional) worlds that are independent of and different from our mundane one, but consistent and logical in their own right (see also Sullivan; Clute and Grant). These worlds have unique histories, mythologies, and religious systems that are often polytheistic. They feature magic or that which is impossible by the standards of "consensus reality" as well as creatures and modes of transportation not present in our world (Hume 21). Mythopoeic YA texts also frequently feature literary maps, that is, visual representations of their worlds, as a means of adding depth and verisimilitude to both world and story (see also Phillips, "Mapping"). Primarily textual, these worlds are created and held together by narrative. As Wolf suggests, "narrative holds a world together at different scales, as it structures individual works that make up a world, links different works set in a world, and occasionally, links separate worlds together into multiverses" (225). Together, these features—being a "feminist project" (Ahmed 14), the fantastic, the formation of a "network of intertextuality" (Wolf 8), and a sense that these worlds are or could be real—shape mythopoeic YA.

In *Building Imaginary Worlds: The Theory and History of Subcreation*, Mark Wolf defines imaginary worlds as dynamic entities superseding both the boundaries of a single text and also single media sources (literature, film, television, games, products) (cf. Jenkins). Imaginary worlds are "transnarrative and transmedial" (2). Indeed, Wolf contends that a multinarrative and multimodal existence is an indispensable feature of "imaginary world" fantasy, as "worlds extend beyond the stories that occur in them," creating depth and immersive opportunity (17). Crucially, the relationship of mythopoeic YA's texts—of whatever form—is not that of series, as series cannot account for how mythopoeic YA appears to offer access to worlds that already exist.[5] Conversely, imaginary worlds are not encountered through the one-time experience of a single text (see also Jenkins), though individual narratives may demonstrate a mythopoeic YA sensibility—Kiran Millwood Hargrave's *The Girl of Ink and Stars*, Sarah Beth Durst's *Vessel*, Natasha Ngan's *The Elites*, Malinda Lo's *Ash* and *Huntress* (both of which are also examples of LGBTQ+ YA). These individual texts lack the depth, sense of history, and verisimilitude created by mythopoeic YA's multiple points of entry. Moreover, the assemblage produced by the "network of intertextuality" forming, and formed by, mythopoeic YA's imaginary worlds is another relationship thwarting the power of binary oppositions (Wolf 8).

Mythopoeic YA's imaginary worlds are frequently pseudomedieval and European, owing to the influence of Tolkien and Lewis and as an effect of the "conceptual centre" of binary opposition under which Western/not is included. As an expression of the West's distant past and the time of heroes (Beowulf, Sir Gawain, King Arthur), the pseudomedieval is the privileged position inscribed by the binaries at the heart of fantasy in its relation to myth.[6] Of the pseudomedieval, Pierce's Tortall offers one excellent example, while Alison Croggon's Edil-Amarandh, accessed primarily through The Books of Pellinor, offers another (2005–2009 and 2016).[7] Edil-Amarandh is home to Bards (have "magical" abilities), Hulls (corrupt Bards), Elidhu (elemental creatures), and Maerad—the female-hero of this world. Set predominantly in Annar and the Seven Kingdoms, The Books of Pellinor follow Maerad as she is rescued from slavery, discovers she is a Bard, and saves the world, following Campbell's basic patterning of separation-initiation-return. Maerad, however, stands in stark contrast to traditional myth and fantasy's women. Not only is she the hero, but Maerad is also not entirely human. She has Elidhu heritage, which gives her the ability to "be wolf" (*Riddle* 426), that is, being-wolf is part of Maerad's being-hero, including both woman and animal within the heroic frame.

Maerad's multifaceted identity, as well as her being-female, is made possible because of the unique articulation of Edil-Amarandh as an example of mythopoeic YA. A high fantasy imaginary world with a highly developed religious system, deeply held beliefs and lore, and an extensive history, as well as a robust collection of maps, Edil-Amarandh gives the appearance that it at least once existed.[8] While the history that gives this world such depth is woven into the narrative, the first four novels also feature appendices, such as "A Brief History of Edil-Amarandh" and "Of Annar and the Seven Kingdoms," that aid in the creation of this imaginary world (*The Gift* 473–79 and 480–91). There are also fragments of lays and poems included before many chapters. These paratextual materials, alongside maps and other accompanying productions, develop the world of Edil-Amarandh beyond the primary narrative, with literary maps—the visual representations of imaginary worlds appealing to cartographic practice—playing a key role.

Graphic maps of imaginary worlds contribute to a world's authenticity in several ways, most notably appealing to the sense that the world is—because it is mapped—"real" (Muehrcke and Muehrcke). These maps also often deepen that sense of the real by insisting, through notes or titles, that they are a product not of the author-creator but of the world itself. *Maresi* by Maria Turtschaninoff demonstrates this through two pretextual maps: the first depicts the layout of The Red Abbey, where most of the story occurs. The second is of Menos, the island location of The Red Abbey. On the island-map, there is a note indicating it was "[d]rawn by SISTER O in the second year of the reign of our thirty-second Mother. Based on the original by GARAI OF THE BLOOD in the reign of the first Mother" (Turtschaninoff 9, formatting original). Both that Sister O drew this map and that it is not the first map of Menos contribute to a sense that this world existed before the glimpse into it we receive in *Maresi*, while also suggesting that it has the potential to continue after we leave it, even if "our island is very small and difficult to find" (15). This method of world-building—of attributing the maps of a place to characters from within the text—both draws readers into the world of the story and contributes to the world's depth, while also indicating the potentially tremendous size and scope of imaginary worlds.

Tamora Pierce: Mythopoeic YA's Founding

The most common manifestation of mythopoeic YA's imaginary worlds is the pseudomedieval and European, owing in considerable part to Tolkien's and Lewis's influence on fantasy for children and young adults (see also Cecire; Phillips, *Female Heroes*). Indeed, Tamora Pierce, a founding mother of mythopoeic YA, frequently declares that "Tolkien is where" she "started with fantasy" (Powell's Books), as is the case for many fantasy writers, YA or otherwise (see Haber). Pierce also cites an absence of female-heroes as the reason she began writing "fantasy with teenaged girl heroes" in the 1980s ("Tamora Pierce Biography"). Indeed, initially written by women and "for" adolescent girls, countering the overwhelmingly male domination of fantasy, mythopoeic YA features female authors and female-heroes as a matter of course, not as an exception.

Pierce's role as a founding mother of this subgenre cannot be understated. Not only is her Tortall Universe one of the most long-standing and well-developed examples of mythopoeic YA, but her influence on the contemporary generation of mythopoeic YA writers is profound. Leigh Bardugo writes, "Pierce didn't just blaze a trail. Her heroines cut a swath through the fantasy world with wit, strength, and savvy. Her stories still lead the vanguard today.

Pierce is the real lioness, and we're all just running to keep pace."[9] Included in the paratextual materials of Pierce's 2017 *Tortall: A Spy's Guide*, Bardugo's statement demonstrates Pierce's lasting influence ("still lead" and "keep pace") on the field of fantasy while also speaking to her intervention within it ("blaze a trail" and "cut a swath").

Pierce's "trail" begins in 1983 with *Alanna: The First Adventure*, the initial book of the Song of the Lioness quartet (1983–1988) and ostensibly the first point of entry into Tortall, though this is not guaranteed.[10] Featuring a cross-dressing heroine who uses her disguise to gain access to the conventionally male space of knighthood (see also Flanagan), this first window in the world of Tortall complicates traditional myth by inserting a female into the role of hero, questioning the gender binary in the process: "[g]irl, boy or dancing bear, you're the finest page—the finest squire-to-be—at Court" (*Alanna: The First Adventure* 215). Despite her female sex, Alanna proves that her abilities at tilting, fencing, archery, and combat—the activities associated with training to become a knight—exceed those of the boys at Court. Indeed, Alanna becomes Alan within the space of her quartet, taking on the masculinity of her cross-dressed persona. She, *as he*, is hero.

Outwardly, Alanna's narrative is a straightforward replication of conventional hero stories, particularly in that she cross-dresses to participate in the male world of knighthood, an issue Robin McKinley's *The Blue Sword* and *The Hero and the Crown* share. While Angharad Crew—the female-hero of this text—may not cross-dress to Alanna's extent, she does insist on being called Harry, implying a masculine identity. The acts of being-Alan (hero) and being-called-Harry are interventions, if only incipient, in the fields of myth and fantasy. Taking on the role of male hero allows the girls scope to be heroes, and Alanna the chance to demonstrate being-hero as she negotiates the binarily opposed identities/roles hero and woman, as I discuss at length in *Female Heroes*. As Victoria Flanagan writes of cross-dressing in children's literature, "the wearing of the clothes deemed socially appropriate for the opposite sex is generally considered to be a transgressive and provocative act" (xv), not a sexual one.[11] The Song of the Lioness quartet—in that it was written by a woman, published in the early 1980s, when fantasy was still overwhelmingly dominated by men, and featured a female-hero, albeit cross-dressed—offers a "transgressive and provocative act," opening doors for further such acts.

Inserting female-heroes into a field structurally requiring male heroes is not easy, nor does it necessarily offer the kinds of diversity of representation we expect today. For example, Alanna is white, upper-class, and able-bodied. She is also ostensibly heterosexual, though her cross-dressing offers the potentiality for a queer reading (see also Phillips, *Female Heroes*; Salter). Despite limits,

Alanna's cross-dressing lays a foundation for others: "[A]n idea made her [Daine's] jaw drop: if she's [Alanna] a legend, and a hero, then anyone could be a hero" (Pierce, *Wild Magic* 61); even when those heroes turn up in the most unlikely of places: "Oh, wonderful. You're [Kel] on a hero's quest to get rid of bullies" (*First Test* 149). Alanna's cross-dressing to become a knight opened a space for other kinds of heroes. As Alanna tells her daughter Aly in *Trickster's Choice*, "the whole point to doing as I did [becoming a knight] was so you could do something else, if you wanted to" (18). Not only does this twenty-first-century window into Tortall demonstrate a more complex engagement with myth by expanding the role of the female-hero through demonstrating her function as a role model and feminist icon, but it also comments on its world-building by explaining the kinds of changes occurring in both Pierce's Tortall and mythopoeic YA more widely. Alanna replicated the (male) hero journey by cross-dressing so that Aly, Pierce's subsequent female heroes, and the many mythopoeic YA heroes since "could do something"—anything—"else."

Diversity in Mythopoeic YA

In the early 1980s, the nascent intervention of a white, able-bodied, upper-class preteen *girl* who trades places with her twin brother so that she (as a he) may train to become a knight was provocative. Indeed, fantasy literature (for adults) was then so dominated by and beholden to the archetype that Pierce—after three rejections and at the suggestion of her agent—transformed Alanna's story from a single novel for adults into "four books for teenagers" ("Tamora Pierce Biography"). YA, as a liminal field of literature outside of the mainstream, offered space to this nontraditional hero, while the Song of the Lioness quartet (the four books for teenagers) set the shape and tone of mythopoeic YA, concomitantly opening the door for increasingly diverse and more-nuanced interventions: *We Hunt the Flame* by Hafsah Faizal features Zafira, a female-hero of color who disguises herself as a man to save her people. Released in 2019, *We Hunt the Flame*, as a potential example of mythopoeic YA, features a cross-dressing female-hero as did the subgenre's founding texts, while also including issues of race and ethnicity (at least) within the heroic frame, more deeply fulfilling the subgenre's interventionist roots.

My definition of diversity aligns with that of Diversity in YA, a blog and social media platform founded in 2011 by YA authors Cindy Pon and Malinda Lo. Diverse YA fiction, including diverse mythopoeic YA, is that which is "set in a non-Western world or inspired by a non-Western world; or with a main character who is non-white, LGBTQ+, and/or disabled" ("Diversity in YA").

Since 2012 a diversity of imaginary worlds, characters, and stories have begun appearing in mythopoeic YA,[12] though representation is far from equal (see Ramdarshan Bold). Indeed, Ebony Elizabeth Thomas's *The Dark Fantastic: Race and the Imagination from Harry Potter to the Hunger Games* explores the absence of racially diverse characters in popular (i.e., mainstream) youth and young adult speculative fiction while also revealing the re-citing of marginalization and hate that overwhelmingly occurs when Black and brown characters do appear in such media. As a subgenre founded on offering that which the mainstream and archetypal refuse, mythopoeic YA has been pushing the boundaries of the "acceptable" since the early 1980s, cultural work that increasingly diverse and intersectional female heroes and imaginary worlds can continue today. In this section, I wish to use my privileged position to highlight some of the excellent recent and forthcoming diverse, as defined above, examples of mythopoeic YA. This section will not include detailed critical engagement, as I believe #OwnVoices scholars should be given the opportunity to perform such readings.[13]

While mythopoeic YA fantasy is foundationally an imaginary world fantasy written by women and "for" adolescent girls, *Shadowshaper*—the first book of Daniel José Older's Shadowshaper Cypher—offers a twist on the obviously mythopoeic in its incorporation of contemporary settings and Puerto Rican traditions. This urban iteration of the mythopoeic YA novel follows the story of Sierra Santiago, a Puerto Rican teenager and shadowshaper, someone who has the ability "to work with spirits" (62), living in Brooklyn. Through her art (street murals) and her shadowshaping power, Sierra can give form to spirits. As Sierra comes to terms with her powers and her place within her family legacy, the novel engages gender, race, and class (and their intersections), as well as the gentrification of neighborhoods. Zoraida Cordova's Brooklyn Brujas (*Labyrinth Lost*) works similarly while also showing the importance of family, heritage, and teamwork. In short, while the pseudomedieval is—hopefully, one day, was—prominent, it is not the only landscape a mythopoeic mind-set may occupy, as the questions of being and life and death supersede this one specific landscape.

Dragons and taverns are key features, and metaphors, in pseudomedieval worlds: dragons are the ultimate foe, and taverns are places of respite. Contemporary mythopoeic YA seems to answer the unspoken plea Deepa Dharmadhikari's "there were no taverns in India" (15). Alwyn Hamilton's Miraji is a pseudo-Arabian imaginary world with an undertone of the Wild West featuring an on-the-run gun-slinging desert girl determined to save herself, a still "snarky" (co)hero, djinns, and ghouls. Renée Ahdieh's imaginary worlds—see

The Wrath and the Dawn and *Flame in the Mist*, as well as concomitant short stories—offer Eastern settings, including feudal Japan in the latter. Other non-Western worlds worth exploring: Nnedi Okorafor's Leopard Society (*Akata Witch*) and Tomi Adeyemi's Orïsha (*Children of Blood and Bone*) offer Nigerian-inspired imaginary worlds, and Rati Mehrotra's *Markswoman* features sisterhoods of elite warriors set in an Asian imaginary world.

As is the case with all mythopoeic YA, the heroes featured in these imaginary worlds reflect their worlds, as their worlds reflect them. From Orïsha, Zélie has dark brown skin and "snow-white hair," marking her a maji (magically gifted and persecuted within this world) (Adeyemi 12), and the Leopard Society's Sunny Nwazue should be "dark brown" like her Nigerian family, but she is albino (Okorafor 3), intersecting a medical condition with gender and race. Dhonielle Clayton's Orléans (The Belles) offers a complex commentary on appearance, class, and race in a world drawing as much from Clayton's own heritage in its fantastical rendering of Orléans as it does Marie Antoinette's court and eighteenth-century Japanese geishas ("The Belles | Dhonielle Clayton"). In Audrey Coulthurst's Northern Kingdoms (*Of Fire and Stars*), Princess Dennaleia falls in love with the Prince of Mynaria's, that is, her betrothed's, sister, and Sarah Glenn Marsh's *Reign of the Fallen* offers gender fluidity as well as fluidity between life and death. Natasha Ngan's *Girls of Paper and Fire*, the first of a promising imaginary world, includes a "forbidden" romance and a non-Western imaginary world, and in Veronica Roth's *Carve the Mark*, Cyra's magical abilities cause her to experience what can only be described as chronic pain, as "the pain was just a part of life now" (Roth 52). These worlds and heroes offer that which the archetypal hero refuses, serving as sites of resistance to hegemonic norms and standards in the process.

Diverse mythopoeic YA is necessary and needed, and it will be until no one questions the existence of nonwhite, disabled, and/or queer heroes—especially if these markers of "otherness" intersect with being-female. There is still work to be done, though with Adeyemi's *The Children of Blood and Bone*—a YA fantasy novel by a person of color featuring a non-Western imaginary world and a dark-skinned female-hero—being called the biggest debut YA novel/ biggest YA fantasy debut of 2018,[14] I have hope that diversity in YA, across the spectrum of genres, is increasing and that mythopoeic YA has a leading role to play in continuing to expose readers to difference, be it landscapes, bodies, sexualities, or something else entirely. Looking at lists such as BN Teen's "50 of Our Most Anticipated YA Fantasy Books of 2019," I am cautiously optimistic that—true to its heritage—the mythopoeic YA of 2019 is continuing to push boundaries by widening perceptions of what it means to be a hero.[15]

Leigh Bardugo's Grishaverse: A Multimodal Imaginary World

With nearly thirty years between the first window into Tortall (Pierce, *Alanna: The First Adventure*) and the first into the Grishaverse (Bardugo, *Shadow and Bone*), the latter takes full advantage not only of the possibilities opened by Pierce and Tortall but also of the potentialities of imaginary worlds when coupled with digital technologies. Indeed, the Grishaverse promises to sit alongside Tortall as a twenty-first-century exemplar of mythopoeic YA, a positioning made even more certain by Netflix's recently announced *Shadow and Bone*, a planned eight-episode series set in the Grishaverse (Andreeva). Modeled on an imperial, tsarist Russia, a trilogy first introduces the Grishaverse, but there are also folktales set within the world, a website offering a multitude of access points, and commodities—jewelry and food—allowing another kind of experience of the Grishaverse. The network of intertextuality, boundary-pushing forms of story as digital capacities, provides increased access to the world, and the diversity of representation reflects the state of mythopoeic YA in 2018.

If following publication order, access to the Grishaverse begins with the Shadow and Bone trilogy (SaB),[16] which follows Alina Starkov as she discovers she possesses the Grisha ability to manipulate matter at its most basic form, in her case the ability to summon light, and is consequently thrust into a battle for power. The next encounter comes through the Six of Crows duology (SoC), in which several characters from the SaB trilogy make appearances and a "crew" of new characters is introduced. In 2019 the King of Scars (KoS) series—focusing on Nikolai Lantsov, who first appears in the initial trilogy as the mysterious military genius Sturmhond—was published. Demonstrating the interaction of narratives within a world, the series follows Nikolai as he rebuilds Ravka after the events of *Ruin and Rising*, the final book of the SaB trilogy—KoS begins six months after the SaB trilogy and two years prior to the SoC duology, frustrating any "easy" linearity offered by publication order. Complicating teleological narrative progression further, *The Language of Thorns* (TLoT)—"a collection of fairy tales and folklore" that the world's inhabitants "would have grown up reading" (Macmillan "Extras")—not only interrupts the publication timeline but also does not advance any narrative; TLoT advances the world.

TLoT's disruption—a clash between publication order and the world's timeline—is present in many of the bigger imaginary worlds, including, for example, Pierce's Tortall, Croggon's Edil-Amarandh, Meyer's Lunar Chronicles, and Maas's Erilea. Moving discontinuously through a world offers narrative depth by filling in gaps related to what occurred before or after a certain point as well as by creating new gaps. Size is, however, not a prerequisite to such disruption. Cashore's Graceling Realm, accessed primarily through a trilogy, uses a nonlinear approach to great effect: *Fire*, published in 2011, is set fifty years before *Graceling* (2009), and *Bitterblue* (2013) picks where *Graceling* ended.

As a collection of fairy tales, TLoT is also an example of extranarrative materials or "information and events which fall outside of the main narrative threads and braids" (Wolf 200). These materials do not specifically advance any story, though they do develop the world through their own, even if only implied, narratives. TLoT, for example, adds depth and verisimilitude to the Grishaverse as the lays, poems, and indices do for Edil-Amarandh (Croggon). Crucially, the material existence of these access points, including their digital incarnations, prevents an enforced reading order. A reader's initial point of entry might be the short fairy tales of TLoT, the SoC duology, or a myriad of other potentialities, as the digital makes explicit.

On Grishaverse.com, there is a range of extranarrative materials contributing to the Grishaverse as a world that somehow exists outside of our consensus reality (yet is also somehow a part of it). For example, there are quizzes to find out your "Grisha order" or which member of the SoC gang you are. There are recipes from the world and downloadable images. Of particular note, there is an interactive, color map of the Grishaverse uniting the novels and this online, digital space: a print—pretextual—version of this map appears in the American versions of SaB and all versions of the SoC duology. Within the novels composing the SoC duology, there are also maps specific to each story, "The Ice Court" and "Ketterdam" respectively. The interactive nature of the online map adds a layer to the world that is not possible with a printed, static map, while also demonstrating Wolf's belief, and I agree, that "even maps can be used to imply narratives; for example, the presence of ruins suggests places that were built and then were destroyed or fell into disuse" (198). SaB is primarily set in and around Ravka, while SoC centers on the island of Kerch, an inset map within the digital offering that zooms into focus when a cursor moves across it.

Many areas on the digital incarnation are also "clickable." For example, the Unsea features in the SaB trilogy and appears on the digital Grishaverse map. On the print map, it is represented as a large void with a monstrous face at its core. On the digital, the Unsea retains the visual representation, but it is also is clickable, offering access to a key passage from *Shadow and Bone* describing the geographical phenomenon and a definition that extends its existence to a time prior to any of the stories (currently existing): "A swath of nearly impenetrable darkness crawling with monsters that feast on human flesh. Hundreds of years ago, its sudden appearance obliterated the Tula Valley, and left Ravka divided and landlocked" ("Welcome to the Grishaverse"). While the print map implies a certain kind of narrative around this feature, the online, digital, interactive map actualizes a narrative—potentially even offering "seeds of new, connected stories, which in turn may extend the world even further" (Wolf 198), while also extending mythopoeic YA's scope and reach.

Countering the individuality of the hero, the heroes of this narrative arc are a motley "crew" of six individuals: at the center, Kaz Brekker. Nicknamed "dirty-hands" for his willingness to take on any job, Kaz is the leader of the "Dregs," one of Ketterdam's biggest gangs, thus offering an alternative to the "class and mastery" requirement of conventional heroes (Hourihan 62–68). He also has haphephobia, a crippling fear of being touched, and uses a cane, demonstrating physical difference. Alongside Kaz, Inej, or "The Wraith," has the dark brown skin of the Suli people, including both a woman and a person of color within the heroic frame. Nina is a Heartrender, that is, one of the Grisha. She is "tall and built like the figurehead of a ship carved by a generous hand" (74), offering readers a female-hero whose body and skills exceed contemporary expectations of and for femininity, or what it means to be a woman. Jesper, a sharpshooter with a gambling problem, Wylan Van Eck, a dyslexic runaway who is good with explosives, and Matthias, an ill-at-ease Fjerdan (a loose adaptation of Germanic peoples), complete the "crew." Together these teenagers—of different races, classes, abilities, and sexualities (Jesper and Wylan fall in love)—seek to end the stratification keeping them in the dregs, paralleling not just the youth activist movements sweeping the USA in light of continued, needless school shootings, but also the current shape of mythopoeic YA.

Conclusion: Digital Frontiers

Mythopoeic YA's defining feature is resistance to dominant discourse; in charting new territories, it offers new ways of being. Elsewhere I refer to this as a mapping sensibility, an ethos of offering alternative frameworks for living and being an adolescent (Phillips, "A Mapping Sensibility"). Here, the mapping sensibility manifests as a tendency for mythopoeic YA to eschew norms and standards, a trait this chapter traces as it explores the narrative arc of mythopoeic YA's journey toward diversity of representation—a journey that it, publishers, and readers are still making. Specifically, this chapter explores how mythopoeic YA has moved from Alanna's "doing as I did [becoming a knight . . .]" to more complex engagements of race, gender and sexuality, and (dis)ability that offer readers—adolescent and more broadly—alternatives to hegemonic norms and standards (Pierce, *Trickster's Choice* 18).

Beginning as a feminist project, mythopoeic YA's growing intersectionality speaks to the needs of contemporary society. Indeed, while it began as a subgenre tied to the pseudomedieval and featuring female heroes quite literally inserted into the heroic narrative by cross-dressing (Pierce's Alanna) or taking on a masculine persona (McKinley's Harry), mythopoeic YA is now much broader in scope and outlook. Moreover, mythopoeic YA's intervention into dominant paradigms is increasingly complex as Leigh Bardugo's Grishaverse demonstrates. In short, mythopoeic YA, as Pierce says of fantasy and science fiction, is "a literature of possibilities" (50), but what are the next possibilities?

In "Theory Rises, Maginot Line Endures," Caroline Hunt suggests the future of YA is "largely digital," declaring that we, as critics, avoid considering e-texts and 'alternative' methods of reading not just at our peril but also to the detriment of readers, especially those who do not align with the imagined "uniformly affluent" 'normal' teen reader (211). While YA fantasy does not typically address issues of literacy—Tracie Chee's extraordinary Sea of Ink and Gold (*The Reader*) is an exception—mythopoeic YA's transmedia imaginary worlds offer significant opportunities for taking up Hunt's call. Indeed, "by expanding the range of narrative possibility rather than pursuing a single path with a beginning, middle, and end," mythopoeic YA offers "new story structures" (Jenkins 119) thus countering the narrative of white, male, able-bodied superiority dominating mainstream, hegemonic discourse alongside how we approach knowledge and information and also the communicating of both to all manner of people.

Notes

1. Mythopoeic YA is related to—though crucially different from—the "mythopoeic literature" endorsed by the Mythopoeic Society (*Mythopoeic Society*), as this chapter demonstrates.

2. Derrida describes binary oppositions as enacting a system of "violent hierarchy," and Gatens observes that binaries are "not a neutral way of dividing up the world," because binaries "contain a set of implicit assumptions that assign a prominence and a dominant value to the term in the position of A at the *expense* of not-A" (93, emphasis mine).

3. Jesse and Jones's reading of masculinity in chapter eight of this collection also describes the hero.

4. "Sheroes" first came into usage on a message board—Sheroes Central—cofounded by mythopoeic YA author Tamora Pierce and children's and YA author Meg Cabot. I prefer "female-heroes," but given Pierce's tie to "shero," as well as how it linguistically offers a critical intervention into the concept of hero, I include it here.

5. Victor Watson offers an excellent reading of series in *Reading Series Fiction: From Arthur Ransome to Gene Kemp*, and I give a more detailed reading of how mythopoeic YA is not series in *Female Heroes in Young Adult Fantasy Fiction: Reframing Myths of Adolescent Girlhood*.

6. Fantasy, especially "high fantasy," is closely tied to myth (see Alexander), but as this chapter will demonstrate, mythopoeic YA is more than high fantasy.

7. The Books of Pellinor are Australian mythopoeic YA, and the first four books were initially published between 2003 and 2008 in Australia with later releases in the UK and the USA. *The Bone Queen* was published simultaneously in Australia, the UK, and the USA.

8. Croggon built Edil-Amarandh so well that she once issued an "Author Note" on her website declaring the world's fictional status: "By the way, over the past few years, so many people have asked me where they can read the Annaren Scripts that I feel obliged to confess that it is a fiction" ("The Books of Pellinor").

9. The same can be said of the, now, women who read Pierce's books as young girls. See Tamora Pierce, "Interview," as well as Ragsdale.

10. I, for example, first encountered Tortall through Pierce's The Immortals quartet (1992–1996), which comes after The Song of the Lioness quartet, according to both Tortall's timeline and publication order.

11. While The Song of the Lioness quartet is YA—and YA is a field of literature related to but also distinct from children's literature—Alanna's cross-dressing, at least at its outset, aligns with Flanagan's reading.

12. As with any shift, there are earlier forerunners, but 2012 seems to mark a concerted turn in the kinds of YA, not just mythopoeic YA, being published.

13. Coined by YA author Corinne Duyvis, #OwnVoices began as a means of identifying if and how authors and characters shared a marginalized identity. For more details, see Duyvis.

14. The success of Children of Blood and Bone is unprecedented. As of September 9, 2018, it has spent twenty-five weeks on the New York Times Best Sellers List (Young Adult Hardcover). With 47 percent of the of the over 100,000 votes cast by (presumably adult) viewers, CoBaB was the 2018 Tonight Show Summer Read, and the book is being adapted to film by Fox 2000.

15. The "Further Reading" section at the end of this chapter includes many of these texts.

16. I give, and use, the abbreviations for these series because doing so is a convention of the subgenre. Acronyms are used, with hashtags, on social media platforms to form another network, or perhaps web, of intertextuality. For example, #ACOTAR is Sarah J. Mass's A Court of Thorns and Roses, and #CoBaB is Tomi Adeyemi's Children of Blood and Bone, both of which can be found on Twitter, Tumblr, Pinterest, and other social media sites.

Works Cited

"10 Recent Diverse* YA Fantasy and Science Fiction Novels." Diversity in YA, 5 Oct. 2015, http://www.diversityinya.com/2015/10/10-recent-diverse-ya-fantasy-and-science-fiction-novels/.

Adeyemi, Tomi. Children of Blood and Bone. Macmillan Children's Books, 2018.

Ahmed, Sara. Living a Feminist Life. Duke UP Books, 2017.

Albert, Melissa. "50 of Our Most Anticipated YA Fantasy Books of 2019." The B&N Teen Blog, 21 Dec. 2018, https://www.barnesandnoble.com/blog/teen/50-of-our-most-anticipated-fantasy-ya-books-of-2019/.

Alexander, Lloyd. "High Fantasy and Heroic Romance." Horn Book Magazine, Dec. 1971.

Andreeva, Nellie, and Denise Petski. "Netflix Orders 'Shadow and Bone' Series Based on Leigh Bardugo's Grishaverse Novels from Eric Heisserer & Shawn Levy." Deadline, 10 Jan. 2019, https://deadline.com/2019/01/netflix-orders-shadow-and-bone-series-leigh-bardugo-grishaverse-fantasy-novels-1202532783/.

Bardugo, Leigh. Shadow and Bone. Henry Holt, 2012.

The Belles | Dhonielle Clayton. https://www.dhonielleclayton.com/the-belles/. Accessed 30 Mar. 2018.

The Books of Pellinor. 13 May 2008, https://web.archive.org/web/20080513083635/http://www
.alisoncroggon.com:80/fantasy/books.html.

Campbell, Joseph. *The Hero with a Thousand Faces.* Princeton UP, 1949.

Cecire, Maria Sachiko. "Sources and Successors." *J.R.R. Tolkien (New Casebooks)*, edited by
Peter Hunt, Palgrave Macmillan, 2013, pp. 32–47.

"Children of Blood and Bone—What We Know So Far." *Pan Macmillan*, https://www
.panmacmillan.com/blogs/fiction/children-of-blood-and-bone-tomi-adeyemi-book-film.
Accessed 5 Sept. 2018.

Clute, John, and John Grant. "Secondary World." *The Encyclopedia of Science Fiction*, 1997,
http://sf-encyclopedia.uk/fe.php?nm=secondary_world.

Croggon, Alison. *The Gift.* Walker, 2004.

Croggon, Alison. *The Riddle.* Walker, 2005.

Dharmadhikari, Deepa. "Surviving Fantasy through Post-Colonialism." *Foundation*, vol. 107,
2009, pp. 15–20.

Diaz, Shelley. "Embracing Diversity in YA Lit." *School Library Journal*, 12 Sept. 2013, https://
www.slj.com/2013/09/teens-ya/embracing-diversity-in-ya-lit/.

"Diversity in YA." *Diversity in YA*, http://www.diversityinya.com/. Accessed 20 June 2019.

Duyvis, Corinne. "#ownvoices • Corinne Duyvis." *Corinne Duyvis*, http://www.corinneduyvis
.net/ownvoices/. Accessed 29 Dec. 2018.

"Extras." *Grishaverse.com*, 2017, /extras/.

Fimi, Dimitra. *Celtic Myth in Contemporary Children's Fantasy.* Palgrave Macmillan, 2017.

Flanagan, Victoria. *Into the Closet: Cross-Dressing and the Gendered Body in Children's
Literature and Film.* Routledge, 2008.

Gatens, Moira. *Feminism and Philosophy: Perspectives on Difference and Equality.* Polity, 1991.

Hourihan, Margery. *Deconstructing the Hero: Literary Theory and Children's Literature.*
Routledge, 1997.

Hume, Kathryn. *Fantasy and Mimesis: Response to Reality in Western Literature.* Routledge, 1984.

Hunt, Caroline. "Theory Rises, Maginot Line Endures." *Children's Literature Association
Quarterly*, vol. 42, no. 2, 2017, pp. 205–17. *CrossRef*, doi:10.1353/chq.2017.0017.

Jenkins, Henry. *Convergence Culture: Where Old and New Media Collide.* New York UP, 2006.

Muehrcke, Philip, and Juliana Muehrcke. "Maps in Literature." *Geographical Review*, vol. 64, no.
3, 1974, pp. 317–38.

Mythopoeic Society. http://www.mythsoc.org/. Accessed 31 Mar. 2018.

Okorafor, Nnedi. *Akata Witch.* Speak, 2017.

Older, Daniel José. *Shadowshaper.* Scholastic, 2015.

Phillips, Leah. *Female Heroes in Young Adult Fantasy Fiction: Reframing Myths of Adolescent
Girlhood.* Bloomsbury, forthcoming.

Phillips, Leah. "A Mapping Sensibility: How Mythopoeic YA (Re)Maps the Terrain of Female
Adolescence." *Modern Language Studies*, vol. 48, no. 1, 2018, pp. 46–63.

Pierce, Tamora. *Alanna: The First Adventure.* Random House, 1983.

Pierce, Tamora. "Fantasy: Why Kids Read It, Why Kids Need It." *School Library Journal*, vol. 39,
no. 10, 1993, pp. 50–51.

Pierce, Tamora. *First Test.* Random House, 1999.

Pierce, Tamora. Interview with Amina Al-Sadi and Lindy West. "Girls Can Be Heroes,
Depending on What Books You Read Growing Up." *KUOW*, 5 Mar. 2018, http://kuow.org/
post/girls-can-be-heroes-depending-what-books-you-read-growing.

Pierce, Tamora. *Tortall: A Spy's Guide.* Random House Books for Young Readers, 2017.

Pierce, Tamora. *Trickster's Choice*. Random House, 2003.

Pierce, Tamora. *Wild Magic*. Random House, 1992.

Powell's Books. "Philip Pullman, Tamora Pierce, and Christopher Paolini Talk Fantasy Fiction." http://www.powells.com/authors/paolini.html. Accessed 31 July 2013.

Prokhovnik, Raia. *Rational Woman: A Feminist Critique of Dichotomy*. Routledge, 2012.

Ragsdale, Melissa. "This Kids' Fantasy Series Is Still Essential Reading for Women in Male-Dominated Fields." *Bustle*, Feb. 2018, https://www.bustle.com/p/this-tamora-pierce-series-helped-me-understand-how-it-feels-to-be-the-only-woman-in-the-room-8090440.

Ramdarshan Bold, Melanie. "The Eight Percent Problem: Authors of Colour in the British Young Adult Market (2006–2016)." *Publishing Research Quarterly*, vol. 34, no. 3, 2018, pp. 385–406. *Springer Link*, doi:10.1007/s12109-018-9600-5.

Reflecting Realities—A Survey of Ethnic Representation within UK Children's Literature 2017, Research. https://clpe.org.uk/library-and-resources/research/reflecting-realities-survey-ethnic-representation-within-uk-children. Accessed 2 Aug. 2018.

Roth, Veronica. *Carve the Mark*. Harper Collins, 2017.

Salter, Anastasia. "Closed Minds: Tamora Pierce's Teenagers and the Problem of Desire." *Supernatural Youth: The Rise of the Teen Hero in Literature and Popular Culture*, edited by Jes Battis, Lexington Books, 2011.

Sullivan, Charles William. "Fantasy." *Stories and Society: Children's Literature in Its Social Context*, edited by Dennis Butts, Palgrave Macmillan, 1992, pp. 97–109.

"Tamora Pierce Biography." *Tamora Pierce*, http://www.tamora-pierce.net/about/. Accessed 5 May 2017.

Thomas, Ebony Elizabeth. *The Dark Fantastic: Race and the Imagination from Harry Potter to the Hunger Games*. New York UP, 2019.

"Tonight Show Summer Reads." *NBC*, https://www.nbc.com/the-tonight-show/exclusives/summer-reads. Accessed 5 Sept. 2018.

Turtschaninoff, Maria. *Maresi*. Pushkin Children's Books, 2016.

Welcome to the Grishaverse. http://www.grishaverse.com/world/#map. Accessed 30 Mar. 2018.

Wolf, Mark J. P. *Building Imaginary Worlds: The Theory and History of Subcreation*. Routledge, 2012.

Yep, Laurence. "Fantasy and Reality." *Horn Book Magazine*, vol. 54, 1978, pp. 137–43.

"Young Adult Hardcover Books—Best Sellers—September 9, 2018—The New York Times." *The New York Times. NYTimes.com*, https://www.nytimes.com/books/best-sellers/2018/09/09/young-adult-hardcover/. Accessed 5 Sept. 2018.

Further Reading

Azul, Mikko. *The Staff of Fire and Bone*. Not a Pipe, 2018.

Belleza, Rhoda. *Empress of a Thousand Skies*. 1st ed., Razorbill, 2017.

Chupeco, Rin. *The Bone Witch*. Sourcebooks Fire, 2017.

Ciccarelli, Kristen. *The Last Namsara*. HarperTeen, 2017.

Daud, Somaiya. *Mirage: A Novel*. Flatiron Books, 2018.

Dennard, Susan. *Truthwitch: A Witchlands Novel*. 1st ed., Tor Teen, 2016.

Elliott, Kate. *Court of Fives*. 1st ed., Little, Brown Books for Young Readers, 2015.

Fine, Sarah. *The Cursed Queen*. Margaret K. McElderry Books, 2017.

Gratton, Tessa. *The Queens of Innis Lear*. HarperVoyager, 2018.

Hartman, Rachel. *Tess of the Road*. Random House Books for Young Readers, 2018.

Jae-Jones, S. *Wintersong: A Novel*. A Thomas Dunne Book for St. Martin's Griffin, 2017.

Khan, Ausma Zehanat. *The Bloodprint*. Harper Voyager, 2017.

Miller, Linsey. *Mask of Shadows*. Sourcebooks Fire, 2017.

Nova, S. B. *A Kingdom of Exiles: Volume 1*. CreateSpace Independent Publishing Platform, 2017.

Oomerbhoy, Farah. *The Last of the Firedrakes*. Wise Ink Creative, 2015.

Parker, Natalie C. *Seafire*. Razorbill, 2018.

Tahir, Sabaa. *An Ember in the Ashes*. 1st ed., Razorbill, 2015.

Taranta, Mary. *Shimmer and Burn*. Margaret K. McElderry Books, 2017.

10

"Tell Me Who I Am": An Investigation of Cultural Authenticity in YA Disability Peritexts

Megan Brown

With the recent push for disability rights and the #weneeddiversebooks campaign, authors, especially those of young adult (YA) fiction, have begun to move away from the pity narrative to attempt to create a wide variety of realistic characters who have disabilities. YA novels such as *Turtles all the Way Down* (Green), *Wonder* (Palacio), and *The Perks of Being a Wallflower* (Chbosky) have been on the forefront of this conversation in the past few years, since the characters in the text demonstrate aspects of disability that were avoided previously. While these texts have received attention, including in film, few others have entered the blockbuster realm, even though there are many more available. These other books also include disabled characters and plots that put intrigue, adventure, and coming-of-age tropes at the fore; however, differences in publishing access, marketing, and writing style keeps many books on the outskirts of conversation. For years, pity had been fully engaged as a narrative prosthesis (Mitchell and Snyder 15) to propel the plot forward for these readers to the detriment of a connection to the disabilities that readers may be experiencing. Characters were placed in stories to facilitate conflict and turmoil in a text. Additionally, these stories were rarely created by authors who had a disability or any personal relationships with people who had disabilities; thus, seldom were they accurate. Ultimately, some of these new YA novels are still being written by people who do not have a great deal of experience with disability; therefore, the story has the potential to further reify the confusions that surround this minority population. They are using the influx of these ideas to support their story but not the actual reality of their readers.

Within this chapter I investigate the ways that authors of a variety of YA texts that have not previously been given much attention in research and popular culture are framed by publishers as having the potential for creating culturally authentic characters who have disabilities in their texts. I argue that an author's experience with disability separates the text for the reader, both disabled and able-bodied, as having the capacity for accuracy that affords a factual reality in the ways that the information is being presented that is not necessarily available when publishers do not inform the readers about certain experiences. Remaining authentic to the accurate culture of disability is not an easy task, but through time spent, experiences, and exposure to disabilities and the people who have them, the author's knowledge aids in their writing, even when the text is not in the realistic genre. Usually framed within the idea of cultural authenticity, this idea presents a challenge for publishers as they seek to share the author's positioning with their purchasing audiences through peritext. They have the power to present narratives that support the population they are describing or to perpetuate stereotypes. Publishers choose to present this information in the peritext that accompanies a book—in full view of the purchaser and reader, whether disabled or able-bodied—to provide validity to the author's authentic portrayal of disability. Readers then can begin their reading with a perspective on the author's knowledge from which they have written the narrative. With increased experience, there is increased potential of the reality of disability being presented within the pages of the book. My discussion focuses on the written peritextual information in thirty YA fiction novels published between 2010 and 2016 that have at least one character who has a disability. Accordingly, the chapter will present the importance of peritextual information in framing a narrative, similar to the work of Sivashankar, Jackson, and Degener, in addition to the ways that positionality statements found within the peritext contribute to the representation of disabilities for young adult readers.

Paratextual Framing

Paratext is a "'vestibule' that offers the world at large the possibility of either stepping inside or turning back" from the narrative itself (Genette 2). Texts, including YA novels, provide paratextual elements to support the narrative as well as market the book to the reader and/or consumer. Paratext is a combination of both peritext and epitext. Within this umbrella term, peritext is the parts of the book that come with publication of the text and are mainly the responsibility of the publisher to design, elicit, and produce, while epitext is the information about the book that is external to the text itself, such as author interviews or reviews. For the purposes of this chapter, I look only at the peritext that directly references the elements within a text itself, similar to the framework employed by Sivashankar Jackson, and Degener in their analysis of African picturebooks (Genette 5). These elements include but are not limited to book covers, dedications, notes, author biographies, acknowledgments, illustrations, diagrams, front and back cover flap information, and the back cover. Genette stresses that "the ways and means of the paratext change continually, depending on period, culture, genre, author, work, and edition, with varying degrees of pressure, sometimes widely varying" (3). In other words, the paratext, and subsequently the peritext, can connect the authors' culture to that of the readers through the enhancement of meaning and the highlighting of the power structures.[1] Appel and Maleckar also share that "paratextual cues can inform recipients about norms and conventions that guided the production of a text and therefore about the likely overlap of story information with real-world story events" (462). Peritext opens the space within a certain context for the sharing of cultural experiences and understandings, while also providing the support for the reasons the narrative is constructed in a certain way (Hearne 24; Sivashankar, Jackson, and Degener). The impact of the peritext on the reading of the text is determined by readers choosing to take the time to include it in their reading experience (Cadden viii; Goffman 9). Therefore, the implied audience for these elements is not always the reader of the narrative itself. In children's literature, the peritext typically gives adults the framework for the text that is provided to children (Higonnet 47; Cadden ix; Jenkins 117), since children's literature is often written with adult intentions in mind (Nodelman 4). YA novels, however, tend to include numerous peritextual elements that are also targeted toward the actual reader to increase the overall marketing of the text, such as images of the authors themselves. Since YA readers reside in the liminal space between child and adult, more often bordering the position of adult (Cart 139), they have a higher chance of employing the peritextual information when reading a text. Since readers are including these peritextual elements within their reading experience, it is vital that publishers present the "overlap" so that readers can choose to engage with the book or "turn away" to another that has the potential for higher authenticity.

Cultural Authenticity

According to Rochman (106), cultural authenticity involves more than just accuracy in writing about a specific topic. When writing authentically, authors present a sensitivity to the realities of the culture itself (Mo and Shen 210). Often citing Bishop's foundational work on mirrors, windows, and sliding glass doors, researchers call for diverse books for children that can give them a picture of their own lives and/or the lives of others. Controversy lies in the ways that authors, as well as the publishers that provide the books to the public, present characters and narratives under the guise of being authentic for their audiences. As Sivashankar, Jackson, and Degener note, this complexity of authenticity within narratives, especially for children, has been an ongoing conversation and point of dissension among researchers. Since cultural authenticity is often discussed alongside discussions of race, Short and Fox share that they are "concerned about how often the debates quickly moved to simplistic insider/outsider distinctions, specifically whether whites should write books about people of color" (3). The cultural authenticity of a text reaches a broader conceptualization than just conversations of race or of insider versus outsider, as all forms of culture, including disability (Hall 31), should be included. One of the biggest questions in this discussion is "Who is allowed to tell whose stories?" Can an author write about an experience, culture, or situation without direct personal experience? Bishop shares that "there is a certain arrogance in assuming that one can incorporate into a work a cultural perspective that is only superficially familiar, and that writers who attempt to do so should understand the difficulties and risks inherent in trying" (32). Ultimately, to be culturally authentic in any area, a text must demonstrate that the author has been successful in portraying the group that they are writing about (Bishop 29). This does not mean that the author necessarily must be a member of the population; however, there needs to be an acknowledgment of the "difficulties of writing outside one's culture" (Bishop 31). Just because someone has had experiences with people who have disabilities does not mean that everything written is naturally authentic. It requires an understanding of the population through more than just surface-level means while also providing space for those within the culture itself to share first whenever possible (Woodson 45), acknowledging that not all people who have disabilities can write authentically about all disabled experiences either. Many times, information about an author's positionality is communicated within the peritextual elements to present them as having some experience with the topic (Sivashankar, Jackson, and Degener). Including these details, according to Jenkins, "serve[s] to give a stamp of authority to the author" and "reflect the determination of those who composed the peritextual material to impress upon adults and children that the books are factually accurate" (118). Within this chapter, "accuracy" means that the aspect of culture is described within the realm of what would be realistically experienced. Without the sharing of experiential details within the peritext, the reader is unaware of the ways their experience or the experiences of others might be presented in the narrative (Sivashankar, Jackson & Degener). The validity of representation could be put into question.

Disability and Authenticity

Historically, people who have disabilities were not provided the space to share their own stories (Hall 32; Mitchell and Snyder 17); the authenticity in texts that included disabled characters was lacking because there was not substantial and documented experience by those writing about disability. Burch and Nielsen cite that many people in this population were also silenced through the perpetuation of institutionalized segregation, demeaning conceptions of human beings, and the constant comparison to the norm (95–98). To provide a platform in the hopes of rectifying this pattern of misrepresentation, texts that include characters who have disabilities have begun to include information about the author's positioning within the peritext. However, Bishop states that even within disability culture, there is the discussion of "who is genuinely 'disabled' and who can legitimately claim to represent the entire group" (31–32). Just stating a disability experience does not necessitate an accurate representation that is shared by any person who has disabilities. Even personal experiences shared in narrative form are retellings of the author's interpretation of events (Goffman 504). In this way, all knowledge is mediated, even when sharing direct experiences. Therefore, it is important to acknowledge that when reading a text written from a certain disability perspective, there is a specific framework that structures the reading of the text. In the end, the importance is accurately representing the disability experience. While not an easy task for those who do not have a disability, because of the "highly relevant" nature of personal experience (Dunn 15), it is also not impossible when significant time spent with people who have disabilities and/or significant research is put at the forefront. The peritext can be the place where this time is documented for the reader's benefit.

Dunn stresses the importance of a critical look at the representation of disability within YA texts because of the ways that authors write about the reality of disabled characters.[2] The remainder of this chapter focuses on analyzing narrative patterns found within peritextual elements written in thirty recently published YA novels that include disabled characters. Seven of the books were chosen from the list of Schneider Family Book Award Teen Book Winners.[3] In order to provide variety of content and peritext elements, the remainder of the books, around three from each year, were chosen from Duyvis and Whaley's (2016) critical post on the *Disability in Kid Lit* blog about the state of disability on book covers. Within this post on one aspect of peritext, they call for better representation. By using some of the texts they mentioned, this chapter focuses on additional ways that disability can be portrayed in the elements that accompany the narrative. Each book was chosen to be a representation of the YA novels published across the past six years; this is not meant to be a full sampling of all texts that include disabled characters that were produced between 2010 and 2016 (see Table 1).

Specific focus is given to the ways that the patterns in these books present author experiences that led them to write about disability in a specific, potentially authentic, way. This discussion is organized into five categories based on the scholarship of Hearne and Sivashankar, Jackson, and Degener's resulting framework: no reference, reference to document research, mention of meetings for research, sustained relationships, and personal experience. This order has been determined with the aforementioned understanding that some categories may provide more strength based on the accuracy within the text itself, since some publishers and authors choose to leave some of their positioning information out of the peritext for reasons outside of those presented in this chapter.[4] Through a thorough investigation of the peritext, the ways that the publishers frame the position of the author's final narrative through the use of peritext is the focus.

No Reference

Out of the thirty texts, almost one-third do not present any support for the author's inclusion of disability within the text, suggesting that there was either no experience that could call into question the accuracy of the text, or the experience was considered unnecessary to share with readers. Some provide a context for their ability to write about other aspects of the narrative, but these do not share any information about any disability research. For example, the book *Somebody, Please Tell Me Who I Am* (Mazer and Lerangis) is a story about a young boy, Ben, who enlists in the army immediately after graduating from high school and returns home with a traumatic brain injury. Throughout the text Ben interacts with his memories of his brother who has autism. Although this narrative focuses on Ben's experiences with a traumatic brain injury and autism, the peritext of the author bio states only that one of the authors was "inspired" to create this story based on "his own experience as an underage enlisted soldier" (Mazer and Lerangis). There is no mention of his understanding of these disabilities beyond his veteran experiences. Additionally, the author of *Schizo* (Nic Scheff), a book about the life experiences of a young man who has schizophrenia, singularly mentions his own "struggles with addiction," and *Love Blind*, which includes a character who is blind, mentions

Table 1: List of YA Novels Used for Analysis

Book Title	Author	Year	Disability Present
Among Others	Walton, J.	2010	Mental disability; Limp; Cane user
Big Girl Small	DeWoskin, R.	2011	Dwarfism
A Blind Guide to Stinkville	Vrabel, B.	2015	Blindness
Blindsided	Cummings, P.	2010	Blindness
Bluefish	Schmatz, P.	2011	Learning disability
Crazy	Reed, A.	2012	Bipolar disorder
Dangerous	Hale, S.	2014	Prosthesis user
Five Flavors of Dumb	John, A.	2010	D/deaf
Girl, Stolen	Henry, A.	2010	Blindness
Girls like Us	Giles, G.	2014	Intellectual disability
Jepp, Who Defied the Stars	Marsh, K.	2012	Dwarfism
Love Blind	Desir, C. & Perry, J.	2016	Blindness
Me, Earl, and the Dying Girl	Andrews, J.	2012	Cancer
Night Sky	Brockmann, S. & M.	2014	Wheelchair user
OCD Love Story	Haydu, C. A.	2013	OCD
OCD, the Dude and Me	Vaughn, L. R.	2013	OCD
OCDaniel	King, W.	2016	OCD
On the Edge of Gone	Duyvis, C.	2014	Autism
One + One = Blue	Auch, M. J.	2013	Synesthesia
Out of My Mind	Draper, S.	2010	Cerebral palsy; wheelchair user
Paperboy	Vawter, V.	2013	Stuttering
Push Girl	Hill, C. & Love, J.	2014	Wheelchair user
Rose under Fire	Wein, E.	2013	Mixed physical disabilities
The Running Dream	Van Draanen, W.	2011	Prosthesis user
Schizo	Sheff, N.	2014	Schizophrenia
The Season of You and Me	Constantine, R.	2016	Wheelchair user
Somebody, Please Tell Me Who I Am	Mazer, H. & Lerangis, P.	2012	Traumatic brain injury; autism
Summer on the Short Bus	Crandell, B.	2014	Mixed
The Unlikely Hero of Room 13B	Toten, T.	2015	OCD

only the author's volunteering as a "rape-victim activist" for a number of years (Desir and Perry). These author biographies that are typically found on the back-cover flap of the text substantiate the other portions of the narrative but not the inclusion of characters who have disabilities. Other texts, such as *Me, Earl, and the Dying Girl* (Andrews), *OCD Love Story* (Haydu), *Night Sky* (Brockmann and Brockmann), *Bluefish* (Schmatz), and *Dangerous* (Hale) do not contain any information that positions the author as knowledgeable about any of the descriptions of disability found within the text. This doesn't necessarily mean that the authors did not attempt to research their written topics or have life experiences that influenced the writing of their novels. Considering the importance of peritext, however, this choice does not provide support for the inclusion of certain characters within the narrative, therefore opening the space for questions concerning the potential cultural authenticity of the text and the importance of being open with readers.

Reference to Document Research

Within the peritext, authors also share the research that they have done on their own to support their ability to write authentically (Marsh; Reed; Wein). These authors, typically, share their references within the peritext at the end of the book so that the reader can add to their knowledge of the topic after or during reading. Research of this form also provides support for those writing historical fiction that cannot necessarily talk to people from the previous time periods. Two examples include *Rose under Fire* (Wein), a story that details an American's experience in the Ravensbruck concentration camp during World War II, and *Jepp, Who Defied the Stars* (Marsh), a narrative about a dwarf in the royal courts of the sixteenth century. Both narratives share stories that have been previously untold within YA literature. Their research is thoroughly explained within the author's note, afterword, and acknowledgments. Wein shares a researched timeline of the experience of the Rabbits, a group of Polish people who were experimented on and ultimately disabled by the researchers at the concentration camp (Wein 349). She also shares about her weeklong stay at Ravensbruck, where she was able to do deeper research into the potential experiences of her characters. In the peritext, both Wein and Marsh share direct sources supporting their potential to write from a culturally authentic perspective. Additionally, in the acknowledgments of *Crazy* (Reed), the author shares appreciation for the book *Living with Someone Who's Living with Bipolar Disorder* by Chelsea Lowe and Bruce M. Cohen, MD, PhD, saying that "this book was invaluable to my understanding of what it's like to love someone with bipolar disorder" (Reed 368). Even this small mention in the peritext positions the author as someone who has taken the time to research an authentic representation of a topic that they may not have any previous personal experience with. However, the breadth of this research reaches only to the pages of research and does not present a willingness to interact with people who have disabilities to further their textual accuracy. Only Wein reports talking with people who have a deeper understanding of the experience at Ravensbruck, although not necessarily the Rabbits' personal experience. This presentation also calls into question the authenticity of the research chosen as support, compounding the complexity of this discussion, especially since Reed references only one text.

Mention of Meetings for Book Research

Another third of the YA texts analyzed for this paper offered a frame of personal connection to the author's work. Most of these texts included short-term personal experiences or contact with individuals who have experience with a disability (Draanen; Henry; John; Cummings; Venkatraman; Toten; Constantine; DeWoskin). This research gives validity to the writing of the narrative while also foregrounding the method of expertise. On the other hand, the amount of research may not necessarily create a culturally authentic narrative if the research choices come from only one certain perspective, often that of able-bodied practitioners who work with people who have disabilities. Within the peritext, some of the authors mention a range of individuals or groups of people whom they contacted with questions about the disabled experience. For example, Constantine in *The Season of You and Me* thanks "Jennifer Moore, a licensed and certified recreational therapist" and "Brock Johnson, board member of Carolina Coastal Adaptive Sports and founder of 'Wheels to Surf'" (346). She includes a person with professional experience but also someone with personal experience. Using these two individuals, she frames her ability to write a culturally authentic text within the social context. However, as Duyvis and Whaley in their *Disability in Kid Lit* blog post point out, "even with so very few wheelchair-using protagonists in YA, even with the possibility of having a groundbreaking cover featuring a sweet scene between a girl and a boy in a wheelchair, they chose to make the character indistinguishable from an able-bodied character." The cover of the book, typically created without author input (Clark and Phillips 142), does not include the character's wheelchair, portraying him sitting on the beach with his arms wrapped around the girl, hiding his disability. While some research was done by the author, the cover art peritext, created by the publisher, distorts the full experience of the disabled characters, presenting a disconnect in the authenticity of the author's presented experience. In *Blindsided* (Cummings), the peritext includes an extensive acknowledgment and references to the year that the author spent "attending school with blind students before writing *Blindsided*." With the statement of time, this research seems to hold more potential for an authentic narrative than a couple short conversations with a few people. The inclusion of the lengthy description as well as a dedication to the students provides a frame that validates the author's text. Additionally, many authors shared appreciation for the people who have disabilities "who read a draft" to validate the included information in the narrative (Venkatraman 312; John 343; Henry 215). Venkatraman, in the acknowledgments after the text of *A Time to Dance*, shares a "heartfelt thanks to the generous medical personnel and differently abled persons who spoke to me and especially to those who read a draft and supported me" (312). After that statement, the author lists over fifty different people and organizations that played a collaborative role in the ultimate production of the text. While meetings can provide some information, especially with those who spent significant time with others and valued their opinions, it is then up to the author to take that information and document it properly in writing. Framing the text in this way, the peritext and henceforth the author demonstrate their position in telling the stories of others but also share their desire for authenticity, including their realities, although not the same as engaging in a sustained relationship with someone who experiences the realities of having a disability.

Sustained relationship

While still not specifically sharing their own narratives, authors who write from their own experiences can position their narrative differently from any of the previously mentioned frames, because their relationship with people who have disabilities occurred outside of the confines of book-writing research. The peritexts that mention some familiarity with disability place the authors in one of two categories: family member (Crandell; Draper; Walton) or teacher (Giles; Vaughn). When writing about family, the authors frame their writing as either slightly autobiographical (Walton) or inspired by their children (Crandell; Draper). In the acknowledgments for *Among Others*, Walton states, "I've found that writing what you know is much harder than making it up" and that "it's easier to research a historical period than your own life" (8). By framing her writing this way, she offers a space for the reader to sympathize with the accounts of the characters, especially her "half-mad" mother in the narrative. Draper, in *Out of My Mind*, and Crandell, in *Summer on the Short Bus*, position their story as culturally authentic but not ultimately biographical.

I suppose the character of Melody came from my experiences with raising a child with developmental difficulties. But Melody is not my daughter. Melody is pure fiction—a unique little girl who has come into being from a mixture of love and understanding. (Draper 303)

It would be easy to assume that *Summer on the Short Bus* was inspired by my special needs daughter, but it wasn't—not really. It's true that elements of her quirky nature were integrated into some of the characters, but the real inspiration for this book had more to do with my own journey in getting to know her. (Crandell 247)

As able-bodied parents, Draper and Crandell are still separated from the personal experience of having a disability. Through their sustained relationships with their daughters, they can learn more than they could with research, but they still position themselves outside of the personal reality of disability. This is like the teachers that write and credit their authenticity to their time spent in the classroom (Giles; Vaughn). While this time provides information about disabilities, they are still writing from their own able-bodied perspective. Both parents and teachers could increase their potential for authenticity by consulting the children/students that they are using as inspiration, an action that is not mentioned in any of these books. By avoiding this step, they could still write from their own uninformed perspective.

Personal Experience

Despite the potential inaccuracy of personal memoirs, authors who frame their narrative with information containing their personal experience with a certain disability have a high likelihood of offering a culturally authentic depiction of their own disability (King; Duyvis; Vawter; Hill and Love). These authors are willing to be direct in their peritext, sharing stories from their own past in an "almost autobiographical" way to compliment the story in the text, while also promoting their authenticity (King 293). One way that this is done is through the telling of their initial knowledge of their disability, such as Vawter's author's note that states "my first recollection of my stutter is just before I was five" (223). Duyvis, in *On the Edge of Gone*, shares that "since my own autism diagnosis in 2004, I've come to accept and embrace it as an inextricable part of myself, but it hasn't been a straightforward journey" (458). The authors position themselves in time relative to the characters in their text, as mentioned by Bamberg (337), directly communicating the ways that they want to be seen by the readers. Additionally, they socially frame themselves as culturally authentic in their writing. Vawter, in *Paperboy*, directly states that "*Paperboy* is my story, then, certainly more memoir than fiction" and is the only YA book to include an image of an individual who has a disability within the peritext. He is directly calling on the reader to understand the "reality" of the depiction in the text while sharing it under the guise of fiction. *One + One = Blue* (Auch 263–268), a narrative about two individuals who have synesthesia, provides an interview between the author and the editor who both have synesthesia. With the inclusion of this peritextual element, the reader is made aware of the positioning of both the creator of the narrative and one of the other participants in the writing process; the interview shares more than one perspective of synesthesia so that the reader can see the multidimensionality of the disability. Finally, some authors also co-write a text with an individual who has a disability to provide an authentic voice to share their own story. Following Woodson's idea of allowing space for people who have disabilities to write their stories, Love writes with Hill, in *Push Girl*, to avoid the chance that an inaccurate representation of the narrative does "not speak the truth about [disability] but rather [tells] someone-on-the outside's idea of who we are" (45). This narrative focuses on the life of a girl who was paralyzed because of a drunk driving accident, which is based directly on the life story of Chelsie Hill, one of the authors. Throughout the peritext, Hill's statements and information are placed on the page before Love's to give the personal experience perspective the strength in the writing of the text. When speaking of Chelsie Hill in her acknowledgments, Love states "thank you for trusting me with your experiences" (vii). The author positions herself alongside of her cowriter and focuses the authenticity on the way that she worked with a person who has a disability instead of writing from her own able-bodied perspective.

Authentic?

While the peritext provides the avenue for examining the ways that the authors frame their texts, there is a need for this information to be investigated in relationship with the texts themselves. The creators of the narratives can be positioned as potentially authentic, but the resulting text will demonstrate whether the position is truly communicating authenticity through the narrative. Since there is such a wide range of experiences within disabilities, there is the potential for debate surrounding the ways that disability is presented within YA novels. The authenticity, however, is vital for the readership to begin to see authentic depictions of disability, without portraying a single, pitied reality. Through research and experiences, authors can begin to produce texts that disabled readers can relate to instead of disregarding and able-bodied readers can read without fear of perpetuating stereotypes. With the potential of more authentic disabled characters with well-researched moments or experience with disability, these books could be more accessible and hold wider appeal for a variety of readers.

My goal with this chapter is not to judge these books as authentic or not. Since each person's experience is different, there is no way to be completely authentic with every page of a fictional narrative. However, those writing from outside of the direct experience of disability need to remember that they occupy a complicated space. By presenting the different ways that authors and publishers position their experiences and research, they demonstrate their desire to situate in a specific position before the reader begins the bulk of the narrative. "The peritext presents the work that the author put into writing so that the reader can understand their perspective" (Sivashankar, Jackson, and Degener). A book becomes a door or a window when an author produces accuracy within the pages (Bishop xi). Through cultural authenticity, stereotypes can be dispelled and the young adults can see the importance of taking time to understand a culture before trying to communicate to others about it. Peritextual statements give more than just facts about the context of the book. They inform the audience about the ways that authors and publishers took specific steps before and during the writing of the text to avoid "cultural thievery," as described by Seto (96). Narratives should not be stolen from the disabled population to serve the purpose of selling books. Instead, they should be presented as pictures of reality based on informed understandings from inside and outside of the culture, with the recognition that being outside carries a heavier weight. As readers take in this information, they see the hard work that the author put into their writing. That leads to informed readers of informed writing who then can engage with the topic knowing that the presentation of information has accuracy beyond the fiction presented. The significance of the peritextual elements in this acknowledgement process needs to be brought to the forefront in the minds of publishers and authors. Readers must be presented with evidence of authenticity, a move that may make these texts more appealing which could potentially place them in competition with some of the more well-known blockbusters already making steps in this direction.

Notes

1. Creating a primary social framework to "locate, perceive, identify, and label" the happenings in the text, the peritext "provide[s] background understanding for events that incorporate the will, aim, and controlling effort of an intelligence, a live agency, the chief one being the human being" (Goffman 22). To see this model deployed in a children's literature context, see Sivashankar, Jackson, and Degener's work on African picture books.

2. For the purposes of this chapter, I will be using person-first and identity-first language interchangeably with the acknowledgment of the weight and problematic nature of both forms of identification, as recognized by Dunn (11).

3. Each year since 2004, the Schneider Family Book Award, awarded through the American Library Association, celebrates authors and illustrators who produce texts that "artistically express the disability experience" (Schneider).

4. Due to space constraints, publisher requirements, and/or disclosure preferences, authors often cannot include all of the information they desire in the peritext of their books. This chapter merely presents the ways these omissions or inclusions may point to authenticity.

Works Cited

Andrews, Jesse. *Me, Earl, and the Dying Girl*. Abrams, 2012.

Appel, Markus, and Barbara Maleckar. "The Influence of Paratext on Narrative Persuasion. Fact, Fiction, or Fake?" *Human Communication Research*, vol. 38, 2012, pp. 459–84.

Auch, M. J. *One + One = Blue*. Square Fish, 2013.

Bishop, Rudine Sims. "Mirrors, Windows, and Sliding Glass Doors." *Perspectives: Choosing and Using Books for the Classroom*, vol. 6, no. 3, 1990, pp. ix–xi.

Bishop, Rudine Sims. "Reframing the Debate about Cultural Authenticity." *Stories Matter: The Complexity of Cultural Authenticity in Children's Literature*, edited by Dana L. Fox and Kathy G. Short, National Council of Teachers of English, 2003, pp. 25–36.

Brockmann, Suzanne, and Melanie Brockmann. *Night Sky*. Sourcebooks, 2014.

Burch, Susan, and Kim E. Nielsen. "History." *Keywords for Disability Studies*, edited by Rachel Adams, Benjamin Reiss, and David Serlin, New York UP, 2015, pp. 95–98.

Cadden, Michael. "Introduction." *Telling Children's Stories: Narrative Theory and Children's Literature*, edited by Michael Cadden, U of Nebraska P, 2010, pp. i–xxv.

Cart, Michael. *Young Adult Literature: From Romance to Realism*. Neal-Schuman, 2016.

Chbosky, Stephen. *The Perks of Being a Wallflower*. Gallery Books, 1999.

Clark, Giles, and Angus Phillips. *Inside Book Publishing*. Routledge, 2014.

Constantine, Robin. *The Season of You and Me*. Balzer + Bray, 2016.

Crandell, Bethany. *Summer on the Short Bus*. Running Press, 2014.

Cummings, Priscilla. *Blindsided*. Dutton Children's Books, 2010.

Desir, C., and Jolene Perry. *Love Blind*. Simon Pulse, 2016.

DeWoskin, Rachel. *Big Girl Small*. Farrar, Straus, and Giroux, 2011.

Draanen, Wendelin Van. *The Running Dream*. Random House, 2011.

Draper, Sharon. *Out of My Mind*. Atheneum Books for Young Readers, 2010.

Dunn, Patricia A. *Disabling Characters: Representations of Disability in Young Adult Literature*. Peter Lang, 2015.

Duyvis, Corinne. *On the Edge of Gone*. Harry M. Abrams, 2016.

Duyvis, Corinne, and Kayla Whaley. "The State of Disability on Book Covers." *Disability in Kid Lit*. 15 July 2016. www.disabilityinkidlit.com/2016/07/15/the-state-of-disability-on-book-covers/. Accessed 13 May 2017.

Genette, Gerard. *Paratexts: Thresholds of Interpretation*. Translated by Jane E. Lewin. Cambridge UP, 1997.

Giles, Gail. *Girls like Us*. Candlewick Press, 2014.

Green, John. *Turtles All the Way Down*. Dutton Books, 2017.

Hale, Shannon. *Dangerous*. Bloomsbury, 2014.

Hall, Alice. *Literature and Disability*. Routledge, 2016.

Haydu, Corey Ann. *OCD Love Story*. Simon Pulse, 2013.

Hearne, Betsy. "Cite the Source: Reducing Cultural Chaos in Picture Books, Part One." *School Library Journal*, 1993, pp. 22–27.

Henry, April. *Girl, Stolen*. Henry Holt, 2010.

Higonnet, Margaret R. "The Playground of Paratext." *Children's Literature Association Quarterly*, vol. 15, no. 2, 1990, pp. 47–49.

Hill, Chelsie, and Jessica Love. *Push Girl*. Thomas Dune Books, 2014.

Jenkins, Elwyn. "Reading Outside the Lines: Peritext and Authenticity in South African Children's Books." *The Lion and the Unicorn*, vol. 25 no. 1, 2001, 115–27.

John, Antony. *Five Flavors of Dumb*. Speak, 2010.

King, Wesley. *OCDaniel*. Simon and Schuster, 2016.

Lerangis, Peter, and Harry Mazer. *Somebody Please Tell Me Who I Am*. Simon and Schuster, 2012.

Marsh, Katherine. *Jepp, Who Defied the Stars*. Hyperion, 2012.

Mitchell, David T., and Sharon L. Snyder. *Narrative Prosthesis: Disability and the Dependencies of Discourse*. U of Michigan P, 2000.

Mo, Weimin, and Wenju Shen. "Accuracy Is Not Enough: The Role of Cultural Values in the Authenticity of Picture Books." *Stories Matter: The Complexity of Cultural Authenticity in Children's Literature*, edited by Dana L. Fox and Kathy G. Short, National Council of Teachers of English, 2003, pp. 198–212.

Nodelman, P. *The Hidden Adult: Defining Children's Literature*. Johns Hopkins UP, 2008.

Palachio, R. J. *Wonder*. Alfred A. Knopf, 2012.

Reed, Amy Lynn. *Crazy*. Simon Pulse, 2012.

Rochman, Hazel. "Beyond Political Correctness." *Stories Matter: The Complexity of Cultural Authenticity in Children's Literature*, edited by Dana L. Fox and Kathy G. Short, National Council of Teachers of English, 2003, pp. 101–15.

Schmatz, Pat. *Bluefish*. Candlewick Press, 2011.

"Schneider Family Book Award." *American Library Association*, 2017, www.ala.org/awardsgrants /schneider-family-book-award. Accessed 13 May 2017.

Sheff, Nic. *Schizo*. Philomel Books. 2014.

Short, Kathy G., and Dana L. Fox. "The Complexity of Cultural Authenticity in Children's Literature: Why the Debates Really Matter." *Stories Matter: The Complexity of Cultural Authenticity in Children's Literature*, edited by Dana L. Fox and Kathy G. Short, Urbana: National Council of Teachers of English, 2003, pp. 3–24.

Sivashankar, Nithya, Sarah E. Jackson, and Rebekah May Degener. "Centering the Margins: Investigating Relationships, Power, and Culture Through Critical Peritextual Analysis." *Childrens Literature in Education* (2019). https://doi.org/10.1007/s10583-019-09395-4.

Toten, Teresa. *The Unlikely Hero of Room 13B*. Delacorte Press. 2015.

Vaughn, Lauren Roedy. *OCD, the Dude and Me*. Dial Books. 2013.

Vawter, Vince. *Paperboy*. Yearling. 2014.

Venkatraman, Padma. *A Time to Dance*. Nancy Paulsen Books. 2014.

Vrabel, Beth. *A Blind Guide to Stinkville*. Sky Pony Press. 2015.

Walton, Jo. *Among Others*. Tom Doherty Associates. 2010.

Wein, Elizabeth. *Rose Under Fire*. Hyperion. 2013.

Woodson, Jacquelyn. "Who Can Tell My Story?" *Stories Matter: The Complexity of Cultural Authenticity in Children's Literature*, edited by Dana L. Fox and Kathy G. Short, Urbana: National Council of Teachers of English, 2003, pp. 41–45.

Further Reading

Andrews, Jesse. *Me, Earl, and the Dying Girl*. Abrams, 2012.

Auch, M. J. *One + One = Blue*. Square Fish, 2013.

Brockmann, Suzanne, and Melanie Brockmann. *Night Sky*. Sourcebooks, 2014.

Chbosky, Stephen. *The Perks of Being a Wallflower*. Gallery Books, 1999.

Constantine, Robin. *The Season of You and Me*. Balzer + Bray, 2016.

Crandell, Bethany. *Summer on the Short Bus*. Running Press, 2014.

Cummings, Priscilla. *Blindsided*. Dutton Children's Books, 2010.

Desir, C., and Jolene Perry. *Love Blind*. Simon Pulse, 2016.

DeWoskin, Rachel. *Big Girl Small*. Farrar, Straus, and Giroux, 2011.

Draanen, Wendelin Van. *The Running Dream*. Random House, 2011.

Draper, Sharon. *Out of My Mind*. Atheneum Books for Young Readers, 2010.

Duyvis, Corinne. *On the Edge of Gone*. Harry M. Abrams, 2016.

Giles, Gail. *Girls like Us*. Candlewick Press, 2014.

Green, John. *Turtles All the Way Down*. Dutton Books, 2017.

Hale, Shannon. *Dangerous*. Bloomsbury, 2014.

Haydu, Corey Ann. *OCD Love Story*. Simon Pulse, 2013.

Henry, April. *Girl, Stolen*. Henry Holt, 2010.

Hill, Chelsie, and Jessica Love. *Push Girl*. Thomas Dune Books, 2014.

John, Antony. *Five Flavors of Dumb*. Speak, 2010

King, Wesley. *OCDaniel*. Simon and Schuster, 2016.

Lerangis, Peter, and Harry Mazer. *Somebody Please Tell Me Who I Am*. Simon and Schuster, 2012.

Marsh, Katherine. *Jepp, Who Defied the Stars*. Hyperion, 2012.

Palachio, R. J. *Wonder*. Alfred A. Knopf, 2012.

Schmatz, Pat. *Bluefish*. Candlewick Press, 2011.

Sheff, Nic. *Schizo*. Philomel Books, 2014.

Toten, Teresa. *The Unlikely Hero of Room 13B*. Delacorte Press, 2015.

Vaughn, Lauren Roedy. *OCD, the Dude and Me*. Dial Books, 2013.

Vawter, Vince. *Paperboy*. Yearling, 2014.

Venkatraman, Padma. *A Time to Dance*. Nancy Paulsen Books, 2014.

Vrabel, Beth. *A Blind Guide to Stinkville*. Sky Pony Press, 2015.

Walton, Jo. *Among Others*. Tom Doherty Associates, 2010.

Wein, Elizabeth. *Rose under Fire*. Hyperion, 2013.

11

Reimagining *Forever*...
The Marriage Plot in Recent Young Adult Literature

Sara K. Day

Since its publication more than forty years ago, Judy Blume's *Forever*... has appeared on "best of" and banned books lists alike, for very similar reasons: the novel's frank treatment of adolescent sexuality has been both celebrated and condemned for breaking with the conventions of juvenile literature that preceded it. As narrator Katherine and her boyfriend Michael navigate their relationship, they reflect the 1970s' increasingly liberal attitudes surrounding sexuality and offer readers an educational—some critics have even said clinical[1]—view of virginity loss, contraception, and the female orgasm. At the same time, and more importantly for the purposes of this chapter, Katherine relates and reflects on her feelings of love for Michael and their mutual belief that their high school romance will naturally continue into college and adulthood. Despite her parents' misgivings and warnings, Kath expresses confidence in her future with Michael, symbolized by the necklace he gives her for her eighteenth birthday with the words "Forever . . . Michael" engraved on the back (124). When they are separated by Kath's job at a summer camp, they sign their letters "love forever," even as their correspondence and Kath's growing attachment to another camp counselor signal that distance is developing between them. By the end of the summer, Kath has decided to end their relationship. After her final conversation with Michael, she reflects, "I wanted to tell him that I will never be sorry for loving him. . . . Maybe if we were ten years older it would have worked out differently. Maybe. I think it's just that I'm not ready for forever" (192).

By allowing her protagonist a first love that does not become a forever love, Blume actively resists didactic messages about premarital sex and instead offers readers a portrayal of young romance that ends happily without an "ever after." In the process, she does more than revolutionize representations of adolescent sexuality in young adult literature; in resisting both the romantic conclusions of much early- to mid-twentieth century literature for teen readers and the longer-standing conventions of the marriage plot, she also rejects traditions that demand that romances end in marriage or, at least, the expression of permanent commitment. Additionally, Blume's novel aligns with larger cultural shifts regarding marriage, particularly in terms of the age of first marriage, which had already started to increase markedly from the decades that preceded the book's publication. And many of those trends have continued into the twenty-first century. As H. Elizabeth Peters and Claire M. Kamp Dush determined in their 2009 study, "[d]ata clearly show that [today] both men and women remain single for a longer period of time. In 2005 the median age of marriage in the United States was twenty-seven for men and twenty-five for women. . . . The age at marriage has increased substantially since the 1950s, when half of women married during their teen years" (xvi).

It is particularly perplexing and potentially troubling, then, to note that one trend in recent YA literature is early marriage, especially in novels for and about adolescent women. That is, novels such as those discussed in this chapter present marriage as the logical and desirable culmination of adolescence. Even when characters do not officially become engaged or married, many texts for adolescent audiences maintain a rhetoric of the permanence of first love, suggesting or asserting that the romances they present will—and should—last forever. As part of a much larger system of messages about matrimony to which women are exposed beginning in childhood, YA novels that feature a sort of twenty-first-century marriage plot telegraph expectations about adolescent sexuality and the transition into adulthood by privileging heteronormative romantic conventions. In this chapter I argue that this trend not only reflects popular misconceptions about the literary marriage plot but also reinforces larger postfeminist influences that seek to reestablish so-called traditional marriage as the key to successful adult womanhood.

The Who, When, and Why of Wedding: Twenty-First-Century Contexts

In *Minimizing Marriage: Marriage, Morality, and the Law*, Elizabeth Brake articulates some of the many questions that surround conversations about marriage in the twenty-first century:

[I]s there good reason for marriage to be structured as it is—monogamous, central, permanent (or aspiring to permanence), with its dense bundle of legal rights and responsibilities? Is such an arrangement really part of the good life, and should it be privileged in the just society? From a secular perspective, does it have any moral significance? Are marriages morally distinct from otherwise similar unmarried relationships? (2)

While Brake's larger project is to examine the legal and moral implications that inform marriage and its role in Western culture, the points she raises here indicate that underlying assumptions about the institution have increasingly been called into question. Modern-day marriage exists within a set of tensions about its importance, and these tensions manifest across culture in a number of ways. For the purposes of this essay, I am particularly interested in the ways that culture at large and YA literature in specific actively minimize or ignore the increasing challenges to "conventional" marriage.

In her 2006 essay "Marriage Envy," Suzanne Leonard asserts that "[i]n popular and political terms, marriage holds an increasingly unassailable position in the twenty-first-century United States" (44).[2] This position, she notes, results from both liberal and conservative attention to the institution, particularly in terms of who should have the right to marry and the manner in which marriage continues to be understood as the main (or only) relationship upon which families can be built. Arguing that women are inculcated to believe that they not only *must* marry but that marriage is a competitive institution, Leonard explains, "This dynamic is perhaps best understood not as an individual pathology, but rather as a product of a contemporary postfeminist moment wherein politics and popular culture have colluded to produce a vision of marriage that is increasingly unassailable, and yet also underpinned by a sense of scarcity" (45). More generally, the "marriage envy" phenomenon acts as a particularly useful lens through which to consider the specific intersection of marriage and heteronormativity, as well as the implications for women that manifest there. Because, historically, marriage has been so closely tied to women's financial and political (in)dependence, "the autonormativity of North American society—hot-housed by the wedding-industrial complex and popular entertainment—sells love and marriage as a valuable commodity for which women are willing to trade more basic goods" (Brake 118).

While marriage envy most obviously affects adult women, the messages and media that perpetuate this phenomenon certainly have wider-reaching effects. Indeed, it is difficult to identify media for even the youngest of audiences that does not rest on assumptions about romantic marriage as the foundation of family and home life. As Mary Catherine Harrison notes,

One need never have read "classic" literary fiction to be influenced by its delin-
eation of courtship and marriage; its cultural significance can be measured by its
reverberations in contemporary popular culture and the stories that have been
told and can be told about fiction and adaptations but also in popular literature,
romantic comedies, sitcoms, soap operas, reality television, romance fiction, and
fairy tales interpreted through Disney films and "princess" culture. (113–14)

Melissa Ames and Sarah Burcon have observed, for example, that the romantic
comedies that have for decades been aimed at twenty-something women have
been retooled for an audience of teens and tweens, so that "these troubling 'how
to date' lessons are being consumed at earlier—and more formative—ages" (59).
Even as questions about the place and value of marriage proliferate, novels such
as those discussed in this chapter tend to offer uncomplicated, optimistic views of
marriage to young readers as part of what Rebecca Munford and Melanie Waters
call "the postfeminist mystique," which "reactivates modes of feminine identity
that were 'proper to a former age' but which seem 'out of harmony' with a present
that has—so we are told—reaped all the benefits of second wave feminism" (10).

The particular role of postfeminism in the development and maintenance of
marriage envy requires a brief consideration of the complex, often contradictory,
perspectives surrounding postfeminsim and its intersection with issues of gender,
age, and class. As Stéphanie Genz and Benjamin B. Brabon note, "Even though
the structure of postfeminism seems to invoke a narrative of progression insisting
on a time 'after' feminism, the directionality and meaning of the 'post' prefix are
far from settled" (3). The implications of this dispute have resulted in a spectrum
of approaches to understanding and applying postfeminist discourse, but for the
purposes of this discussion, I will be working within a view of postfeminism as a
problematic and frequently misleading resistance to second-wave feminism. As
Munford and Waters note, because it has been "[r]eadily appropriated by a media
culture eager to announce feminism's demise, 'postfeminism' has also provided a
focus for contemporary feminist debates about femininity and empowerment" (13).
Though more positive views of postfeminism certainly exist and have useful elements, I am primarily interested in the ways that a resistance to feminism or—perhaps more troubling—a belief that the work of feminism has been completed can
complicate discussions about marriage for twenty-first-century adolescent women.

Misreading the Marriage Plot

For many modern readers, the words "marriage plot" conjure up images of
Mr. Darcy or Rochester, the romantic heroes of nineteenth-century novels that
continue to occupy an important place in popular culture. To some degree,

such associations are useful, as the works of Jane Austen, Charlotte Brontë, and other novelists certainly engage with some of the most prominent tropes of the marriage plot, from the growing awareness of mutual desire to the obstacles that serve to postpone the inevitable union at the end of the novel. In "Reading the Marriage Plot," Harrison notes, "Novels center on the heroine's path to marriage; the conventional focus on the female's perspective signals its particular relevance to a woman's life. The conspicuous lack of interest in events following marriage establishes getting married as the primary fictional and life goal" (116). In keeping with Munford and Waters's "postfeminist mystique," the continuing popularity of many nineteenth-century marriage plots indicates an anachronistic desire for the trajectory of courtship and matrimony these novels document. In turn, noting that contemporary authors struggle with the potentially feminist underpinnings of Austen's works as they rewrite them for modern readers, Maria Lorena Santos has asserted, "Austen's enabling 'silence' and arguably ambiguous feminism appeal to many contemporary women and . . . the spinoffs they produce or consume similarly engage with earlier first- or second-wave feminist movements in non-confrontational ways" (Santos 4).

Furthermore, the ease with which a small subset of novels has come to represent the trend at large indicates the degree to which certain elements have been ignored or erased over time. As Talia Schaeffer has noted, the popular view of the marriage plot as strictly romantic fails to acknowledge the frequency with which women in marriage plots are faced with the option of what she calls "familiar marriages," or matches based on questions of community, financial security, and so on, issues that are likewise frequently ignored in YA literature's representations of relationships. Additionally, the assumption that the marriage plot's conclusion is necessarily a happy one ignores the many ways in which authors use the conventional arc in order to question or subvert cultural norms rather than condoning and reinforcing them. That works such as Brontë's *Jane Eyre* and George Eliot's *Middlemarch*, with their conventional marriage plot conclusions, have been read as "disappointing" on one hand or subversive on the other indicates the possibility of engaging with the marriage plot as a (proto)feminist tool, even if modern takes on these novels do not always leave room for them to function as such.

In her examination of marriage envy, Leonard notes the role that literature has played in reinforcing this phenomenon, highlighting so-called chick lit and its subgenres "bride lit" and "wedding fic" as spaces that particularly explore marriage as a competitive institution.[3] Likewise, literary marriage plots from the nineteenth century continue to echo through representations of marriage in much YA literature and culture. There are a number of recent adaptations of Austen's novels, including Elizabeth Eulberg's *Prom and Prejudice* and Claire

LeZebnik's *Epic Fail* (both 2011), as well as various takes on *Jane Eyre* and *Wuthering Heights*, suggesting that teen readers are engaging with these novels' plots, if not directly with the texts themselves. Joy Penny's *A Love for the Pages* (2014) actively combines a number of Austen and Brontë novels—all of which are beloved by protagonist Jane Eyermann—in order to offer a romantic arc that precisely follows the stories she adores. Even novels that do not necessarily borrow their stories from these nineteenth-century texts make explicit references to them as a sort of shorthand for epic romance. For example, Lennie, the narrator of Jandy Nelson's *The Sky Is Everywhere* (2010), carries around a weathered paperback copy of *Wuthering Heights* and maps her own developing romance onto Cathy and Heathcliff's. After her boyfriend breaks up with her, she responds by destroying the paperback, potentially suggesting that she has begun to distinguish between the novel's portrayal of romance and her own experiences. However, when she and Joe reunite near the end of the text, she declares, "I want to be with you forever!" before reflecting to the reader, "You can chop the Victorian novel to shreds with garden shears but you can't take it out of the girl" (Nelson).

Lennie's statement might be expanded to describe YA literature as a category, which has frequently turned to romance as one of its central genres or modes. As Michael Cart notes, Maureen Daly's *Seventeenth Summer* and many similarly titled tales that followed in the 1940s and '50s focus on adolescent women's introduction to romance, with an implicit or explicit drive toward eventual marriage. Likewise, Cart writes, the late twentieth century witnessed a resurgence of romantic novels for young readers, potentially signaling a desire to "escape from life's cares and woes" (43). Though the twenty-first-century novels I discuss do not all fit neatly into the category of romance as a genre, many do adhere to the general trajectory of the marriage plot in ways that echo their literary ancestors. It is also worth noting that while I focus here on realistic literature, the trend also extends to fantasy novels like Nancy Werlin's *Impossible*, steampunk novels like Cassandra Clare's The Infernal Devices trilogy, and dystopian fiction like Ally Condie's Matched trilogy and Keira Cass's The Selection series.

Of course, many YA novels that feature the marriage plot *are* romances. Together, the three novels of Stephanie Perkins's trilogy, made up of *Anna and the French Kiss* (2010), *Lola and the Boy Next Door* (2011), and *Isla and the Happily Ever After* (2014), constitute what An Goris calls a hybrid serialized romance, which combines a focus on a small group of recurring characters and a larger romantic narrative arc.[4] Although all three novels feature young couples in love, Anna's is the story that extends across the trilogy as a whole. When she begins her senior year of high school as a new student at the School of America in Paris, Anna meets and immediately develops a crush on Etienne St. Clair, despite the fact that she is sort of dating a guy back home in Atlanta and he is involved in a long-term relationship of his own. Lola, the eccentric narrator of the second novel, likewise finds herself in a romantic pickle when her next-door neighbor and first real crush, Cricket, returns after years away. Though she believes herself to be desperately in love and destined to spend forever with her boyfriend Max, Lola quickly realizes that she still has feelings for Cricket, who is not shy about revealing his own romantic attachment to her. Finally, quiet Isla narrates her relationship with Josh, St. Clair's best friend. At the beginning of their senior year, Isla and Josh finally embark upon a relationship after years of mutual but unspoken interest; it quickly escalates, with Josh suggesting that Isla apply to Dartmouth, a school near the college he plans to attend. Predictably, all three novels end happily, despite obstacles and, in Isla and Josh's case, a dramatic breakup and reunion. More importantly, all three young couples insist that they will be together forever, a point which is most clearly illustrated by St. Clair's proposing to Anna in front of the other two couples at the end of the aptly titled third novel. While only one of the couples is officially betrothed, then, all three novels participate in a larger effort to establish young love and teen relationships as permanent.

"Last First Kiss[es]": Romance and Sex in the YA Marriage Plot

Although not all of the novels discussed here feature all aspects of the conventional marriage plot, they frequently engage with key elements of that genre in ways that reinforce often outdated expectations about romance and sexuality. Indeed, one component of the twenty-first-century marriage plot for young adults that certainly and directly harks back to its nineteenth-century predecessor is the emphasis on young women's virginity. Harrison points out that "[t]he marriage plot served to contain sexuality, at least in theory, within heterosexual marriage. . . . Women were increasingly defined as nonsexual, nondesiring, and nonsinful, with the attendant belief that women who did exhibit sexual desire or behavior outside of marriage were 'fallen' and, as such, irredeemable" (118). Some novels note a character's virginity as a more general symbol of inexperience and to locate that character on a path toward marriage and, thus, sex. For example, in Rainbow Rowell's *Fangirl* (2013), protagonist Cath struggles with her reluctance to show physical affection to her boyfriend Levi:

> Was she waiting for marriage? At the moment, it was hard to think beyond Levi
> . . . whom she was nowhere near marrying. That fact only made her want him

more. Because if she didn't end up marrying Levi, she wouldn't have lifetime access to his chest and his lips and whatever might be happening in his lap. What if they married other people? She should probably have sex with him now, while she still could. (Rowell)

Cath's concerns about her own expressions of desire are gradually resolved through her increasingly serious relationship with Levi, who makes it possible for her to move at her own pace while also reassuring her about the strength of his feelings for her. While *Fangirl* ends with the last days of Cath's freshman year and not technically with her marriage to Levi, the two have by that point expressed an unwillingness to be apart. And Rowell does, in her later novel for adults *Landline* (2014), reveal that Levi and Cath get engaged, thus cementing their relationship beyond the bounds of *Fangirl*'s pages. Cath's virginity and her decisions about pursuing a physical relationship are therefore comfortably resolved in her eventual betrothal to the boy who makes her question her own stances on sex.

Other marriage-oriented novels allow their female protagonists to pursue their sexuality in limited ways but generally recuperate their virginity through marriage. For example, Abby Abernathy, the narrator of Jamie McGuire's 2012 novel *Beautiful Disaster*, establishes her sexual purity early in the novel; in contrast, her love interest Travis Maddox is known for his casual one-night stands. When the two eventually pursue a relationship, the novel emphasizes that their monogamous connection is significant for both parties. In fact, when their first kiss leads immediately to the loss of Abby's virginity, Travis Maddox declares it her "last first kiss," and even though she hesitates to pursue a relationship afterward, he remains committed to her, deciding that he will not have sex with anyone else (McGuire). Their relationship is tumultuous and marked by multiple separations, yet within months Abby finds herself proposing to Travis, who reveals that he has already bought her a ring; the novel's conclusion finds them eloping to Vegas. The intensity of the couple's passion—both emotional and physical—as well as Travis's moral reform upon becoming involved with Abby underscores the more general suggestion that Abby's decision to have sex with Travis is a necessary and reasonable step on the path to inevitably becoming Mrs. Maddox.

In addition to protecting a woman's virtue, many texts that uphold the YA marriage plot retain old-fashioned ideas about love and marriage as fate. Indeed, Christine Seifert finds that many YA novels link sexuality and soul-mates, asserting that "the fated nature of [some] relationships allows them to operate in a sort of marital state" and thus remain "pseudovirgins forever" (38). While the idea that a couple is "meant to be" may be appealing in some ways, the assumption that marriage is necessarily the culmination of a couple's romantic destiny actually works to eliminate the role of choice and freedom in relationships. In *We'll Always Have Summer* (2011), the third novel of her Summer series, Jenny Han positions her protagonist Isabel "Belly" Conklin as destined to an early marriage to one of two very specific suitors. The first two novels follow Belly's lifelong relationships with brothers Conrad and Jeremiah Fisher, beginning with the intense crush she developed on Conrad as a young girl. Over the course of the series, she first dates brooding Conrad and then, when he distances himself after his mother's death, his younger, more cheerful brother Jeremiah; at the outset of the final novel in the trilogy, she has followed Jeremiah to college, where they become engaged. In the opening pages of this novel, Belly reflects on their shared past, concluding, "I think I always knew I would be Belly Fisher one day" (Han ii). Her conviction that she "always knew" she would marry one of the brothers seems to inform not only her acceptance of Jeremiah's proposal but also her more general willingness to quickly marry at the age of nineteen. After a series of conflicts—including Conrad's last-minute confession that he still loves her—Belly and Jeremiah's engagement ends abruptly on their intended wedding day, and the novel concludes just pages later with the revelation that, after finishing college, Belly has married Conrad. While this ending highlights the enduring quality of first love, it also underscores that Belly's belief that she is destined to marry a Fisher brother becomes a self-fulfilling prophecy that allows her to ignore or reject other possible futures.

While believing in soulmates might be understood as a primarily feminine impulse, it is important to note that a number of YA novels, such as Jennifer Smith's *The Statistical Probability of Love at First Sight* (2012) and Sarah Dessen's *This Lullaby* (2002), actively flip the script in this regard, framing their female protagonists as skeptics. One notable example occurs in Nicola Yoon's *The Sun Is Also a Star*, which introduces its teen protagonists on the morning of the day that will change their—and several other people's—lives: Daniel is meant to be interviewing for admission to Yale, while Natasha is following any lead she can find to prevent her family's imminent deportation. By that afternoon, following a few "magic" kisses, both teens are grappling with the potential of a relationship in very different ways. Poetry-loving Daniel insists that they are "meant to be" (188), while science-minded Natasha reasons *"meant to be* doesn't have to mean *forever"* (334). When Natasha is, in fact, forced to return to her native Jamaica, it appears that she has been right all along, especially as the young lovers' efforts to remain connected fail over time; however, the novel's epilogue apparently reunites Natasha and Daniel ten years later. Thus, Daniel's belief in destiny seems to be upheld by the novel's conclusion, undermining Natasha's skepticism and reinforcing the romantic notion that the two are "meant to be." These texts ultimately emphasize their male characters' confident acceptance of destiny as a means of changing the heroines' minds about romance and commitment, suggesting that even when young women attempt to challenge traditional narratives, their suitors' refusal to do so limits their options.

The problem of limited choice also appears as a feature of another common trope: romantic competition, including the now ubiquitous love triangle, which functions as a specific means of directing the protagonist toward a seemingly inevitable commitment to one of only two apparent options. Molly McAdams's *Taking Chances* (2012) offers a fairly typical portrayal of an adolescent love triangle: when virginal Harper gets to college, she immediately meets and finds herself struggling to choose between two boys. Chase is the stereotypical "bad boy," who drinks heavily and has casual sex, while Brandon is a clean, respectful prepster. By positioning Harper between these two seemingly opposed romantic options, McAdams perpetuates large-scale stereotypes about the choice between passion and security, suggesting that women can only have one or the other. And like many other young female protagonists trapped in love triangles, Harper responds not by questioning these oppositions or seeking a happy medium, but by attempting to determine which can be sacrificed so that the other can be embraced. Indeed, the novel underscores this point when Chase, attempting to turn a new leaf in order to meet Harper's desires, tells her, "Meeting you changed my world. Even when I thought you would never be mine, I couldn't continue to live a life I knew you hated" (McAdams). Despite his efforts, their relationship remains tumultuous and, ultimately, tragic: Harper discovers that she is pregnant, and they plan to marry; but after the couple has a dramatic fight, Chase dies in a car accident. Quickly, Harper and Brandon reconcile, with Brandon declaring his intention to marry her and act as the father of her unborn child. In the process, Harper reveals to Brandon that despite her relationship with Chase, "I had already known way before that, that I wanted to marry you" (McAdams), suggesting that her own attempts to navigate the love triangle inevitably would have led to the same conclusion.

Though McAdams's protagonist ends up marrying the conventional good guy, Harper's willingness to marry Chase despite their apparent incompatibility gestures toward another variation in the marriage plot—specifically, marriage as a means of resolving conflict. For example, Colleen Hoover's *Slammed* and its sequel *Point of Retreat* present the romance between eighteen-year-old Layken and twenty-one-year-old Will, who face a series of obstacles that prevent their relationship from developing smoothly, beginning with their realization, days after their first date, that he is student teaching at the high school she now attends. Over time, additional complications threaten their relationship: both are orphaned and act as guardians for their much-younger siblings; their school schedules prevent them from spending much time together; and the reappearance of Will's high school girlfriend makes Layken jealous. Despite these problems, Will reflects that "it's almost unbearable for me to take things slowly. If I left my head out of it and followed my heart, I'd marry her today" (Hoover, *Point*). Ultimately, in an effort to overcome the rift that his ex-girlfriend has caused, Will decides not to "take things slowly" anymore; his proposal to Layken results in their rushing to the courthouse less than two weeks later, believing that their marriage will function as a means of smoothing over their other difficulties.

It is also worth noting that not every YA novel that culminates in the protagonists' marriage frames that decision in terms of romance and passion; instead, some YA novels feature a (at times naive) consideration of marriage as a stable, secure means of moving into adulthood. While romance is not necessarily absent from such representations, it takes a backseat to more pragmatic concerns; these relationships in some ways more closely resemble the "familiar marriages" Schaeffer discusses than the happy endings of much conventional "chick lit." John Cusick's *Cherry Money Baby* (2013), for example, follows its decidedly unromantic protagonist Cherry as she faces the end of high school and the beginning of her adult life. Early in the novel, as Cherry and her long-term boyfriend Lucas consider the future together, he casually but sincerely proposes marriage; though she is caught off guard, Cherry accepts, reflecting that "really there was no question because there was only one place she wanted to go, an inner place, a place with Lucas" (Cusick). Though their relationship faces challenges when Cherry suddenly becomes swept up in a friendship with a movie star, Cherry and especially Lucas are portrayed throughout the novel as committed, reasonable, and well-suited partners. In the end, they happily respond to an unplanned pregnancy by moving forward with their simple, affordable wedding plans. It's also worth noting that recent novels like Sandhya Menon's *When Dimple Met Rishi* (2017) offer young readers a view of modern-day arranged marriages, highlighting the often positive—if not always completely welcome—role of family in guiding young people's romantic choices. Such representations, though much less common than the texts discussed earlier, reveal the possibility for more nuanced and potentially subversive uses for the marriage plot in YA literature.

Steps Back and Steps Forward

As novels such as those discussed here demonstrate, the prevalence of the marriage plot in contemporary YA literature functions as a means of reviving conventional attitudes about matrimony and implicating young readers in the "marriage envy" that perpetuates many cultural ideas about marriage. In contrast to conversations that suggest that young women might actually benefit from delaying marriage, such novels enact a set of postfeminist messages about sexuality, stability, and the successful transition into adulthood. Moreover, the at-times regressive ideas that seem to be motivating such portrayals of adolescent romance as permanent are underscored by the absence of similarly permanent relationships in queer YA literature; considering that same-sex marriage is now legal in many Western countries and that there has been a notable increase in YA novels featuring LGBTQ+ characters in the past few years, the absence of such marriage-centric storylines in queer YA suggests that the trend depends on and actively perpetuates heteronormative conventions and expectations.

Ultimately, the resurgence of the marriage plot in texts about and for adolescent women seems to signal a decidedly postfeminist impulse tied to ongoing cultural debates about marriage as an institution and calls into question the potential of YA literature as a potentially feminist space. Ames and Burcon, in their examination of some of the most prominent female protagonists of young adult literature, find that "[t]here are hundreds of YA titles that can be labeled as feminist, and even within these texts conflicting messages abound" (57). Usefully, though, they reframe these messages as a space for optimism: "perhaps if teenage girls can learn to weed through the confusing directives that are launched at these characters—and, by extension, them—the didactic messages they receive about gender and sexuality . . . will have less lasting impact as they pass on to the adult years where new texts eagerly wait to train them yet again" (Ames and Burcon 57).

Indeed, while it is certainly tempting to see the contemporary YA marriage plot as a danger to young readers and their sense of romantic destiny, I share Ames and Burcon's hope that novels such as those I discuss here may in fact equip readers to navigate and engage critically with this trope on a larger scale—not dooming them to unrealistic expectations or disappointed hopes, but preparing them to critique and question the seemingly endless series of messages they will receive as they move into adulthood. That is, even if these novels offer young readers models of romance that frequently prize regressive or outdated models of marriage, it remains possible that teen readers confronting the pressures of "marriage envy" will find these models limited or problematic, potentially questioning the need to conform to this idea of "forever" themselves.

Notes

1. Michael Cart, for example, asserts that "it too often seems that Blume has written not a novel but a scarcely dramatized sex manual" (178).

2. Leonard's claim has more to do with the perception of marriage than its literal, statistical nature. As Steven L. Nock has noted, "Current trends indicate that marriage in the future will be less central as a defining event in the life course of adults than it is in the present" (301). Perhaps more importantly for the purposes of this chapter, young women's ideas and expectations about marriage might currently be in flux, especially because of the increasing acceptance of cohabitation and divorce.

3. Though Leonard distinguishes chick lit from the larger genre of romance fiction, the latter genre continues to play an important role in reinforcing attitudes about marriage in contemporary American culture. Notably, Jade McKay and Elizabeth Parsons have found that "[m]arriages and their ceremonies remain highly fashionable in these apparently postfeminist times and represent a lucrative industry," but that "the trope is no longer unequivocally the herald of oppression or the conclusive end to a romance heroine's exciting life."

4. Although a more in-depth discussion of serialized narratives is beyond the scope of this project, it is worth noting that many of the texts discussed here are part of series. Goris's discussion of the increasing popularity of serialization in adult romance fiction is potentially helpful here, as she notes that "while serialization may stretch the romance's narrative possibilities to the breaking point, the serial form also offers the genre a new space in which to articulate romance fantasies that might particularly appeal to its contemporary reader." That is, seriality postpones or fundamentally changes expectations about a conventional "happily ever after" conclusion, but in doing so, it potentially opens up new ways of understanding the marriage plot for twenty-first-century readers (Goris).

Works Cited

Ames, Melissa, and Sarah Burcon. *How Pop Culture Shapes the Stages of a Woman's Life: From Toddlers-in-Tiaras to Cougars-on-the-Prowl*. Palgrave Macmillan, 2016.

Blume, Judy. *Forever*. 1975. Simon Pulse, 2007.

Brake, Elizabeth. *Minimizing Marriage: Marriage, Morality, and the Law*. Oxford UP, 2012.

Cart, Michael. *Young Adult Literature: From Romance to Realism*. 3rd ed., Neal-Schuman, 2016.

Cusick, John. *Cherry Money Baby*. Nook ed., Candlewick, 2013.

Genz, Stéphanie, and Benjamin B. Brabon. *Postfeminism: Cultural Texts and Theories*. Edinburgh UP, 2009.

Goris, An. "Happily Ever After . . . and After: Serialization and the Popular Romance Novel." *Americana: The Journal of American Popular Culture*, vol. 12, no. 1, 2013, http://www.americanapopularculture.com/journal/articles/spring_2013/goris.htm.

Han, Jenny. *We'll Always Have Summer*. Simon and Schuster BFYR, 2012.

Hoover, Colleen. *Point of Retreat*. Nook ed., Atria Books, 2012.

Hoover, Colleen. *Slammed*. Nook ed., Atria Books, 2012.

Leonard, Suzanne. "Marriage Envy." *Women's Studies Quarterly*, vol. 34, no. 3 & 4, 2006, pp. 43–44. *JSTOR*, http://jstor. org/stable/40003526.

McAdams, Molly. *Taking Chances*. Nook ed., Harper Collins, 2012.

McGuire, Jamie. *Beautiful Disaster*. Nook ed., Simon and Schuster, 2012.

McKay, Jade, and Elizabeth Parsons. "Out of Wedlock: The Consummation and Consumption of Marriage in Contemporary Romance Fiction." *Genders*, 1 Aug. 2009, http://www.colorado .edu/gendersarchive1998–2013/2009/08/01/out-wedlock-consummation-and-consumption -marriage-contemporary-romance-fiction.

Menon, Sandhya. *When Dimple Met Rishi*. Simon Pulse, 2017.

Munford, Rebecca, and Melanie Waters. *Feminism and Popular Culture: Investigating the Postfeminist Mystique*. Rutgers UP, 2014.

Nelson, Jandy. *The Sky Is Everywhere*. Nook ed., Dial, 2010.

Nock, Steven L. "The Growing Importance of Marriage in America." *Marriage and Family: Perspectives and Complexities*, edited by H. Elizabeth Peters and Claire M. Kamp Dush, Columbia UP, 2009, pp. 301–24.

Perkins, Stephanie. *Anna and the French Kiss*. Nook ed., Speak, 2010.

Perkins, Stephanie. *Isla and the Happily Ever After*. Nook ed., Speak, 2014.

Perkins, Stephanie. *Lola and the Boy Next Door*. Nook ed., Speak, 2011.

Peters, H. Elizabeth, and Claire M. Kamp Dush. "Introduction." *Marriage and Family: Perspectives and Complexities*, edited by H. Elizabeth Peters and Claire M. Kamp Dush, Columbia UP, 2009, pp. xv–xxix.

Rowell, Rainbow. *Fangirl*. Nook ed., St. Martin's Griffin, 2013.

Santos, Maria Lorena. "A Truth Universally Acknowledged? Rewriting Jane Austen's Marriage Plot." *Journal of English Studies and Comparative Literature*, vol. 14, no. 1, 2014, pp. 1–33.

Schaeffer, Talia. *Romance's Rival: Familiar Marriage in Victorian Fiction*. Oxford UP, 2016.

Seifert, Christine. *Virginity in Young Adult Literature after* Twilight. Rowman and Littlefield, 2015.

Yoon, Nicola. *The Sun Is Also a Star*. Random House, 2016.

Further Reading

Cannon, Katie. *And Then We Ran*. Stripes, 2017.

Cass, Kiera. *The Crown*. HarperCollins, 2016.

Cass, Kiera. *The Elite*. HarperCollins, 2013

Cass, Kiera. *The Heir*. HarperCollins, 2015.

Cass, Kiera. *The One*. HarperCollins, 2014.

Cass, Kiera. *The Selection*. HarperCollins, 2012.

Castrovilla, Selene. *The Girl Next Door*. West Side Books, 2010.

Clare, Cassandra. *Clockwork Angel*. Simon and Schuster, 2010.

Clare, Cassandra. *Clockwork Prince*. Simon and Schuster, 2011.

Clare, Cassandra. *Clockwork Princess*. Simon and Schuster, 2013.

Condie, Ally. *Crossed*. Dutton, 2011.

Condie, Ally. *Matched*. Dutton, 2010.

Condie, Ally. *Reached*. Dutton, 2012.

Coutts, Alexandra. *Young Widows Club*. Farrar, Straus, and Giroux, 2015.

Crane, Shelley. *Accordance*. Kiss Me, 2011.

Crane, Shelley. *Defiance*. Kiss Me, 2011.

Crane, Shelley. *Independence*. Kiss Me, 2012.

Crane, Shelley. *Significance*. Kiss Me, 2011.

Crane, Shelley. *Undeniably Chosen*. Kiss Me, 2015.

McCahan, Erin. *I Now Pronounce You Someone Else.* Arthur A. Levine, 2010.
Oppel, Kenneth. *Every Hidden Thing.* HarperCollins, 2016.
Werlin, Nancy. *Impossible.* Dial, 2008.
Williams, Nicole. *Clash.* HarperCollins, 2012.
Williams, Nicole. *Crash.* HarperCollins, 2012.
Williams, Nicole. *Crush.* HarperCollins, 2013.

12

"No Accident, No Mistake": Acquaintance Rape in Recent YA Novels

Roxanne Harde

"Rape is not committed by psychopaths or deviants from our social norms—rape is committed by *exemplars* of our social norms," Andrea Dworkin argued in 1976. "Rape is no excess, no aberration, no accident, no mistake—it embodies sexuality as the culture defines it" (45–46). As a society, we have come to understand that the face of the rapist is most often a face we know, a friend, a schoolmate, a date; as the RAINN website notes, 93 percent of sexually assaulted juveniles know their attackers (RAINN). We are learning that sexuality, as we have defined it, that the social codes surrounding male sexuality, mean that a frightening proportion of women, particularly young women, will be raped by an acquaintance, someone who moves in their social circles. It comes as no surprise, then, that young adult literature reflects this growing understanding, and that contemporary debates about consent, alcohol and drug abuse, and sexual violence drive the plots of dozens of recent YA novels. These novels—listed below and all published within the last seven years—generally follow the themes of Laurie Halse Anderson's germinal rape novel, *Speak*, even as they support Dworkin's contention that rape is not anomalous but paradigmatic, that it enacts and reinforces shared cultural understandings about gender and sexuality. In these views the core dynamic of patriarchal sexuality is the normalizing and sexualizing of masculine control and dominance over the feminine, which finds expression in a number of beliefs about what is natural, acceptable, and even desirable in male-female sexual interaction: that the male will be persistent and aggressive, the female often reluctant and passive; that "real men" (young men in this case) are entitled to sexual access to women when, where, and how they want it; that sexual intercourse is only an act of male conquest; that women are men's sexual objects or possessions. As Joan McGregor summarizes the situation, "men are taught to be the aggressors and to be persistent, and women are taught to be passive and appear reluctant" (7). As a group, these YA novels about acquaintance rape engage with the dominant discourse about sexuality, with the ways in which it constructs teenagers who rape and a society that rarely holds them accountable. Jody Raphael asks that "readers come to understand that there are many acquaintance scenarios, not just one, and that our response to it must encompass all the varied situations in which women and girls are subjected to rape" (5). The scenarios in these novels offer readers alternate discourses about culpability and shame, detail options for survivors, and give readers access to voices too often silenced, helping them toward understanding the social codes that lead to and the circumstances that arise from acquaintance rape.

This chapter examines these common themes in several novels about acquaintance rape. Anderson's *Speak* laid the thematic foundations on which these texts build. Melinda, Anderson's protagonist, can barely bring herself to tell the reader about her rape; silent to the point of muteness, she hides in her closet screaming herself hoarse and chews her lips into a bloody mess. Her rapist, an older and popular jock, spreads rumors about her promiscuity even as he pressures other girls for sex, then attacks her a second time when she finally tells and challenges his masculinity. Anderson thus outlines issues concerning when, how, and whom to tell about the rape; the ways in which the survivor reacts to the rape, including self-harm; the ways in which the survivor is both shamed and blamed; and ways to understand the rapist. In focusing on these themes in a handful of contemporary YA novels, I consider their cultural significance and pedagogical value. The ways in which they embody sexuality, male and female, and how they represent acquaintance rape might have lasting implications.

Telling: "This Thing, It Touches Everyone"

Rape, in these novels, takes up very little space; what comes after—coping with the trauma, learning how to live with a drastically changed worldview, rebuilding the ability to trust, and testing the connections with family and friends—forms the bulk of these narratives. Susan Brison suggests that the trauma resulting from incidents like sexual violence "not only shatters one's fundamental assumptions about the world and one's safety in it . . . it also severs the sustaining connection between the self and the rest of humanity . . . one can no longer be oneself even to oneself, since the self exists fundamentally in relation to others (40). Survivors of acquaintance rape in these novels, often but not always the protagonist and/or speaker, begin to cope with, if not work through, the trauma, trying to recover from this shattering immediately after the rape; their very survival depends on it. However, this set of texts almost uniformly positions real recovery as beginning at the point of telling. At the beginning of *Speak*, long before Melinda reveals the rape to the reader, she wishes she could tell her former best friend: "If there is anyone in the entire galaxy I am dying to tell what really happened, it's Rachel. My throat burns. . . . My lip bleeds a little. It tastes like metal" (5). When Melinda finally works up the courage to tell, Rachel refuses to believe and calls her jealous and sick. Nonetheless, this telling is, as are they all, cathartic. Melinda begins to heal, commits to artistic outlets for her pain, and prevails against the rapist when he attacks her again. The novel ends with a scene in which Melinda's art teacher comments that she has been "through a lot," and she confidently begins to speak with "Let me tell you about it" (198). Telling in the novels under study comes in one of three ways: as in *Speak*, the survivor struggles with the rape throughout the text, remaining silent until near the end of the narrative; or the survivor tells—family or friends—after the rape; or the survivor has no choice about it. In the first two scenarios, these authors depict the survivors coming to terms with sexual assault, often in negative ways, as their protagonists engage in self-harm or other self-destructive behaviors. Real healing, they collectively suggest, comes only after the people closest to the survivor know and can begin to help. The problem, of course, is that the novels with this narrative, like *Speak*, do not engage with the difficulties survivors face after the point of telling.

For example, in Courtney Stevens's *Faking Normal*, fifteen-year-old Alexi is raped by her older sister's boyfriend and does not tell because he has long been a part of their family; throughout the narrative she refers to how long she has kept her secret: "Faking normal is a skill I learned seventy-seven days ago" (93). Her suffering worsens until she tells a friend, who gives her the courage to tell her sister, confront the rapist, and then tell her parents. In Colleen Clayton's *What Happens Next*, sixteen-year-old Sid is drugged and raped by a "college guy" she met on a high school ski trip. Because she can't remember the rape, and because she refuses to tell her mother, Sid keeps the assault a secret until the end of the novel, when she sees the rapist's picture in the newspaper after he is charged for several similar crimes. Her mother responds with full support and love: "You're going to get through this. *We* are going to get through this." Sid responds by "choos[ing] to believe that I will be okay" (309–10). In Amber Smith's *The Way I Used to Be*, at the start of her freshman year, Eden is brutally raped by her older brother's best friend. He threatens to kill her if she tells;

she keeps her secret through her four years of high school, around which the novel is structured, finally telling in her senior year, after he rapes a girl in his college dorm. Eden's brother complains that the girl couldn't have really been raped because she waited two days to tell, and Eden thinks, "Compared to how long I've waited, two days seems nearly instantaneous" (314). Eden tells a friend, then her brother; as they go together to tell the police and their parents, she understands that "this isn't all about me. This thing, it touches everyone" (359). As each of these protagonists considers telling, each understands that her family and friends also will be profoundly affected by what has happened to her.

Just as with *Speak*, there are problems with the way these narratives unfold toward the moment the survivor tells about the rape. First, and Anderson foregrounds this fact, people tend not to believe that an assault took place. In a study of the law and acquaintance rape, Raphael points out that the "more acquaintance rapes are reported—and the more acquaintance rape claims are taken seriously by prosecutors, judges, and juries—the more people clamor that women are falsely claiming they've been raped" (2). In these three novels, the first persons told are friends or boyfriends close enough to the survivor to understand that she is struggling with trauma. While they believe and are supportive, each author makes clear that peers are simply not enough to help a young survivor of sexual assault. I don't disagree, but I'm not sure how helpful it is to so fully connect disclosure with healing. Telling one's parents or any authority figure might not be the one thing that will help a young adult who has been sexually assaulted work through their trauma. Parents aren't infallible, and the parents of these three young women are depicted with flaws: Eden's parents clearly prioritize their son and his friend over their daughter; Alexi's mother is dealing with grief over the murder of a close friend, and her father sees the rapist as a son; Sid's mother is single and trying to support two children on her own. Ending with telling might suggest to young readers that telling means a suddenly happy ending.

Even if these parents have the resources to fully support their assaulted children—and this is my second point—each of these young women has been dealing with her trauma in self-harming ways, developing habits and practices that will not be easy to break. Sid, partly blaming her buxom figure for the assault, develops an eating disorder; between running, starving, and forcing herself to throw up when she does eat, she manages to lose most of the curves that she thinks attracted the rapist. When she finally faces her naked self in the mirror, she hates that she has become that girl "who pukes and runs and starves herself to death because she can't deal with her pain" (291). Nonetheless, she understands the "mental effort" it will take for her to stop reshaping her body (291). Alexi responds in a Melinda-like fashion, playing a "blame game," compulsively hiding in her closet, counting the slits in the air vent over her bed, and gouging the back of her neck with her fingernails. Like Sid, she articulates that her methods for coping will be hard habits to break. Eden's coping mechanisms, developed over four years instead of the roughly one that it takes Melinda, Alexi, and Sid to tell, may have more lasting effects. She responds to the violent assault and her family's failure to notice that she has been traumatized with drastic changes to her personality and behavior. She goes from being a stereotypical "good girl," excellent student, and member of the school band, to becoming a party girl. When her parents fail to notice those dramatic changes, and her brother finds out and exacerbates her behavior, she progresses from drinking and smoking pot to casual sex. This narrative emphasizes telling the police over telling the parents, but the response sounds the same, as a female detective assures Eden, "Everything will be okay" (364). In all three cases, ending with telling suggests that a survivor can easily stop self-harming behavior and get on with her life. And while I understand the value in delineating the ways in which youths come to terms with sexual assault before they can tell someone about it, by moving the telling to the end of the novel, these authors extend the immediate trauma of rape into a seemingly endless cycle of pain and guilt. Their inability, as Eden phrases it, "to say a word I just cannot say," means that readers are not shown the struggles these survivors, their friends, and families will face after disclosure (341). Whether these young women choose to report the crime or not, something these texts make clear should be their choice and no one else's, "this thing," as Eden notes, "touches everyone" (349).

Two novels in which the disclosure happens earlier offer some insight into what survivors might face. Valerie, in Alina Klein's *Rape Girl*, tells her mother the day after she was raped while hungover and semi-unconscious by a boy she had liked. Her mother immediately calls the police and takes Valerie to the doctor. When she tells her best friend, Valerie begins to understand how the charge will be perceived at school and in her town when Mimi doubts her: "Are you *sure* you want to go through with this, Val? . . . The whole . . . *rape* thing. . . . Adam said it was totally consensual and I know how much you like him," and later criticizes her: "[T]hat's no reason for you to wreck Adam's life" (34, 44). These themes of both disbelieving the rape and blaming the survivor for its effect on the perpetrator's life run through the novel as Valerie is ostracized at school, moved out of the classes Adam is in, verbally attacked by more than a dozen boys who are ready to testify that they had sex with her, and finally forced by the principal into a meeting with Adam after the prosecutor's office drops the rape charges (37). Advised by her uncle to move on, that "this is just a bump in the road," Valerie nonetheless continues to defend herself and work toward healing (49).

In Laurie Gray's *Maybe I Will*, Sandy, whose gender is never identified, is sixteen, brilliant, artistic, privileged, and best friends with Cassie. Sandy is sexually assaulted by Cassie's boyfriend, Aaron, a wrestler. The assault is clearly about control: Aaron suddenly pins Sandy to the floor, saying, "Try to get up," covering Sandy's mouth with one hand while anally penetrating Sandy with the other (39). Sandy is haunted by Cassie saying Aaron "didn't assault you" and copes by drinking (60). Sandy's journal leads to telling, and Sandy's parents involve both the police and a psychoanalyst. While the prosecutor believes Sandy's story and that of Shanika, a friend Aaron date-raped a year earlier, he chooses to not proceed because of the improbability of getting a conviction. Sandy's mother, a lawyer, agrees and concludes, like Valerie's uncle, "Sometimes it's better to just move on" (183).

Both Klein and Gray juxtapose the difficulties these traumatized young people face against the callous or indifferent treatment they receive. It will be clear to readers that being told by loved ones to "just move on" causes Valerie and Sandy as much pain as being openly tormented by other people. It was made clear to each of the women in Raphael's study that if she was "not lying, then she [was] responsible for the incident by drinking and being sexually promiscuous, her actions resulting in sexual penetration that, though unwanted, cannot be considered serious or harmful" (2). In the case of sexual assault, art must reflect life, and both texts gesture toward the social implications of charging someone, in or out of the courts, with sexual assault. As pedagogical messages, both novels also emphasize the importance of telling as a preventative measure. After her rapist is charged with another assault, Eden feels guilty for not reporting him, but both Valerie and Sandy are congratulated for at least registering a formal complaint and putting their attackers on notice: Valerie's school guidance counselor says, "I'm proud of you—for reporting what happened to you. . . . Did you know less than a quarter of rapes are reported?" (89). When Valerie questions her actions because of their impact on Adam's life, the teacher points out that "it is nobody's fault but his own. . . . By telling, you may have prevented the same thing from happening to another girl" (89–90). Klein also demonstrates Valerie's resilience when she confronts Adam in the meeting she was forced to attend; she is strong and persistent, repeatedly referring to the ways in which she told him no. Likewise, Sandy's psychoanalyst stresses that "all things considered, Sandy has made some very positive choices in dealing with an incredibly stressful and difficult situation. . . . Some kids never, ever find the courage to tell" (145). Instead of ending their narratives at the point of telling, Klein and Gray offer a realistic array of challenges that rape survivors face, both in and outside of the legal system. Whereas Smith, Stevens, and Clayton delineate the internal struggles and subsequent behaviors of a traumatized young person, Klein and Gray move readers into the array of possibilities of what can happen when family and friends, schools and other institutions become part of the rape narrative. In these cases, telling becomes a necessary, but incredibly difficult, step that the survivor must take, and these novels both evade the problematic aspects of telling even as they imply that if telling means courage, then not telling simply means cowardice.

No Telling: "It's Easier Not to Make a Fuss"

What happens, then, when telling is not an option, when the survivor's control over telling is taken away from them along with the control over their person-hood that they lose during the rape? Chloe Angyal argues that when "we forget that rape is about power, when we choose instead to imagine that it is about sex, we make a terrible mistake. It's a mistake that worms into every aspect of how we deal with the phenomenon of rape. It affects how we think about and talk about rape, perniciously affecting how we treat rape victims, how we prosecute rapists and how we try to prevent future rapes from occurring." In several YA novels about acquaintance rape, the plot removes from the victim control over telling; other people tell, sometimes concerned friends or family tell when the unconscious victim is found undressed and bleeding; sometimes the perpetrator publicizes the rape as consensual sex through social media before the victim can even consider reporting it as rape. In both cases the removal of control over telling facilitates mistaking the rape for sex and fitting the assault into the social codes that define the rapist as a player, a model of ideal masculinity, and the victim as promiscuous, an example of aberrant femininity and subject to the phenomenon of "slut-shaming."

Two novels depict the unconscious-victim scenario. In *Exit, Pursued by a Bear*, E. K. Johnston's rape plot reads like a test case for appropriate social responses to rape. Hermione, a virgin and all-around good girl, is drugged and raped during a dance at a regional cheerleader camp, then left naked and half submerged in a lake, where she is found by her friends and taken to a hospital. Even as she points out that this "is not standard procedure," Johnston notes that it was important for her protagonist to "have an excellent support system. Her parents, teachers, coach, minister, and community rally around her. She receives the medical care she requires. The police are gracious and helpful." Moreover, because the rapist drugged her and she has no memory of the assault, Hermione feels "like it never happened in the first place" (152). This survivor may not have to cope with trauma like that suffered by Eden and the other characters discussed above, but neither is she treated by many of her peers like the victim of a nongendered crime, a mugging, for example. At cheer camp, Hermione, newly elected captain of her large and successful cheer squad, is organized, assertive, and fully in control of her team; she also mingles with the other teams to help devise the best strategies to beat them during the season's competitions. After the rape, rumors circulate about her "flirting" with boys from the other teams; all her actions are called into question, and many of her peers think she "brought it on [her]self" (126). The control Hermione worked so hard to maintain is taken from her during the rape, and again after when she cannot control the narrative of the assault. Johnston brings continued focus on issues of power and control at the end, when Hermione recognizes the rapist at a cheer competition and spends several moments deciding what to do about it, understanding that his future depends on "what I choose to do next. . . . the choice is mine" (240). Even though she dreads a trial, after concluding that he "took away my ability to choose last time," Hermione decides to press charges (242).

Grace, the protagonist of Patty Blount's *Some Boys*, is raped while passed out at an outdoor party, by Zac, her school's "golden boy." Found by Ian, Zac's friend and the boy with whom she later forms a relationship, and taken to a hospital, Grace decides to press charges. However, Zac posts a thirty-second video of her on Facebook, showing what looks like her willingness to have sex with him. Though she was a virgin and had not dated much previously, the situation immediately devolves into "the *entire* school" against Grace (1). He is the star of the lacrosse team; she is a slut who "likes it on [her] knees" and might get him kicked off the team (3). The police won't press charges, and the only help she receives at school is a pamphlet from the Rape Crisis Hotline that a librarian slips into her book. She is ostracized, verbally and physically abused, and even her father thinks she is responsible for being raped. Understanding that she doesn't "have a damn thing left because Zac McMahon took it all," Grace devises a plan to prove that it was rape and not consensual sex. Blount depicts Grace as strong and stubborn, willing to forgo a normal life to find justice. However, if her courage and tenacity offer readers a positive role model, then a plot that has Ian find the evidence to have Zac expelled and charged diminishes that agency.

In any case, Grace, like Hermione, struggles against social codes that would see her completely at fault for being assaulted. By structuring these plots after the rape becomes public, Blount and Johnston offer readers characters who deal with far more than trauma and telling. Both girls see the effects of the rape on their families; they suffer social stigma at school, and they engage with medical and judicial systems that may or may not be supportive. Both girls resist the perception that they are at fault for their attacks, and both narratives show how the dominant discourse surrounding male sexuality is at fault for much of what happens to these girls. Noting that "rape is an instance in which discourses of power produce the feminine body as violable and weak," Holly Henderson draws on Michel Foucault to argue that "resistance to this constitutive discourse of power is also located with the feminine body. . . . If the feminine body is a surface on which the tenets of a sexually hierarchical culture are written, Foucault suggests that it is also the site where those tenets may be fought" (229). The bodies of Hermione and Grace become surfaces on which Johnston and Blount write resistance as they move from losing both control of their bodies and the narrative of their rapes to reclaiming agency and dignity.

However, I want to complicate that rosy summary with two more novels in which the victim of acquaintance rape is denied the right to tell. In *Asking for It*, Louise O'Neill places eighteen-year-old Emma and her friends firmly in the grip of a virulent rape culture. Emma's school is in a small city in Ireland, but it could be anywhere. Emma is sexually active, but largely not by choice. She thinks back to a recent party: "Kevin throwing me against a wall at the party, his teeth sharp. . . . It seemed easiest to go along with it" (27). She seems far more concerned that her partners not tell anyone than about the number of times she and her friends are raped by the boys in their group; as Dylan describes them, "Girls are all the same. . . . Get wasted and get a bit slutty, then in the morning try to pretend it never happened because you regret it" (27). Early on, Emma remembers counseling her friend Jamie to keep quiet about being raped by Dylan. Soon after, she watches Jamie drink at the next party, thinking, "She should take it easy. She should know what happens when you drink too much," and being unsurprised that Jamie "scored with Colin Daly" in a scenario that looks like another rape (65, 82). O'Neill pauses over the scene in which Jamie criticizes Emma for her advice: "You said it would be better. . . . It's not better, Emma. It's not better," and Emma explains again, "It's happened to loads of people. It happens all the time. You wake up the next morning and you regret it or you don't remember what happened exactly, but it's easier not to make a fuss" (85). Emma, worn down by sexual and social codes, by demands that she look perfect, behave like a lady, and hide her own desires while satisfying those of others, drinks heavily and takes drugs at a party. Her friends are surprised, noting, "It's not like her though, you know what a control freak she is" (95). Emma blacks out completely and is gang-raped, but telling isn't her option; she is dumped on her front porch and regains consciousness only when her parents find her. She has no memory of what happened, but the photos on Facebook tell the story of a gang rape in which she is violated multiple times and in many ways. Unsurprisingly, the entire community sides against Emma and her family, and charges against the boys, all from a winning sports team, are dropped. Emma becomes depressed and suicidal, wishing, "I could tell Jamie that I did her a favor. I wish I could explain to her that she is the lucky one. If I could go back, pretend like nothing happened, I would" (230). Emma concludes that she has lost everything, including herself: "I belong to those other boys, as surely as if they have stamped me with a cattle brand" (315).

Ben is the speaker in C. Desir's *Fault Line*, a star athlete and all-around good guy. When he falls in love with Ani, they are deliberate about adding sex to their developing relationship. Then Ani goes to a raver party with her friend Kate, is drugged and gang-raped. She is left torn, needing surgery to remove a foreign object, refusing to tell her mother or press charges. As word gets around their high school, exacerbated by Kate who informs everyone that Ani "was acting like a complete slut. A lot of people heard her say she was going to hook up with all those guys," Ani is tormented by most of the student body (105). Ben reacts badly, using physical force against those abusing her verbally. He wavers between understanding that the drugs she was given made her act that way and wondering if she was just drunk. Ben also listens to a conversation about date-rape drugs, learning from knowledgeable-sounding teenagers about how those drugs made girls behave: "Could've been roofies, though. I've also seen chicks act that way when they're buzzing on Special K. There was a bunch of E going around the party too" (139). Nonetheless, he feels disgusted when he realizes he "was dating the Manhole" (140). Their relationship falls apart as Ani begins engaging in casual sex with several men, finally telling him, "Don't you see? If I don't hate myself, I don't feel anything at all. At least disgust feels better than nothing" (225). The novel ends with Ben telling Ani's mother, suggesting she may get help and begin to heal, but thereby further taking control from her.

These novels have several problematic aspects in common, and their authors seem haunted by the rape culture narrative that insists on the inclusion of sexual history as a factor in sexual assault cases. Both feature girls who are sexually active and then gang-raped. Their similarly unhappy endings, though not unrealistic, seem to suggest to readers that unless you were a virgin when you were raped—as was each of the other survivors depicted in the novels I've discussed thus far—you have no future: you are now only the "It" Emma now thinks herself, or the "Manhole" that Ani is called. Henderson argues that we must not see "rape as a fate worse than death," because this view "participates in the reduction of the core of one's being to sexuality; thus, to be raped is to be stripped of all sense of oneself, of some inner, private, and intimate space" (251). Each of the four white, middle-class girls discussed in this section woke to a new version of her life, one in which she had been violated while unconscious, but only the virgins are allowed the resilience that enables recovery.[1] Each has been stripped of the right to say no, and the right to tell her own story, but only Emma and Ani are repeatedly violated by the actions of others. McGregor argues that rape expresses "the message of the inferiority of women. The rapist . . . sends the message that this woman is for his enjoyment, an object to be used for his pleasure. His actions express her inferiority to him since he does not feel the need to bother to investigate whether she is really consenting, even in the face of evidence that she was not" (230). Understanding that she is "supposed to set an example," "to be brave for other victims" by prosecuting the rapists, Emma knows that her friends' witness statements will say, "She was drunk, she was high, she was asking for it," and she drops the charges (301, 284, 285). The treatment of Emma and Ani after their rapes—by family, friends, institutions, the media—makes clear this perceived inferiority and supports this objectification.

In her germinal study of rape culture, *Against Our Will*, Susan Brownmiller could, on the one hand, be describing the teenagers who raped Emma and Ani: "On the shoulders of these unthinking, predictable, insensitive, violence-prone young men there rests an age-old burden that amounts to an historic mission: the perpetuation of male domination over women by force" (209). On the other hand, when she writes about date rape specifically, Brownmiller aligns with Emma's friends: "Upon hearing such cases, even with my feminist perspective, I often feel like shouting, 'Idiot, why didn't you see the warning signs earlier?'" (257). However, as Brownmiller continues, "that, of course, is precisely the point. As debatable as the case may appear when one tries to apply objective standards, it is the subjective behavioral factors that may determine a rape," and she bolsters her point with a study of juries, in which acquaintance rapes of women who drank with their rapists and were alleged to be "promiscuous" "were assessed by juries . . . as having taken an undue risk and morally not worth a conviction for rape" (257). These novels seem to reinforce the social codes that say that because they had sex and partied, both Emma and Ani are deemed "morally" not worth it by the people closest to them and the institutions that should have helped them. Both characters are depicted as especially beautiful young women, both are intelligent and high achievers, and both are self-aware personalities with high degrees of control of themselves and their social situations, descriptions that cumulatively emphasize privilege and power. Therefore, these plotlines seem to work exceptionally hard at showing how young women can lose, but never regain, power, and I find it especially bleak that O'Neill and Desir position these rapes as the "fate worse than death" that Henderson describes. McGregor notes that because "sex, sexuality, our bodies and control over them are central to who we are," rape "transgresses this central zone for our identity it exposes us and makes us a tool or thing for someone else's sexual ends" (221, 222). Rape "transgresses"; it does not, and should not, necessarily destroy. Foucault argues that "resistance is never in a position of exteriority in relation to power. . . . one is always 'inside' power, there is no 'escaping' it, there is no absolute outside where it is concerned" (95). If he is right and power is not something that is possessed but something that is exercised, then O'Neill and Desir might realistically have found ways for Emma and Ani to recover from the trauma they suffered, might have contested slut-shaming, and shown readers that sexually active young women have the same resilience and rights as virgins.

Raping: "Was There Something So Terrible in What He Had Done?"

And what about the rapist? In the novels discussed thus far, the young male who rapes is either excluded or is an undeveloped and stereotypical character: all those described are popular and athletic, models of stereotypical masculinity. Aiyana Altrows argues that YA rape novels "in which the rapist is excluded ultimately demonstrate a surrender to patriarchal systems of power, as they are incapable of appropriately assigning fault"; she goes on to note that novels including the rapist as a character reject those patriarchal controls (53). In *The Word for Yes*, Claire Needell includes the rapist as a developed secondary character. Needell features three sisters; the youngest, fifteen-year-old Melanie, is confident and spoiled, often arrogant and obnoxious, and treats her close friend Gerald callously. At one point she agrees with others that her "hair is more important than any part of Gerald" (64). Melanie knows that Gerald would "do anything to be close to her" (122). With her sister and their friends, they attend a Halloween party, "filled with bodies—smoking, drinking, groping teenage bodies" (75). Gerald gets drunk and is picked on by older classmates; he makes his way to Melanie, thinking that they would stop laughing at him if they knew he was with her (76). A very drunk Melanie stumbles into him, where she clearly feels safe: "Oh, Gerald . . . it's just you" (77). Gerald takes her to an empty room, where he rapes her after she passes out. Needell uses Melanie and Gerald to consider the aftermath of rape: Melanie is furious. She threatens and attacks her sister, and the thought of Gerald brings revulsion and hatred: "She wished she had hit him when she had the chance, hit him hard, so his mouth swelled, his nose bled. She wished it was him who had been found on the stupid white rug, bloody, in pain. . . . She wasn't going to let a stupid boy like Gerald . . . make her feel worthless" (133). She also continues to masturbate and fantasize about boys she likes. When she finally confronts him, she asserts both her right to consent ("I remember I told you to stop. . . . I told you no . . . you must have known I was too drunk") and her autonomy ("he had lost any right to complain. He didn't even have the right to look at her") (208, 209).

As rumors of the rape circulate, instead of shaming Melanie, the whole school ostracizes Gerald. He finally asks his older brother if he "ever, you know, messed around with a girl when maybe he shouldn't have—when maybe they were both too drunk?" (178). Gerald desperately wants his drunkenness to absolve him, even as he notes that his decision was conscious. His brother's response, a punch to his jaw, seems an adequate answer. Up to the point of the rape, Needell draws Gerald as a sympathetic, if inept, character, a boy whom girls like platonically, who gets along at home and school. But this ordinary boy turns into a rapist at the first possible opportunity, and his interior monologue makes clear that his crime includes his desire for Melanie's passivity, his need to have power over this strong-willed girl. If Altrows is correct that including the rapist allows readers to assign responsibility and interrogate "the rapist's motivations [which] can reveal the social conditions which facilitate rape," then readers of this novel can draw the conclusion that because of the rape culture we have constructed, our society has managed to turn every boy into a potential rapist (63). Readers are given to understand that he has been badly treated and used by Melanie, but that treatment and his drunkenness, even the kisses they share, are shown to be no excuse for raping an unconscious girl. Arguing that "to ignore men, to believe that women alone will transform a rape culture, freezes men in a posture of defensiveness, defiance, and immobility," Michael Kimmel points out that rapists are "overconformists to destructive norms of male sexual behavior. Until we change the meaning of manhood . . . conquest will remain part of the rhetoric of masculinity" (156, 152). Raping gives Gerald a stereotypically masculine control over this strong-willed girl. In drawing both rapist and survivor, Needell adumbrates Altrows's conclusion that including the rapist shifts the narrative away from "the trauma of the victim" (63). Juxtaposing Melanie's strength and fury with Gerald's cowardly assault, Needell figures "everyboy" as rapist even as she makes clear that rape survivors can reclaim the right to manage their bodies.

Writing: "I Have a Story"

When considering acquaintance rape, theorists like Joan McGregor focus rightly on issues of consent: a universally taught and understood idea of consent would expand "women's sexual autonomy, and women would have more freedom and control over their sexual lives" (99). However, just as Altrows justifiably wants authors to focus more fully on the young men who rape, I suggest that these authors should also engage more explicitly with issues of consent, a theme Klein, Blount, and O'Neill introduce but don't develop.

Instead, these authors have, as do their characters and all survivors of rape, difficulty looking past the rape. Many of the authors discussed here include afterwords that consider their experiences of acquaintance rape and/or their interest in helping rape survivors. Alina Klein writes, "As a sixteen-year-old rape survivor I pressed charges, but I wasn't alone in the proceedings: five other girls stepped forward with similar stories. I'd like to thank them, now, for telling the truth" (124). Courtney Stevens concludes with a letter to the reader, emphasizing, "Alexi's story is not my story, but I have a story," and giving her readers a list emphasizing that rape is not the survivor's fault. Patty Blount wants to bring to light how "victims of rape aren't just victims of rape" (319). Louise O'Neill notes, "When I was writing this novel, friend after friend came to me telling me of something that had happened to them. A hand up their skirt, a boy who wouldn't take no for an answer, a night where they were too drunk to give consent but they think it was taken from them anyway. We shared these stories with one another and it was as if we were discussing some essential part of being a woman" (320). And Claire Needell concludes, "I can guarantee you that a woman you love and respect has been raped" (237). While I agree that their stories, fictional or not, are important to bring acquaintance rape of girls and young women to a place where the public, and judicial and educational institutions, can no longer ignore it, I would like to see stories that engage more fully with the issues of rape denial and consent. As Raphael argues, we all have a role to play in reforming rape denial: "We can correct friends who minimize acquaintance rape. We can complain to the appropriate authorities when we notice that a rape report in our college or workplace is being minimized or handled incorrectly. We can protest rape jokes" (191). Placing rape on a continuum of power that begins with social constructions of the female body, Henderson argues that "rape prevention requires that rape not be theorized as a foregone conclusion; rather, feminism must learn to view rape as a sequence or process that can be undermined *before it occurs*" (229). That change will be harder, involving first a change in the way we understand and enforce consent, and second, a change, as Kimmel contends, in the meaning of manhood. Authors writing fiction for young adults must begin to make clear that rape is no accident or mistake, to imagine new ways in which to rewrite rape and rape culture, and to redefine male and female sexuality.

Note

1. Of the dozens of recently published YA rape narratives I have found, only two feature protagonists who are other than white, including *Gabi, a Girl in Pieces* by Isabel Quintero and *One Night* by Melanie Florence, which feature Mexican American and Indigenous Canadian girls, respectively.

Works Cited

Altrows, Aiyana. "Rape Scripts and Rape Spaces: Constructions of Female Bodies in Adolescent Fiction." *International Research in Children's Literature*, vol. 9, no. 1, 2016, 50–64.

Anderson, Laurie Halse. *Speak*. Puffin, 1999.

Angyal, Chloe. "Sex and Power, from North Carolina to Congo." *Huffington Post*, 11 March 2010, www.huffingtonpost.com/chloe-angyal-sex-and-power-from north_b_495296.html.

Blount, Patty. *Some Boys*. Sourcebooks Fire, 2014.

Brison, Susan J. *Aftermath: Violence and the Remaking of a Self*. Princeton UP, 2002.

Brownmiller, Susan. *Against Our Will: Men, Women, and Rape*. Bantam, 1975.

Clayton, Colleen. *What Happens Next*. Poppy/Little, Brown Books for Young Readers, 2012.

Desir, Christa. *Fault Line*. Simon Pulse, 2013.

Dworkin, Andrea. *Our Blood: Prophecies and Discourses on Sexual Politics*. Perigee Books, 1976.

Foucault, Michel. *The History of Sexuality*. Vol. 1. Translated by Robert Hurley. Penguin, 1978.

Gray, Laurie. *Maybe I Will*. Luminis, 2013.

Henderson, Holly. "Feminism, Foucault, and Rape: A Theory and Politics of Rape Prevention." *Berkeley Journal of Gender, Law, and Justice*, vol. 22, no. 1, 2013, 225–53.

Horvath, Miranda, and Jennifer Brown. *Rape: Challenging Contemporary Thinking*. Willan, 2009.

Johnston, E. K. *Exit, Pursued by a Bear*. Dutton Books for Young Readers, 2016.

Kimmel, Michael. "Men, Masculinity, and the Rape Culture." *Transforming a Rape Culture*, edited by Emilie Buchwald, et al., rev. ed. Milkweed, 2005, pp. 139–57.

Klein, Alina. *Rape Girl*. Namelos, 2012.

McGregor, Joan. *Is It Rape? On Acquaintance Rape and Taking Women's Consent Seriously*. Ashgate, 2005.

Needell, Claire. *The Word for Yes*. HarperTeen, 2016.

O'Neill, Louise. *Asking for It*. Quercus, 2016.

RAINN: Rape, Abuse, & Incest National Network. https://www.rainn.org/. Accessed 13 July 2018.

Raphael, Jody. *Rape Is Rape: How Denial, Distortion, and Victim Blaming Are Fueling a Hidden Acquaintance Rape Crisis*. Lawrence Hill Books, 2013.

Smith, Amber. *The Way I Used to Be*. Margaret K. McElderry, 2016.

Stevens, Courtney C. *Faking Normal*. HarperTeen, 2014.

Further Reading

Alpine, Rachele. *Canary*. Medallion Press, 2013.

Blakemore, Megan F. *Good and Gone*. HarperTeen, 2017.

Brooks, Kevin. *iBoy*. Scholastic, 2010.

Burkhart, Kiersi. *Honor Code*. Carolrhoda Lab, 2017.

Carlson, Melody. *Damaged: A Violated Trust*. NavPress, 2011.

Cassidy, Anne. *No Virgin*. Hot Key Books, 2016.

Costigan, Suzanne. *Empty Cup*. Rebelight, 2014.

Deriso, Christine H. *Thirty Sunsets*. Flux, 2014.

Downham, Jenny. *You against Me*. David Fickling Books, 2011.

Florence, Melanie. *One Night*. Lorimer, 2017.

Glover, Sandra. *Fallout*. Andersen, 2011.

Goobie, Beth. *The Pain Eater*. Second Story Press, 2017.

Halbrook, Kristin. *Every Last Promise*. HarperTeen, 2015.

Hartzler, Aaron. *What We Saw*. HarperTeen, 2015.

Krossing, Karen. *Punch like a Girl*. Orca Book, 2015.

Lindroth, Malin, and Clem Martini. *Train Wreck*. Annick Press, 2010.

Lynch, Chris. *Inexcusable*. Simon and Schuster Books for Young Readers, 2005.

Lynch, Chris. *Irreversible*. Simon and Schuster Books for Young Readers, 2016.

Maciel, Amanda. *Lucky Girl*. Balzer + Bray, 2017.

Marcus, Kimberly. *Exposed*. Random House, 2011.

Moore, Stephanie Perry, and Derrick C. Moore. *Settle Down*. Saddleback Educational, 2012.

Myers, Jason. *Dead End*. Simon Pulse, 2011.

O'Neill, Louise. *Only Ever Yours*. Quercus, 2015.

Padian, Maria. *Wrecked*. Algonquin Young Readers, 2016.

Payne, Mary J. *Enough*. Orca Book, 2016.

Quintero, Isabel. *Gabi, a Girl in Pieces*. Cinco Puntos Press, 2015.

Ramsey, Jo. *High Heels and Lipstick*. Harmony Ink Press, 2015

Reed, Amy L. *The Nowhere Girls*. Simon Pulse, 2017.

Shelton, Donna. *Sticks and Stones*. Turtleback Books, 2016.

Smith, Sharon B. *The Short Life of Moths*. OakTara, 2013.

Summers, Courtney. *All the Rage*. St. Martin's Griffin, 2015.

Tillit, L. B. *Edge of Ready*. Saddleback Educational, 2012.

Walton, K. M. *Empty*. Simon Pulse, 2013.

Watson, Cristy. *Epic Fail*. Lorimer, 2017.

Webber, Tammara. *Easy*. Penguin, 2013.

Wells, Maggie. *Jasmine*. Epic Press, 2016.

Whitney, Daisy. *The Mockingbirds*. Little, Brown, 2012.

Wolf, Jennifer S. *Breaking Beautiful*. Walker, 2012.

Wolf, Sara. *Love Me Never*. Entangled: Teen, 2016.

York, Kelley. *Modern Monsters*. Entangled: Teen, 2015.

Zhang, Amy. *This Is Where the World Ends*. Greenwillow Books, 2016.

13

Eliminating Extermination, Fostering Existence: Diverse Dystopian Fiction and Female Adolescent Identity

S. R. Toliver

While dystopian literature has been consistently taught in the classroom (*Fahrenheit 451* by Ray Bradbury, *1984* by George Orwell, and *Brave New World* by Aldous Huxley), the popularity of the genre has been revived in the past few years (Scholes and Ostenson, par. 1) with the influx of new, young protagonists who are fighting to save the world from oppressive forces. More importantly, though, the rejuvenation of the genre has brought young female characters to the frontlines of the action. Specifically, modern dystopian stories include prominent female characters who work to "claim their identities . . . [and] attempt to recreate the worlds in which they live, making their lives more egalitarian, more progressive, and ultimately, more free" (Day, Green-Barteet, and Montz 2).

However, although the speculative fiction world—which includes science fiction, fantasy, and horror as well as dystopian literature—has opened its doors to women in strong lead roles, narratives that reflect the experiences, cultures, and histories of Indigenous people and people of color (IPOC) continue to be limited in the publishing arena (Baxley and Boston 4). This means that the progressive picture of young adolescent womanhood is restricted to a view that lacks the representation of diverse populations. It promotes the idea that white female adolescent protagonists of the future get to experience freedom, equality, and societal progress, while adolescent females of color get to remain ignored as they continue to struggle for mere existence.

There is danger in this limited, constricted narrative, for if the view is not widened, the reification of the stereotypical oppressed, silent, or nonexistent girl of color could become the identifying trope in young adult dystopian fiction (YADF), creating the impression that young women of color have a dismal future existence. The issue, however, is not that diverse women should never be a sidekick or die in a story. The problem is that if these characteristics are the only ones depicted in the literature highlighted in English and literature classrooms, this view of adolescent girls of color could become imprinted in readers' minds as the only story available for diverse young women (Tschida, Ryan, and Ticknor 31). Thus, the narrowed lens created by the singular storyline is dangerous in that it limits the expansion of identity traits beyond the majority group, showing diverse young women's progress as stagnant.

In this chapter I aim to unsettle the hypercanon by introducing various YADF texts with young women of color featured as the protagonists. Specifically, I conduct a comparative analysis of books that represent young women who are Asian, biracial, Black, Indigenous, and Latinx. Yet, instead of focusing solely on the differences inherent in these texts, I align themes within the texts with universal adolescent identity themes, noting how the race of the characters does not eliminate some of the universal themes educators discuss when teaching mainstream texts.

YADF and Identity Construction

Researchers have found that adolescents of color explore their racial and ethnic identities earlier and more often than their white counterparts, and they often absorb the belief that the dominant culture is better, because they are socialized in a world where the "models, lifestyles, and images of beauty represented by the dominant group [are valued] more highly than those of their own cultural group" (Tatum 55). Therefore, it is important for teachers to use literature that reflects all human experiences, ensuring that the texts provide nuanced and accurate representations of diverse populations (Bishop, par. 1). This is especially important during the time of adolescence because if children of color constantly see images that are "distorted, negative or laughable, they learn a powerful lesson about how they are devalued in the society of which they are a part" (par. 4). They begin to internalize the negative imagery and take on the burden of monolithic stereotypes that plague society and obstruct their identity possibilities.

To combat singular portrayals of identity and present stories of diverse populations, many educators rely on multicultural literature, which works to include representations of marginalized populations who have been ostracized because of race, ethnicity, gender, religion, social class, ability, sexual orientation, and other identity characteristics (Baxley and Boston 19). However, although many studies promote the prevalence and necessity of students' ability to see representations of themselves and others, multicultural literature is often reduced to "a mirror-like understanding whereby young people of color are expected to find primary—if not exclusive—significance in literature that reflects their racial/ethnic/cultural backgrounds" (Sciurba 309), which means that some educators may believe that just because there are characters of color, students should be able to identify with them.

For example, a study completed by Gibson presents the negative conclusion that urban fiction can relate to all African American girls because the girls are looking for representations of themselves, regardless of whether the depiction is positive or negative (568). Specifically, the author posits that Black adolescent women "are not afforded the luxury to discriminate against readings that contain negative and stereotypic portrayals," and therefore, because they do not get the luxury of choice, they are often forced to accept any portrayal present in texts (569). Brooks posits, however, that the use of diverse elements, even with students who have the same identity characteristics, cannot be taken for granted or presumed similar (390). That is, just because there are parallels between the character and the student, that does not mean that the student will identify with the character. Essentially, the author suggests that a diverse student population requires diverse forms of literature that have diverse and intersecting characters in leading positions, specifically because literature is not one-size-fits-all.

Ultimately, it is important to analyze representations of girls of color in YADF because of the necessity for racially diverse young women to see themselves depicted in this genre. Yet it is also important to examine multiple examples, because one dystopian story cannot represent every girl within the diverse populace. Thus, in the following sections, I provide a content analysis in which I analyze fifteen books representing female adolescents of color, with three books examined for each racial designation. Of course, the fifteen books selected are not comprehensive, and they will not represent every girl of color. However, it is a starting point to begin a necessary conversation about the ways in which girls of color are represented in YADF.

Method of Content Analysis

Various websites and blogs are dedicated to diverse populations in speculative fiction, and I relied on the ones I use most often for personal recommendations to find books for this analysis. Because dystopian literature is often situated within speculative fiction, I used the following websites to expand my search for YADF with female protagonists:

- All Our Worlds: Diverse Fantastic Fiction: Large searchable database that highlights indie publishers, small presses, self-publishers, and larger publishing houses
- Charlotte's Library: Blog providing book reviews specifically for kids and teens
- Diverse Dystopias—Lee & Low List: Catalog of diverse SFF on the Lee & Low website
- The Illustrated Page: Blog dedicated to reviewing SFF books with diverse characters

From these websites, I looked for texts that included diverse adolescent women from different racial and ethnic backgrounds. I found numerous dystopian books with diverse protagonists, but there were few with female protagonists of color, resulting in a small list of texts for analysis. I then restricted the results to books published after 2006 to ensure that the books included were disseminated around the same time as other dystopian texts with female protagonists (e.g., *The Hunger Games* in 2008, *Divergent* in 2011, and *The 5th Wave* in 2013). This eliminated certain highly recommended dystopian fiction by notable authors such as Octavia Butler. After eliminations, fifteen books were included for this analysis. These books are listed in the chart below.

Protagonist Identity	*Books*
Asian	*The Abyss Surrounds Us* (Emily Skrutskie) *Dove Arising* (Karen Bao) *Legend* (Marie Lu)
Biracial	*On the Edge of Gone* (Corinne Duyvis) *Partials* (Dan Wells) *Pure* (Julianna Baggot)
Black	*Orleans* (Sherri Smith) *Panther in the Hive* (Olivia Cole) *Tankborn* (Karen Sandler)
Latinx	*Bluescreen* (Dan Wells) *Future Shock* (Elizabeth Briggs) *The Summer Prince* (Alaya Dawn Johnson)
Indigenous	*The Interrogation of Ashala Wolf* (Ambelin Kwaymullina) *Killer of Enemies* (Joseph Bruchac) *Trail of Lightning* (Rebecca Roanhorse)

Santoli and Wagner state that YA contains the "same themes that the classics do: alienation from one's society or group, survival or meeting a challenge; social and/or political concerns about racial or ethnic discrimination; [and] . . . problems resulting from family conflicts; fear of death; and the issue of political injustice" (68). The YADF books in this study were no different. Particularly, the protagonists were often on a journey of inner growth that forced them to make choices that altered the trajectories of their lives. They also had to make decisions to conform to societal rules and regulations or ignore those rules and create their own ways of life. In growing and making difficult decisions, they went against the values instilled by their parents because traditional ways of being no longer suited them, and they also learned to critically think about the "facts" they had been socialized to believe.

Additionally, because these are dystopic books, the protagonists often navigated new societal changes, highlighting technology and its possible future impact. Within this new society, they became leaders of a revolution, where they had to work with others to ensure that those who are marginalized persist even in the face of adversity. Although there are times that the protagonists are steadfast in their determination to help the people and ensure the success of the revolution, the protagonists often experienced the death of friends, family members, and loved ones, causing them to think about how much they owe the society when they really just want to protect themselves and those they love. However, even though they were often seen as leaders, that did not save them from dealing with microaggressions, explicit derogatory name calling, or systemic institutional oppression.

Each of the novels analyzed includes a racially diverse protagonist, yet many universal YA themes are prevalent, regardless of the character's race. The dystopian genre plays a large role in the characters' portrayals. As writers in a subgenre within the larger genre of speculative fiction, dystopian authors are granted the ability to go beyond the current reality while also extrapolating about events occurring in modern times (Serafini and Blasingame). Thus, although IPOC are often stereotyped as possessing certain traits and characteristics in modern society, dystopian authors are able to critique these roles and provide characters that break the confines created by these stereotypes. They have the capacity to prompt engaging, critically focused discussion on themes relating to all adolescents, and their inclusion of diverse characters offers a confirmation and validation of identity that challenges social expectations.

The ubiquity of common adolescent-centered themes within the novels suggests that the dystopian authors contest the reification of the stereotypical oppressed, silent, or nonexistent girl of color by ensuring that their characters are complex. They disrupt the stereotypes by placing girls of color in lead roles, thereby breaking contrived identity positions that would bind them just because they are not white. They ensure that the protagonists are agentic leaders who are striving to make change in the world, subverting ideas of silence and eternal oppression. Moreover, by establishing the pervasiveness of adolescent themes in the novels, the YADF authors show how the intersectional identities of the characters position them as young people who deal with more than just prejudice. In other words, YADF depicts young girls of color as people who find community, critique society, become leaders, sustain agency, love unconditionally, and grow steadily while also living in a world that tries to deny their existence. They are experiencing common facets of adolescent growth while also coping with the various ways that their race and age intersect

To illustrate the intricate ways in which YADF authors position girls of color, I expand upon these statements in the subsequent sections. However, to provide an in-depth analysis of each text is beyond the scope of this chapter. Therefore, in each section, I provide a detailed analysis of one book and briefly highlight aspects of other books that contain similar themes.

Unbound by Gender, Bound by Prejudice

Unconventional choices are vital for diverse identity development, because some theorists assert that "individuals who can abandon culturally imposed definitions about their racial or gender groups, respectively, have more positive mental health," and are thus more able to have a positive adjustment to adolescence through higher levels of self-esteem and psychological well-being (Buckley and Carter 658). Each of the novels analyzed had a female character of color as the protagonist who did not conform to stereotypical conceptions of gender or race; instead, they were individuals who rejected others' ideas about what they could or could not do.

This depiction of girlhood is important because teenage girls spend large amounts of time trying on various roles and searching for role models by which to define themselves (Jacobs 20). In traditional YA, girls are often described in binaries: beautiful and happy or ugly and miserable; obtaining a boyfriend and being successful or being alone and hopeless. Therefore, YADF distorts this ideal by highlighting characters that do not fall within these binaries. For example, Maria in *Bluescreen* is a poor girl who is also a technologically savvy computer hacker and gamer who works with her friends to stop another hacker from remotely controlling humans through their brain-implanted computer chips. Additionally, Kira from *Partials* is a medical assistant who risks her life battling human-robot hybrids to find a cure for her sister's unborn child. Thus, the young women are not confined to "gender-appropriate" roles, presenting diverse and complex options for girls of color.

However, the character's unbound gender does not protect her from various prejudices. Specifically, in *Panther in the Hive*, Tasha is a highly intelligent young woman who works at a pet store to earn money to support her expensive lifestyle. Yet she is accused by a wealthy customer of stealing a ring. Even though the ring was given to her by her mother, she was forced to relinquish the ring for further investigation because stereotypes of thievery often follow Black women and girls. Elena in *Future Shock* has an eidetic memory that some would consider a trait of genius. Yet she is constantly relegated to the sidelines, unable to follow her dreams, because she is a Latinx foster child. Lozen in *Killer of Enemies* is an Apache hunter who kills extraordinary beasts single-handedly, yet the Ones who rule the community and murdered her father believe her to be unintelligent and savage. Moreover, Denise, the protagonist of *On the Edge of Gone*, is determined to save her family by securing their place on an escape ship after a comet hits the Earth. However, various characters doubt her ability to be "of use" on the ship, not only because they do not believe that an autistic person can be a productive community member, but also because she stands out as one of the only Black people on the ship.

Hood notes that race in speculative stories subverts binaries, suggesting that the authors who write stories in this genre often embrace the possibilities of the future, while also enabling the diverse characters to have "intact family units, intergenerational support and relationships" and to be "gifted and talented protagonists who can take on the world without carrying it on their shoulders" (85). In the above examples, every character possesses some form of intelligence, strength, or natural ability that helps them to thrive in the world, but they also face prejudice from dominant societal members who wish to tyrannize, silence, and surveil them. However, the YADF authors present the characters as having a life that is more than just oppression. It is a part of their lives, but it does not define their existence.

Essentially, all the characters referenced decide to embrace their individuality, but they also struggle against individual and societal prejudice. To provide a more in-depth depiction of these themes, I focus on Fen, the protagonist of *Orleans*. In this story a number of hurricanes have ravaged the Gulf Coast, resulting in a virus called Delta Fever that affects the inhabitants' circulatory systems at varying rates. Specifically, although people with A and B blood types are greatly affected by the virus and die quickly without a transfusion, those with type O are able to survive for longer periods of time, causing them to be targeted for their blood. Therefore, the increased risk of death for the As and Bs creates a natural separation of people as the O blood types fight for survival.

Fen is the fifteen-year-old protagonist of the story and a member of the O-positive tribe, led by the pregnant matriarch, Lydia. She does not describe herself as beautiful or defenseless; instead, she considers herself to be a fierce warrior whose physical features are insignificant. Additionally, when her chieftain is killed in a battle between two blood tribes, Fen decides to take care of Lydia's child. Yet Fen does not possess the motherly instinct. In fact, when she is flustered by how slow and vulnerable she is with the child, she contemplates abandoning the child in order to ensure her own safety. Fen does, however, show her ability to care, not only because she never leaves the child, but also because she helps an outsider survive Orleans when she could have left him to die. Thus, Fen is characterized as not particularly eye-catching, selfish, caring, loyal, and protective, and although she must deal with the institutional racism that caused Orleans to exist in the first place, her identification as a Black character is not the main conflict. In other words, Fen is not bound by gender roles, as she is not particularly motherly or girly according to societal conceptions of girlhood. She is also not bound by her racial identity, as the storyline is more focused on her ability to complete her duty than on the fact that she is Black.

Coming of Age in Dystopia: Navigating a New World

In the last fifteen years, the advancement of technology has skyrocketed, the number of people who use the technology has amplified, and the time it takes for new technology to reach the masses has exponentially decreased. According to Giedd, thirty-eight years passed before the world caught on to the new phenomenon of radio, but it took only eighty-eight days for Google+ to reach this level of societal dispersion, showing the enhanced speed of new technological innovation (101). Of course, Google+ is now dated, and new technologies are invented every day, yet this influx of technological innovation is a concern for many adults, especially because the pervasiveness of technology has not only changed the way young people interact and learn, but also how they navigate the tasks of development (101). Thus, many YADF texts include characters who are adapting to technological and societal change.

For instance, Phaet Theta in *Dove Arising* is a member of a colony of scientists who immigrated to the moon when they decided that Earth was no longer an inhabitable place. In *The Summer Prince*, June Costa lives in a matriarchal pyramid society filled with miniature surveillance bots that monitor citizens and act as paparazzi, hypodermic LEDs that replace tattoos, and body modifications that allow humans to speak and become one with technology. Also, in *Pure*, the rich members of society build a dome capable of withstanding a nuclear bomb and release an explosive so great that millions are killed, the environment is forever scarred by nuclear residue, and many outside the dome—including Pressia, the main protagonist—become fused to the objects around them.

The technological advancements prevalent in the stories impact how the characters navigate adolescence, and modern adolescent girls will face similar technological possibilities. For this theme, I highlight Cassandra Leung (Cas), the protagonist of *The Abyss Surrounds Us*. In the novel, the modern world has been altered due to climate change that caused floods that submerged most of the Earth. Because of this, the world government decides to rearrange national boundaries so that smaller governments can optimize the care they provide for citizens. With the influx of water on the planet, however, pirates have taken to the seas, choosing to live outside of government rule. To combat this new societal threat, the government creates a weapon called a Reckoner, a metal-plated genetically engineered monster infused with animal DNA that is larger than a semi-truck and trained to destroy anything that threatens the ship they're imprinted to protect.

Cas wanted to be a Reckoner trainer, but although she began learning to train the monsters as a child, she never had full control of them. At seventeen Cas finally gets her chance and becomes the trainer of a large cruise ship Reckoner. Sadly, Cas's Reckoner, *Durga*, is poisoned on her first job, and Cassandra is captured by a pirate ship helmed by Santa Elena and her crew of mutineers. Somehow, Santa Elena captured a Reckoner of her own, and she wants Cas to raise it. However, what should have been a frightening event for Cas becomes an eye-opening situation that alters her life completely. She learns that the pirates may not be evil, and her society may be more malevolent than she ever anticipated. Pirates kill only those who fight back, but Cas was raised to use a technological advancement to kill and justify killing, rather than using technology for the benefit of humanity.

In this story Cas's adolescence is upended by climate change, technology, and society. Environmental change causes the floods that result in the prevalence of pirates. Although Cas is raised in this society, she is sheltered because of her family's occupational status and allegiance to the government. Specifically, the existence of Reckoners is not just for protection: their creation stems from the government's desire to govern those who have chosen to live a life of piracy rather than be controlled. Yet Cas would never have known about the nuances of Reckoner training and use had she not been captured by Santa

Elena in the first place. Once captured and forced to learn the ways of those who were not privileged with technology, Cas is obligated to critically analyze the society she's always known.

Cas's story represents an example of an adolescent being forced to critique technology's impact on society and on the adolescent. In trying to survive, she must question her level of comfortability with her family's values; she must deal with the loss of her family and the world she thought she knew; she must work with people whom she once believed to be morally beneath her. For diverse adolescents coming of age in a changing society, this text presents a glimpse of future possibilities, and it also provides an imaginary world that reflects characteristics of modern society. Just as Cas had to reconsider the purpose and use of Reckoners, adolescent readers will also need to critically think and "interrogate subjective positions within our current techno-global existence" as well as ask important questions about who owns, who develops, who benefits, and who is oppressed by technology (Zigo and Moore 88). Of course, access to technology is disparate, but regardless of accessibility, all teens will come of age in a world greatly affected by these advances; thus, YADF can assist them in navigating questions about the potentials and pitfalls of advancement.

Leadership, Teamwork, and Critiquing Accepted Truths

Ames notes that young adults have an interest in "current events, global politics, environmental concerns, and ethical debates involving scientific invention, human trafficking, and social equity" (3). Biological differences and growth are no longer the main concern as adolescents begin to notice more causal relationships and see an increase in their probabilistic reasoning, which assists them in the development of cognitive complexity (Kroger 65). These reasoning skills are necessary if adolescents are to form new ideas, to create distinct opinions, and to question authority and societal standards to discover their personal truths. This scholarship suggests that during adolescence, young people begin questioning the society in which they live, and forming their own opinions even if they do not understand the larger impact of societal actions.

YADF gives readers the opportunity to question the current world and themselves. The problems faced by YADF characters resonate with young readers because the novels replicate aspects of modern society with surprising accuracy, as the authors write to "extrapolate on current social, political, or economic trends," prompting adolescents to critically analyze facets of the society in which they live to promote a more positive future existence (Serafini and Blasingame 147). Particularly, Ames states that "teenage readers are drawn to the way these texts repackage societal concerns from reality, displacing them into the safe comforts of fiction where they are addressed recurrently with more favorable results" (17).

As with the other elements highlighted in this discussion, each book includes facets of this theme, with authors presenting situations involving digital access, digital footprints, artificial intelligence, genetic modification, digital warfare, virtual reality, and even time travel. For example, Kayla from *Tankborn* is a genetically engineered nonhuman raised to believe that she was only made to work for humans because of the futuristic caste system, but she later realizes that the government she serves is corrupt, and she works with others to subvert it. Maggie from *Trail of Lightning* hunts monsters to protect her home, but she later has to decide who is and who is not a monster. Also, June from *Legend* is a member of a police state known as the Republic. She is born to one of the wealthiest families and has been guaranteed a leadership position because of her family's monetary gains. However, even though she is certain to live a life of luxury, she begins to uncover the harsh reality that others face in the world, ultimately causing her to rebel against the government with the help of a new friend. Essentially, although socialized into the societal ways of thinking, these characters work to uncover the intricacies of their respective governments, form new opinions and ideas about their worlds, and rebel against their socialization with the help of new and old friends.

A more intricate example of these themes is represented in *The Interrogation of Ashala Wolf*, a story set far in the future, after the world has flooded, washing away most of society. To avoid another world catastrophe and maintain "the balance," the government has begun identifying children and young adults with special abilities and containing them in detention centers away from their families and friends. The young people in these camps wear special collars to prevent them from accessing their skills, and although the centers are touted as humane institutions, the children are imprisoned in high-security areas and sometimes tortured for information about the whereabouts of other special children. Although manipulated by the government, people in this society tolerate the imprisonment after the disaster because they believe it will keep them safe. They believe that by eliminating the threat of difference, the balance of the world could be preserved.

However, the main character of the story, Ashala, does not accept this belief. She believes it is wrong to force children into seclusion because they are different, and she knows that all people are a part of the balance, because a balance does not mean saving one group and destroying another. Because of her beliefs, she runs away from home before the government has a chance to test her for her abilities, and she forms a tribal group of runaways who do not believe in society's regulations. In doing this, she creates a utopia inside of a dystopia, one where children can live with the freedom to express their humanity. Therefore, instead of accepting "truths" constructed by the government to constrain children with abilities, Ashala chooses to survive by rejecting forceful conformity. However, she notes her position as a leader, understanding that she has a duty to society and to herself to lead other young people to a safer environment and work with them to create a space that is more inclusive. Essentially, Ashala is not apathetic toward societal conceptions of social and moral integrity. She is a fictional representation of an adolescent who questions society and refuses to believe in superficial laws that result in the subjugation of any population.

Implications

During adolescence an analysis of self takes place, where young adults try to figure out what beliefs they hold, how gender and sexuality impact their identities, what influence race has on who they are, what vocational direction they wish to pursue, and/or whether their religious or spiritual affiliations define how they think (Kroger 63). Additionally, while the young people are discovering who they are in the present, they must also be able to imagine what life will be like for them in the future, analyzing the different paths they may or may not take (66). Narrative texts, YADF in this case, can assist adolescents in this analytical process, because many young adults can conduct a form of identification that often happens through an "imaginative process of spontaneously assuming the identity of a character in a narrative and simulating that character's thoughts, emotions, behaviors, goals, and traits as if they were [their] own" (Kaufman and Libby 1). In other words, YADF has the ability to assist young people in "trying on" possible selves as they navigate this important time in their lives, helping them to figure out who they are, who they are not, who they want to be, and who they have the potential to become.

However, although YADF can assist all female adolescents in expanding their identity possibilities, it is crucial for racially diverse students to be centered in literature discussions, not only because there is a need for them to access broadened identity possibilities, but also because racially diverse adolescent females have historically been invisible in the English/language arts curriculum unless the perspective is centering a stereotypical deficit (Boston and Baxley). In each of the diverse dystopian stories highlighted in this chapter, however, there are prominent female characters who are strong, intelligent, empathetic, independent, confident, creative, and complex, traits that expand social identity possibilities beyond stereotypical notions of diverse womanhood

(Rubinstein-Avila 366). They work to re-create their worlds, creating innovative options for themselves that are not restricted by what society says they can or cannot do. They grow up in advanced societies, but they do not accept the world at face value. Instead, they critique the world, go against conformity, forge their own path, and lead others to do the same. Thus, the highlighting of YADF stories with diverse female protagonists creates new identity possibilities for the real adolescent females of color who read these texts, showing them that they do not have to remain invisible and that they can move beyond societally prescribed stereotypes.

Yet, even though the adolescents in the stories are racially diverse, many of the experiences they have while coming of age within these texts represent adolescent identity themes that are relevant to all young people working to define who they are and who they want to be. As Bishop notes, books "can introduce readers to the history and traditions that are important to any one cultural group, and which to invite comparisons to their own," so these stories can enable young women from various racial designations to not only notice their differences but also see similarities that connect all adolescents. Thus, as some YADF with mainstream characters discuss many of the same themes highlighted, the texts represented in this chapter specifically address racial difference and adolescent similarity. In other words, they provide windows through which all adolescents can see depictions of racially diverse young women as well as mirrors where adolescent females of color can see themselves.

Conclusion

Heroine role models in YADF are unique individuals who embrace their differences and question society to create a more egalitarian world for all people. It is a genre that provides a different view of female adolescence by offering examples of rebellion, small or large scale, that transform oppressed girls guided by the system to young women who can take charge of their futures (Green-Barteet 49). Specifically, the heroines in these stories try to change the monolithic view of culture within their worlds, a task that many young women of color face daily.

Although gender differences in identity development are minute, racial identity requires more affirmative representations of difference to promote positive identity development. Specifically, longitudinal research indicates that adolescents who have positive ethnic group identification have a more positive adjustment in terms of identity development (Quintana 264). This means that different genres, ones that are less constrained by stereotypical portrayals of identity, should be used in classrooms, particularly because narratives affect how adolescents relate to others and how they see themselves, which can greatly affect the positive or negative direction of their identity development (Kokesh and Sternadori 141).

YADF is one such genre, not only because of its increased popularity in society but also because these stories often feature female protagonists in possible futures, providing young women with the chance to take on the personas of the characters and discover new options of identity. With racially diverse female representatives expressing identity through nontraditional modes, adolescent girls of color can see characters who look like them who are strong, clever, insightful, creative, and dynamic. Thus, the constricted narrative reifying stereotypical oppressed, silent, or nonexistent women of color can be subverted through the centering of diverse characters in YADF, expanding identity possibilities and highlighting the young women's existence and experiences as a part of the future of humanity.

Works Cited

Ames, Melissa. "Engaging 'Apolitical' Adolescents: Analyzing the Popularity and Educational Potential of Dystopian Literature Post-9/11." *High School Journal* 97, no. 1, 2013, 3–20.

Baggott, Julianna. *Pure.* Grand Central, 2012.

Bao, Karen. *Dove Arising.* Penguin Young Readers Group, 2016.

Baxley, Traci, and Genyne Boston. *(In)visible Presence: Feminist Counter-Narratives of Young Adult Literature by Women of Color.* Sense, 2014.

Bishop, Rudine. "Mirrors, Windows, and Sliding Glass Doors." *Perspectives: Choosing and Using Books for the Classroom* 6, no. 3, 1990.

Briggs, Elizabeth. *Future Shock.* Albert Whitman, 2016.

Brooks, Wanda. "Reading Representations of Themselves: Urban Youth Use Culture and African American Textual Features to Develop Literary Understandings." *Reading Research Quarterly* 41, no. 3, 2006, 372–92.

Bruchac, Joseph. *Killer of Enemies.* Tu Books, 2013.

Buckley, Tamara R., and Robert T. Carter. "Black Adolescent Girls: Do Gender Role and Racial Identity: Impact Their Self-Esteem?" *Sex Roles* vol. 53, no. 9–10, 2005, 647–61.

Cole, Olivia. *Panther in the Hive.* Fletchero, 2015.

Day, Sarah K., Miranda A. Green-Barteet, and Amy L. Montz. "Introduction: From "New Woman" to "Future Girl": The Roots and the Rise of the Female Protagonist in Contemporary Young Adult Dystopias." *Female Rebellion in Young Adult Dystopian Fiction.* Routledge, 2014.

Duyvis, Corinne. *On the Edge of Gone.* Amulet Books, 2016.

Gibson, Simone. "Critical Readings: African American Girls and Urban Fiction." *Journal of Adolescent & Adult Literacy,* vol. 53, no. 7, 2010, 565–74.

Giedd, Jay. "The Digital Revolution and Adolescent Brain Evolution." *Journal of Adolescent Health,* vol. 51, 2014, 101–05.

Green-Barteet, Miranda A. "'I'm Beginning to Know Who I Am': The Rebellious Subjectivities of Katniss Everdeen and Tris Prior." *Female Rebellion in Young Adult*

Dystopian Fiction, edited by Sarah K. Day, Miranda A. Green-Barteet, and Amy L. Montz. Routledge, 2014, 33–50.

Jacobs, Katherine. "Gender Issues in Young Adult Literature." *Indiana Libraries*, vol. 23, no. 2, 2001, 19–25.

Johnson, Alaya Dawn. *The Summer Prince*. Scholastic, 2014.

Kaufman, Geoff, and Lisa K. Libby. "Changing Beliefs and Behavior through Experience-Taking." *Journal of Personality and Social Psychology*, vol. 103, no. 1, 2012, 1–19.

Kokesh, Jessica, and Miglena Sternadori. "The Good, the Bad, and the Ugly: A Qualitative Study of How Young Adult Fiction Affects Identity Construction." *Atlantic Journal of Communication*, vol. 23, no. 3, 2015, 139–58.

Kroger, Jane. *Identity Development: Adolescence through Adulthood*. Sage, 2007.

Kwaymullina, Ambelin. *The Interrogation of Ashala Wolf*. Candlewick, 2014.

Lu, Marie. *Legend*. Penguin Young Readers Group, 2013.

Quintana, Stephen. "Racial and Ethnic Identity: Developmental Perspectives and Research." *Journal of Counseling Psychology*, vol. 54, no. 3, 2007, 259–70.

Roanhorse, Rebecca. *Trail of Lightning*. Simon and Schuster, 2018.

Rubinstein-Avila, Eliane. "Examining Representations of Young Adult Female Protagonists through Critical Race Feminism." *Changing English*, vol. 14, no. 3, 2007, 363–74.

Sandler, Kat. *Tankborn*. Tu Books, 2011.

Sciurba, Katie. "Texts as Mirrors, Texts as Windows: Black Adolescent Boys and the Complexities of Textual Relevance." *Journal of Adolescent and Adult Literacy*, 58, no. 4, 2015, 308–16.

Serafini, Frank, and James Blasingame. "The Changing Face of the Novel." *Reading Teacher* 66, no. 2, 2012, 145–48.

Skrutskie, Emily. *The Abyss Surrounds Us*. Flux, 2016.

Smith, Sherri. *Orleans*. Penguin Random House, 2013.

Tatum, Beverly. *"Why Are All the Black Kids Sitting Together in the Cafeteria?" And Other Conversations about Race*. Basic Books, 1997.

Tschida, Christina M., Caitlin L. Ryan, and Anne Swenson Ticknor. "Building on Windows and Mirrors: Encouraging the Disruption of 'Single Stories' through Children's Literature." *Journal of Children's Literature*, 40, no. 1, 2014, 28–39.

Wells, Dan. *Blue Screen*. HarperCollins, 2016.

Wells, Dan. *Partials*. HarperCollins, 2013.

Zigo, Diane, and Michael Moore. "Serious Reading, Critical Reading." *English Journal*, 94, no. 2, 2004, 85–90.

Further Reading

Baggott, Julianna. *Pure*. Grand Central, 2012.

Bao, Karen. *Dove Arising*. Penguin Young Readers Group, 2016.

Briggs, Elizabeth. *Future Shock*. Albert Whitman, 2016.

Bruchac, Joseph. *Killer of Enemies*. Tu Books, 2013.

Chapman, Elsie. *Dualed*. Penguin Random House, 2013.

Cole, Olivia. *Panther in the Hive*. Fletchero, 2015.

Duyvis, Corinne. *On the Edge of Gone*. Amulet Books, 2016.

Hopkinson, Nalo. *The Chaos*. Simon and Schuster, 2012.

Johnson, Alaya Dawn. *The Summer Prince*. Scholastic, 2014.

Kang, Lydia. *Control*. Penguin Young Readers Group, 2015.

Knutsson, Catherine. *Shadows Cast by Stars*. Simon & Schuster, 2012.

Kwaymullina, Ambelin. *The Interrogation of Ashala Wolf*. Candlewick, 2014.

Lu, Marie. *Legend*. Penguin Young Readers Group, 2013.

Mandanna, Sangu. *The Lost Girl*. HarperCollins, 2012.

Okorafor, Nnedi. *Who Fears Death*. DAW/Penguin, 2010.

Roanhorse, Rebecca. *Trail of Lightning*. Simon and Schuster, 2018.

Sandler, Kat. *Tankborn*. Tu Books, 2011.

Skrutskie, Emily. *The Abyss Surrounds Us*. Flux, 2016.

Smith, Sherri. *Orleans*. Penguin Random House, 2013.

Wells, Dan. *Blue Screen*. HarperCollins, 2016.

Wells, Dan. *Partials*. HarperCollins, 2013.

14

Sharpening the Pointe: The Intersectional Feminism of Contemporary Young Adult Ballet Novels

Sarah E. Whitney

Laced delicately with ribbons, pointe shoes—pink slippers of burnished satin—epitomize the grace, beauty, and strength of classical dance. When *en pointe*, ballerinas balance their body weight at the tips of extended feet, executing magical leaps, turns, and kicks. Contemporary YA ballet novels present girls who are both *en pointe* and "on point," the pop culture phrase that signals grace, beauty, and strength.[1] Combining dramatic narrative, lush imagery, and powerful social commentary, these texts display loving respect for the heritage, discipline and emotional power of dance. Yet they depart from earlier, more sentimental ballet narratives portraying individual dancers' journeys to meritorious success. In keeping with other feminist intersectional work in YA, contemporary ballet novels interrogate how structural prejudices of racism and sexism create barriers to the center stage.

Focusing primarily upon works authored by women of color or told through queered perspectives, I examine here how YA narratives in varied melodramatic, thriller, and paranormal forms deconstruct the pink, pretty, and postfeminist "music box ballerina" image. Sona Charaipotra and Dhonielle Clayton's series *Tiny Pretty Things* (2015) and *Shiny Broken Pieces* (2016) use a multicultural cast of characters to dispel the assumption that ballet "belongs" to white bodies. Nova Ren Suma's gothic *The Walls Around Us* (2015) questions the ease with which a white, privileged façade can insulate ballerinas. Brandy Colbert's *Pointe* (2015) and Sharon M. Draper's *Panic* (2014) utilize the woman-in-peril structure to spotlight the trauma of sexual exploitation and abuse perpetrated upon ballerinas of color. Finally, Amber Keyser's paranormal *Pointe, Claw* (2017) features a ballerina creating feminist choreography in response to a queered interspecies encounter. Amidst sumptuous descriptions of velvets, jewels, and glimmering tiaras, these novels offer frank new discussions of ballet's darker side, including body image disorders, rape culture, and racism. Within their pages adolescent readers find young women refusing objectification and reclaiming dance on their own terms.

First Position: On YA, Ballet, and Pink Princesses

YA offers, Meghan Lewit writes, "the opportunity to disappear into the lives and adventures of strong-willed young women," which is "a kind of feminist victory." Arguably, the most totemic female presence in recent years is *The Hunger Games*'s Katniss Everdeen, an "extremely competent, tomboyish young woman who is athletic, focused, responsible, and able to take care of herself" (Berlatsky). While the gossamer world of tutus and pointe shoes might seem far removed from Katniss's dystopian landscape, ballet novels figure into a larger battle over the politics of identification in girls' YA. Online discourse often invokes Katniss as a corrective to Bella Swan, the *Twilight* series' shy, lovesick, and physically inept heroine. While many feminist critics rightly interrogate *Twilight* concerning gender politics, others diagnose a troubling "discomfort with femininity" in the venomous responses to Bella (Berlatsky).[2]

Katniss's and Bella's role model battle asks larger questions about the relationship of "soft" or heavily feminized spheres of culture to American liberal feminist traditions, which deemphasize gender differences in order to advocate for women's political and social equality. In popular culture both the 1990s Riot Grrl movement and its commercialized successor, Girl Power, brought together traditional totems of femininity—like Barbie, tight skirts, or the color pink—with empowerment rhetoric. Alternatively, some feminized subcultures, such as gymnastics and figure skating, deemphasize "girliness" through new scoring systems that emphasize raw athleticism over glitter and sparkle. YA ballet novels strike a balance here, retaining respect for the discipline, traditions, and visual accoutrements of dance while seeking ways to renovate its hierarchies. This, though, is no small task, for many feminist critics reserve Bella Swan–like levels of disdain for ballet.

George Balanchine, arguably the most famous choreographer and artistic director in modern memory, emphasized ballet's essential feminine nature. "Woman," mused Balanchine. "Everywhere else man is first. But in ballet, it's the woman. All my life I have dedicated my art to her" (qtd. in Croft 202). But who counts as "the" woman, and what does this woman do? Feminist critics of ballet have looked askance at the most well-known ballets' portrayal of women as sleeping beauties, sylphs, and princesses; the popular "dying swan" showcase, comments Alexandra Carter, is "a sitting duck for an exposé of how ballet constructed images of women which embodied the oppressive hegemonies of patriarchy" (227). While ballet requires extraordinary strength and flexibility, ballerinas onstage often provide the illusion of being dependent agents who are frequently lifted, carried, and otherwise twined "like valuable necklaces around" the "manly bodies" of their partners (Jowitt, quoted in Croft 205). Furthermore, only exceedingly slender bodies perform ballet. "Ballet is the perfect space for ideal femininity," Jennifer M. Miskec neatly summarizes. "Thin bodies, frilly skirts, speechlessness; graceful movements making it all look easy while hiding the pain, physical anguish for beauty" (240).[3]

Some feminist dance critics resist this rather dim view of ballet.[4] Anna Aalten argues for increased attention to embodiment, or how the sheer athleticism of ballet provides "women with a place where ambitions can be realized and physical excellence is valued" (274). World-famous ballerina Misty Copeland celebrates the personal satisfaction of dance, how "the exhilaration of perfor-mance, the ecstasy of losing yourself in movement" creates "the most joyful moments" (161). Nevertheless, young adult novels enter the conversation at a vexed moment, when ballet is lumped into a popular aesthetic that Miskec labels "hyper-feminine ballerina/fairy/pink princess" (224). Today's parents cannot escape the princess marketing juggernaut, which offers hundreds of diverse goods in sparkly pink. Most feminist critics resist the princess craze, deeming it a white, heteronormative narrative that encourages girls to value unearned wealth and looks, and the attention of boys above all.[5] While a glass slipper is not necessarily the same as a ballet slipper, there is convergence between representa-tions of dance and princess culture. Disney's early films used "regally denotative ballet styles" to represent princesses, observes Rebecca-Anne Do Rozario (46). Simultaneously, Disney's princess line regularly stamps "generic tutus" upon non-balletic products ranging from swimwear to pajamas (Turk 486).

Thought not necessarily pink and tutu-like, earlier ballet stories echo princess-like narratives of aspirational success and spectacular visibility. The "mother" of children's ballet books is unquestionably Noel Streatfeild, the Carnegie Medal–winning British author whose "Shoes" books of the 1930s and 1940s remain beloved. In these well-researched but formulaic books, plucky heroines are "always stimulated and never defeated by adversity" (Kuznets 149).[6] Streatfeild's most famous work, *Ballet Shoes* (1936), centers on three female orphans raised by a mysterious and often absent benefactor. The spirited

Posy boasts to a renowned Eastern European legend that "it would be a mistake not to see me [dance]" and is rewarded with a balletic career (274).[7]

Streatfield's accounts of girls' virtue, discipline, and self-sacrifice en route to meritorious success have become ballet novel staples. Pamela Knights finds that twentieth-century young girls' ballet novels open "with the young dancer at a liminal point (her first steps, early lessons, or first encounter with ballet), moving into a trajectory of discovery, dedication, growth, and control, as she works to conquer that dangerous space" (87). This sort of straightforward, bildungsromanic portrayal is still around today, primarily in children's series such as *Angelina Ballerina*. Indeed, children's author Annie Barrows, author of the popular *Ivy and Bean* series about two spirited preteens, has noted that for girls, a ballet setting is "the perfect wrapping for the 'work hard and you'll succeed' story, because it's both true and pretty" (quoted in Miskec 239).

Second Position: Ballerinas of Color Claiming the Stage

The quality of prettiness, however, is not part of YA literature's dominant aesthetic. It is no surprise, then, that young adult ballet novels have taken a less glossy view of the world on and off stage. Former teen librarian Dhonielle Clayton and journalist Sona Charaipotra's series *Tiny Pretty Things* and *Shiny Broken Pieces* chronicle the changing fortunes of three high schoolers competing for treasured company positions. The authors, who cofounded a packaging company for diverse young adult novels, weave tales of privileged, white Bette; African American newcomer Gigi; and June, a half-Korean ballerina always relegated to supporting roles. The narratives reflect some of the authors' own experiences; Clayton worked as a teacher at a private ballet academy, while Charaipotra, a dancer in childhood, remembers "how much racism there was in that world, even for little girls. We never got asked to be in the recital. I was the only brown girl in the class" (Diaz 2015).

The novel *Tiny Pretty Things* opens on selection eve for the iconic *Nutcracker* showcase. June confides in the audience that the newest ballerina, Gigi, will be cast "as Arabian Coffee, just like the other brown girl from two years ago," since their teacher is "predictable enough to put minorities in ethnic roles" (26). The prized Sugar Plum Fairy appears reserved for the ice-cold blonde Bette. However, when Gigi wins the role instead, she is made to feel unwelcome. Clayton and Charaipotra employ loaded language to show misogynoir's coded language within ballet's white patrician world. In real life African American female performers often find their contributions attacked through racialized and masculinized epithets. Tennis star Serena Williams, for instance, has been

caricatured as a "gorilla," as "savage," and as "manly" (Blay). Within the ballet world, meanwhile, Sierra Leone–born international ballet star Michaela
DePrince was labeled a "real brute" who "should leave the classical ballet to
white girls" (DePrince 123–24). A dance professional even invoked the stereotype of "big thighs and behinds" to justify to DePrince's mother why he
didn't "waste a lot of time, money, and effort on the black girls" in ballet (124).
The fictional Gigi faces similar linguistic assaults. Bette's recollection of Gigi's
entrance is worth unpacking at length:

> I remember her first ballet class with us. She stuck out. It made me realize,
> for the first time ever, just how white the ballet world is. Even the Asian girls
> sort of blend in at initial glance, with their pale little arms and tiny frames and
> quiet personalities. But not Gigi. She barreled into the room, her hair a burst of
> *wild* curls, pins between her teeth as she wrestled it into a bun, and she wore a
> hideous, multicolored leotard, totally ignoring the very specific ballet class uni-
> form instructions. . . . I close my eyes and can see her dancing. I see how *loud*
> it was. How riveted everyone was. How much *fire* she had in her movements."
> (*Shiny* 39, emphasis added)

Bette's portrayal of Gigi as "wild," "loud," and fiery invokes loaded words that
discipline African American women's behavior and distinguish it from the
norms of white femininity (Bette accomplishes this in part through another
racist dig at Asian American women, whose purported silence and white
skin signal an "acceptable" level of diversity). The collective weight of these
stereotypes—too raucous, too noisy, too big—follows Gigi around the ballet
school. "*The black girl. The new girl. She's no Sugar Plum Fairy,*" the whispers
say within Gigi's earshot. "*Her feet are bad. Her legs are too muscular*" (*Tiny* 31).
Recognizing the racially specific ways in which her body is stigmatized, Gigi
muses, "I hate that being *different* can be a code word for being black" (152).

Within the world of ballet, where identical body types populate the corps,
any form of difference is particularly visible. Misty Copeland, arguably the
most famous ballerina of the twenty-first century and one of very few African
American soloists, has written that while "in nearly every way, my body was
molded for dance . . . ballet isn't just about ability or strength. You must also
look the part" (163). Copeland, possessed of "full breasts, muscular limbs, and a
curve to [her] hips," was ostracized early in her career (162). She recounts racist
objections to her participation in *Swan Lake*, as well as uncomfortably painting
and powdering her face "a completely different color" to "appear ethereal and
ghostlike" in *ballets blancs*, or productions which feature snowy-white clothing
and magical characters (175).[8]

Shiny Pretty Things echoes this moment when a teacher lambastes Gigi for being "too dark for the white" tights. "White swans have white legs," she grumbles (271). The iconic ballet *Swan Lake*—disproportionately featured in YA ballet novels as the ultimate test of physical strength—has itself been deemed a racially politicized narrative. The dance showcases a ballerina who embodies both Odette, the "pristine, virginal White Swan," and Odile, "her aggressive and sexualized Black counterpart" (Marston 702). To displace privilege, Charaipotra and Clayton reverse these roles; the sympathetic Gigi dances Odette, while devious Bette schemes against her as Odile. June, however, triangulates this battle for elite status, and her body is also a flashpoint for intersectional discussion.

As a supporting character, June also contributes to Clayton and Charaipotra's project to show the "hidden diversity" of ballet beyond "the people who get the main roles and those who are primarily photographed in the major magazines and programs" (Diaz 2015). Lacking Bette's connections and wealth, or Gigi's eye-catching talent, June is literally and metaphorically the understudy. Her character is shown depriving herself of everything, including food and interpersonal connection, in pursuit of stardom. "I do nothing but study and dance," June complains after another day of endless run-throughs. "I am [a] good little girl" (45). To avoid the scrutiny of her cutthroat classmates, June cultivates no friendships. "Never show how you feel about a particular role," she advises the audience. "People are watching. Always. They'll take what you want" (28). Furthermore, June punishes her anorexic body with starvation. "For my height, I should be 110 pounds, a hippo in tights," she sneers. Instead, she says, "I do what I have to do" (101).

Yet June is well aware that despite her extraordinary self-discipline, institutionalized roadblocks limit her potential. There "are no Asian dancers featured" in the school's gallery, but, she wryly observes, "the school will happily take their money" (206). Indeed, professional companies misread June's quietude as the "inscrutable Asian" stereotype.[9] "June, your technique is very nice," a scout hedges, but "look like you're enjoying it. I need to see passion" (82). Furthermore, there are racialized consequences for June's disordered eating. While many characters in the series perform extreme feats of dieting, including the abuse of metabolism-boosting prescription drugs, June *alone* fails to win roles, and she is further stung when a company rejects her thin body as a potential medical liability. The novel thus both critiques the stereotype of Asian American women as inherently slender and suggests June's body is uniquely pathologized so as to deny her entrance to ballet's white world. Through June's thwarted narrative, Charaipotra and Clayton caution readers that beyond the successes of individual ballerinas of color, many racial barriers still bar the way to center stage.

Third Position: The Ghostly Mask of White Femininity

While Charaipotra and Clayton's novels disrupt ballet's snowy landscape and confront the barriers facing young women of color in dance, Nova Ren Suma's ghost story *The Walls around Us* asks readers to explore the potentially dangerous relationship between white femininity and the socially constructed ballerina persona. In this narratively complicated novel told by multiple voices in alternating flashbacks, Violet, a young white woman who employs a façade of "princesslike" docility, falsely accuses her best friend, the ballerina of color Ori, of committing a double murder. Sentenced to a girls' correctional facility, Ori and her fellow inmates die by accidental food poisoning. Years later, Violet returns to the now-shuttered jail, where supernatural justice is served.

Every young dancer confronts the conundrum, writes Pamela Knights, of becoming "the cleverest, hardest-working, most ruthlessly focused" girl while simultaneously appearing onstage as "the most fragile, graceful, and beautiful" (84). Suma's prima ballerina Violet embodies this tension; she does not seem to dance for the love of it, but rather for self-display. Violet yearns "to have the spotlight on me and have no one able to pull their gaze away from the gorgeous shape of me under the bright-hot, mesmerizing beam of light" (249). Offstage, Violet is a hypersensitive narcissist who masquerades as wholesome and nonthreatening. "So much is about how you look on the outside. That's what matters to most people," she confides in the reader, offering the following advice: "Smooth your hair and bobby-pin it down. Use as many pins as you need. Be sure to flick the eyeliner crumble out of from the corners of your eyes. Wear your prettiest clothes. Pale noncolor colors help, like powder pink. Keep that good-girl mask on and no one can see past it to the bad, unstable girl inside" (70). Her mask slips when she murders two fellow dancers who have never accepted her.

Violet's façade of beauty, whiteness, wealth, and privilege proves powerful enough to insulate her from criminal repercussions; she successfully frames her orphaned, darker-skinned best friend, Ori, for the murders. Suma connects Ori's injustice to wider stories of race and class disparity in girls' incarceration. Judges, rues one girl, condemn "ten seconds in. If you're poor. If you're brown. If you're black. If you've got an accent. If your skirt's too short" (223). Justice is miscarried for Ori and her companions in life; after their accidental deaths, though, the girls enact it and reclaim the stage for ballerinas of color.

Perhaps because they are ghosts, the dead inmates are able to discern Violet's true nature when she visits the now-rotting jail. Having fantasized about ballerinas as tinkly golden beings on charm bracelets, the girls notice Violet is not "pretty like her outside parts" or "made of tinkling gold," but rather "rotten" (60–61). The girls' recognition denies Violet the masquerade of balletic feminine appearance she so cares about. In an act of posthumous retribution, the girls bludgeon her with a shovel, and Violet "drops into the dirt with a hard thump" and a "clatter"; this pointedly undignified ending denies her the "full of grace" ballerina title (310). Orianna, the truly gifted ballerina, magically comes to life, and choreographs a dance expressing the inmates' loss and pain.

sj Miller has suggested that fantastical young adult stories can "hold open a transparent window that provides access to a world out there filled with new opportunities for growth and understanding, a world not bound to conventional social norms, mores, or dichotomies" (70). Suma uses dark fantasy to open such windows, by undoing the gold-charm-bracelet image of the ballerina, a stereotype of gender conformity and white privilege. Ori becomes a sort of social justice ballerina, if such a thing exists, and her graceful spins and twirls capture the rage, grief, and loss of the girls who applaud her from the grave.

Fourth Position: The Ballet Thriller and Bodies under Siege

The ballerina's body, writes Peter Stonely, is both "powerful and erect and "deliberately and completely vulnerable to the gaze of the audience" (141). YA authors Brandy Colbert and Sharon M. Draper capture this vulnerability in mystery form. Their respective novels *Pointe* and *Panic* repurpose the conventional white-woman-in-jeopardy form, spotlighting the specific isolation and vulnerability of girls of color. In Colbert's novel *Pointe*, a pedophile abuses a high-achieving ballerina of color named Theo. Shuttling between a narrow world of school and dance, the socially isolated Theo idolizes Misty Copeland. Well aware of her minority status in ballet, Theo nonetheless believes the force of her technical gifts will combat prejudice, leading companies to "judge me based on my talent instead of my skin color" (63–64). She believes that restricted eating will improve her chances and survives on only a few hundred calories a day. "Everyone tells you 'a spoonful of this' or 'a little bite of that' won't hurt, but those spoonfuls and bites could be the difference between sixteen fouettés and thirty-two," she advises (170). Into this airless environment steps Chris, an older man posing as an eighteen-year-old boy. Warning Theo to secrecy, he pursues sexual intimacy with her despite her clear reluctance.

Colbert pairs two scenes involving dance's iconic pointe shoe to demonstrate Chris's pedophilic gaze. Pamela Knights has observed that many ballet texts connect pointe work to sexuality; the shoes arrive "when girls are 'ready,' at around twelve, the age of puberty" (87).[10] In Colbert's novel Chris asks to see Theo's new pointe shoes soon after meeting. "I slowly pulled them out of my dance bag . . . and slipped one onto his lap," she recalls; they were "still unmarred; a soft, sweet pink," and he "slid his hands around the satin almost wonderingly" (8). The eroticized innocence of this passage sharply contrasts with a later one after Chris has taken Theo's virginity and tired of her. When "Chris saw my pointe shoes again," muses Theo, "they were almost dead; the satin was dirty and starting to rip . . . dried brown spots decorated the toe, and when I waved the shoe jokingly in front of his face, he pushed it away from me, told me not to be gross" (21). This passage emphasizes the eroticized infantilization of the ballerina body; it also highlights rape culture's victim-blaming rhetoric, as Theo perceives her own abused body as "dirty" and "gross." Thankfully, Theo is able to summon the strength *through* dance to recognize her abuse and move forward. While practicing Swan Lake's turns *en pointe*, painful memories break through and cause her to "crash down and nearly tumble to the floor" (207). Knocked off balance in a literal and metaphorical sense, Theo recognizes Chris's actions as rape and agrees to testify against him.

Colbert creates a layered interpretation of ballet as powerful and problematic; her heroine's isolation, fueled by her drive to overcompensate as a person of color in a white field, makes her vulnerable to a predator who fetishizes the prepubescent dancing body. Well-known young adult author Sharon M. Draper addresses similar themes in the sex trafficking thriller *Panic*. Gifted young African American dance student Diamond devotes all her time to dance and as a result is somewhat socially naive; as in *Pointe*, an older man capitalizes on her vulnerability. When she encounters a trafficker who claims to be casting a film version of the *Peter Pan* ballet, she is lured by the promise of a part that is no longer "in the back row" (28).[11] Consequently, Diamond appears at a fake "audition" center, where she is drugged, confined, and raped nightly in front of internet audiences. The kidnapper comments upon the sexualized ballerina body when he leers that "the last few nights have been simply glorious. It never occurred to me how much more . . . ah, flexible . . . dancers could be" (157). The trafficking of Diamond is an extreme experience of sexual trauma. Yet Draper draws parallels between Diamond's ordeal and a more common, peer-based experience of assault to suggest the unfortunate ubiquity of rape culture's claim to female corporeal ownership. Back at home, Diamond's best friend, fellow ballerina Layla, endures the threats of a violent boyfriend. The boyfriend isolates Layla, objects to her dance work with other men, demands sex, and eventually commits image-based abuse (more commonly known as "revenge pornography" in the United States, image-based abuse involves the nonconsensual taking and/or distributing of intimate images for the purpose of harm and humiliation; it is a criminal offense in many states). Significantly, he captions his photos "Layla 4 Sale" (211). By layering these ballerinas' narratives,

Draper critiques rape culture's perceived entitlement to view, buy, and sell the female body—in any format.

Though dance-derived pressures may galvanize these abuse narratives, *Panic*, like *Pointe*, also emphasizes ballet's power to rescue, heal, and create new forms. The physical discipline of ballet training aids Diamond's eventual escape; she leaps over a ditch and evades her assailant by doing "what she's done a hundred times on the dance floor," leaping "into the air and across the gulf" (234). Furthermore, dance assists the emotional recovery of both Diamond and her friends to process their traumatic emotions. Upon her escape, Diamond creates an expressive ballet, her "heavy-toed pointe shoes barely making a sound as she embrace[s] the music. . . . her body an arrow of beauty" (259). Draper writes that "dance and music swirl throughout" *Panic* "as colorful decorations" that "help the characters express complicated feelings while they work through the demons in their lives." ("Intro, Summary"). These choreographic pieces infuse new texts into the ballet canon and place agency into the hands of dancers rather than professionals.

Fifth Position: Something Wild in the Ballet Paranormal

Whereas *Pointe* and *Panic* explore captivity *literally*, in narratives of kidnapping, Amber Keyser's overtly feminist *Pointe, Claw* uses the captivity metaphor for two young women trapped by patriarchal demands. The teenage Jessie performs hyperfemininity within her tightly controlled ballet academy. Meanwhile her friend Dawn, whose queer identity is condemned by her gender-conforming family, struggles with unexplained blackouts, olfactory sensitivity, and other bodily changes. Through their friendship both stifled girls help each other to move differently in the world. Dawn literally escapes her body through shapeshifting, while Jessie jettisons her "pretty ballerina" identity and pioneers a new, more egalitarian form of dance.

Dawn is both species and gender nonconforming; she is slowly changing form, gaining muscles, hair, and increased sensitivity to scent. She welcomes her changes even as they frighten her, as they release her from a feminine body that, she says, "constantly betrays me" (7). The masculinized Dawn is more comfortable "dressed like a boy . . . thick-limbed, and chunky" with "no makeup [and] jaggedly cut hair" (95). She "sits like a guy, thighs spread," Jessie remarks. "I half expect her to scratch her balls" (100). While her sexuality and gender orientation are not fixed, Dawn displays erotic longing for Jessie. The novel also evokes queerness through unsupportive parental response. Dawn's fundamentalist Christian father prays for her soul constantly; her mother pathologizes Dawn as a sick girl in need of a diagnosis. "Fix," Dawn muses, examining herself in the mirror. "I function. But . . . not to specifications, not the daughter they intended" (108–09).[12]

Society ostracizes Dawn for *not* fitting feminine paradigms; for the lithe ballerina Jessie, the cost of fulfilling them is a constant leering male gaze. Dawn depicts Jessie as a music box ballerina, the "kind of girl that men want" (99). Readers, however, understand how being this "kind of girl" inflicts constant harassment. Teenaged star dancer Michaela DePrince has commented on the damaging effects of this "ballerina mystique," which assumes that dancers are "seductresses" possessed of "womanly charms" no matter what their actual age (3). The fictional Jessie is subject to the ballerina mystique by men who view her disciplined body as sexually available. Jessie's own accompanist grabs his crotch and propositions her. On the street, strangers watch her butt through the studio glass. One approaches her "with a hard-on in his khaki trousers" to ask if she is a dancer. He does not mean "the Sugar Plum Fairy," Jessie realizes. "When he says *dancer* he doesn't mean ballet" (103). At several places in the novel, Keyser links the ballerina mystique to the presumption of sexual availability forced upon exotic dancers, suggesting that all female artists within the world of dance are subject to a controlling patriarchal gaze.

Jessie's music box world is further constrained by unequal gender politics; her artistic director does all "the choosing" for elite roles, and the ballerinas are "are all trying to be exactly what he wants" (36). *Pointe, Claw*'s exploration of gendered power relations within the dance profession also reflects reality. Famous ballerinas like Gelsey Kirkland have documented the complex sexual politics between "muses" and their choreographers.[13] Coercion can also occur offstage; Moscow's iconic Bolshoi Ballet recently faced the "sexual skeletons" of sponsorship scandals, and Joy Womack, the only American ballerina contracted with the company, quit over the "very blurred" personal and professional lines (Shuster, "American").[14]

In *Pointe, Claw* the constraints of feminine performativity hold both young women captive. Freedom, for Jessie, presents itself in her new, unconventional ballet showcase that upends traditional partnering roles. Initially disdaining the approach as lacking ballet's traditional "grace" and "beauty," she instead finds agency and rediscovers her love of movement (56). "This time I move [my partner] as much as he moves me," she recounts. "My body presses against his. Every movement is bigger, more carnivorous than the last. . . . I feel as big as he is. Bigger" (56). The dance moves her from ballerina-as-object to a more embodied subjectivity and feminist understanding.[15]

Jessie now casts a critical eye upon the traditional restrictions of ballet. She derides a ballerina cupcake topper made in "an unnatural shade of pink." "All she can do is spin around and around," mocks Jessie. "Dance, little girl. Spin, little doll. Be pretty. Be sweet. I wonder why I ever wanted to be her" (256–57). Unleashing her own choreographic potential has now fundamentally altered Jessie's perspective on her body as tool. "Instead of seeing a myriad of tiny flaws that must be beaten into perfection, I see myself claiming the territory of the body," Jessie reflects. "I have never, until this moment, understood what dance could be. *I am far bigger than the skin that holds me*" (168, emphasis added). Through that realization and others, Keyser linguistically links the unbridling of Jessie's spirit to Dawn's metamorphosis. Just as Dawn becomes feral in the novel's ending, Jessie rejects the "china ballerina" persona, claiming she is not one of "those girls any longer . . . by a long shot" (271).

At its heart, argues Jennifer Homans, ballet offers "the idea of human transformation, the conviction that human beings could remake themselves in another, more perfect or divine image" (548). While *Pointe, Claw* literalizes the idea of human transformation, all of these young adult ballet novels rewrite the rules for women in dance. *Tiny Pretty Things* and *The Walls around Us* diversify the bodies featured onstage. *Pointe, Panic,* and *Pointe, Claw* challenge the objectification and sexualization of girls' ballerina bodies. Displaying a frankness that is characteristic of YA in general, ballet novels do not hold back about the dark underside of dance, from blisters and bloody toe shoes to the perils of substance abuse, disordered eating, and sexual exploitation. Yet these works do not simply critique; they also *persist*, portraying heroines bulldozing their way through institutional barriers in pursuit of the passion and pleasure that ballet provides. On point and *en pointe*, these ballerinas, to use Theo's words, "can do damn near anything" (52).

Notes

1. See also Allen and Lindeman regarding the phrase usage and connections.

2. See also Berlatsky, Christakis, and Firestone on critical disdain for Bella.

3. See also Carter on changing historical "ideal bodies" in ballet.

4. See also Fisher on the ballerina as "powerhouse."

5. See also Forman-Brunell and Hains; Orenstein; and Orr.

6. See also Stokes on Streatfeild's critical merits.

7. See also Kuznets on Streatfeild's pressure to capitalize upon the popularity of *Ballet Shoes*.

8. See also Woodard on *ballets blancs*.

9. See also *TV Tropes*' "Inscrutable Oriental" for historicizing of the stereotype.

10. See also Miskec on the eroticized foot in children's ballet stories.

11. Draper chose *Peter Pan* because "it is really a harsh story of someone who sneaks into a bedroom at night and steals three children! It's an abduction worthy of an Amber Alert" ("Intro, Summary").

12. See Miller for more on the werewolf metaphor in gender-non-conforming YAL.

13. See Kirkland; Homans.

14. See also Shuster, "Raising."

15. See Aalten, Carter, and Fisher in particular on embodied feminist subjectivity.

Works Cited

Aalten, Anna. "The Moment When It All Comes Together: Embodied Experiences in Ballet." *European Journal of Women's Studies* vol. 11, no. 3, 2004, pp. 263–76.

Allen, Shundalyn. "'Is It 'On Point' or 'En Pointe'?" *Grammarly*. https://www.grammarly.com /blog/is-it-on-point-or-en-pointe/. Accessed April 27, 2017.

Berlatsky, Noah. "'Twilight' vs. 'Hunger Games': Why Do So Many Grown-Ups Hate Bella?" *Atlantic Monthly*, 15 November 2011, https://www.theatlantic.com/entertainment/archive /2011/11/twilight-vs-hunger-games-why-do-so-many-grown-ups-hate-bella/248439/. Accessed 3 May 2017.

Blay, Zeba. "When We Attack Serena Williams' Body, It's Really about Her Blackness." *Huffington Post*, 13 July 2015, http://www.huffingtonpost.com/entry/serena-williams -policing-of-black-bodies_us_55a3bef4e4b0a47ac15ccc00. Accessed 2 May 2017.

Carter, Alexandra. "Staring Back, Mindfully: Reinstating the Dancer—and the Dance—in Feminist Ballet Historiography." *Proceedings of the Society of Dance History Scholars. Twenty-Second Annual Conference. University of New Mexico: 10–13 June 1999.* The Printing House, 1999, pp. 227–32.

Charaipotra, Sona, and Dhonielle Clayton. *Shiny Broken Pieces*. HarperTeen, 2016.

Charaipotra, Sona, and Dhonielle Clayton. *Tiny Pretty Things*. HarperTeen, 2015.

Christakis, Erika. "The Harsh Bigotry of Twilight Haters." *Time*, 21 Nov. 2011, http://ideas.time .com/2011/11/21/the-harsh-bigotry-of-twilight-haters/. Accessed 16 April 2017.

Click, Melissa A., Jennifer Stevens Aubrey, and Elizabeth Behm-Morawitz, editors. *Bitten By Twilight*. Peter Lang, 2010.

Colbert, Brandy. *Pointe*. Speak, 2014.

Copeland, Misty. *Life in Motion: An Unlikely Ballerina*. Simon and Schuster, 2014.

Croft, Clare. "Feminist Dance Criticism and Ballet." *Dance Chronicle*, vol. 37, no. 2, 2014, pp. 195–217.

DePrince, Michaela, with Elaine DePrince. *Taking Flight: From War Orphan to Star Ballerina*. Alfred A. Knopf, 2014.

Diaz, Shelley. "Ballerinas Behaving Badly: Sona Charaipotra and Dhonielle Clayton on *Tiny Pretty Things*." *School Library Journal*, 26 May 2015, http://www.slj.com/2015/05/interviews /ballerinas-behaving-badly-sona-charaipotra-and-dhonielle-clayton-on-tiny-pretty- things/#. Accessed 2 May 2017.

Do Rozario, Rebecca-Anne C. "The Princess and the Magic Kingdom: Beyond Nostalgia, the Function of the Disney Princess." *Women's Studies in Communication*, vol. 27, no. 1, 2004, 34–59.

Draper, Sharon M. "Intro, Summary and General Questions." *Sharondraper.com*. http://sharon draper.com/bookdetail.asp?id=73. Accessed 2 May 2017.

Draper, Sharon M. *Panic*. New York: Atheneum, 2013.

Firestone, Amanda. "Apples to Oranges: The Heroines in Twilight and The Hunger Games." *Of Blood, Bread, and the Hunger Games*, edited by Mary Pharr, McFarland, 2012, pp. 209–18.

Fisher, Jennifer. "Tulle as Tool: Embracing the Conflict of the Ballerina as Powerhouse." *Dance Research Journal*, vol. 39, no. 1, 2007, pp. 3–24.

Forman-Brunell, Miriam, and Rebecca C. Hains, editors. *Princess Cultures: Mediating Girls' Imaginations & Identities*. Peter Lang, 2015.

Homans, Jennifer. *Apollo's Angels: A History of Ballet*. Random House, 2010.

Keyser, Amber J. *Pointe, Claw*. Carolrhoda Lab, 2017.

Kirkland, Gelsey. *Dancing on My Grave*. 1986. Berkley Books, 1992.

Knights, Pamela. "Still Centre Stage? Reframing Girls' Culture in New Generation Fictions of Performance." *Girls, Texts, Cultures*, edited by Clare Bradford and Mavis Reimer, Wilfrid Laurier UP, 2015, pp. 75–110.

Kuznets, Lois R. "Family as Formula: Cawelti's Formulaic Theory and Streatfield's 'Shoe' Books." *Children's Literature Association Quarterly*, vol. 9, no. 4, 1984–1985, pp. 147–201.

Larsson, Mariah, and Ann Steiner, editors. *Interdisciplinary Approaches to Twilight*. Nordic Academic Press, 2011.

Lewit, Meghan. "Why Do Female Authors Dominate Young-Adult Fiction?" *Atlantic Monthly*, 7 August 2012, https://www.theatlantic.com/entertainment/archive/2012/08/why-do-female -authors-dominate-young-adult-fiction/260829/. Accessed 2 May 2017.

Liberman, Mark. "Ask Language Log: On Point." *Language Log*, 22 Nov. 2010, http://languagelog .ldc.upenn.edu/nll/?p=2066. Accessed 2 May 2017.

Marston, Kendra. "The Tragic Ballerina's Shadow Self: Troubling the Political Economy of Melancholy in *Black Swan*." *Quarterly Review of Film and Video*, vol. 32, no. 8, pp. 695–711.

Miller, sj. "Hungry like the Wolf: Gender Non-Conformity in YAL." *The Critical Merits of Young Adult Literature*, edited by Crag Hill. Routledge, 2014, pp. 55–72.

Miskec, Jennifer M. "Pedi-Files: Reading the Foot in Contemporary Illustrated Children's Literature." *Children's Literature*, vol. 42, 2014, pp. 224–45.

Nick, Stacy. "Ballet Programs Look for More Boys to Step up to the Barre." *NPR*. 22 Aug. 2015. http://www.npr.org/2015/08/22/433264225/ballet-programs-look-for-more-boys-to-step -up-to-the-barre. Accessed 3 May 2017.

Orenstein, Peggy. *Cinderella Ate My Daughter: Dispatches from the Front Lines of the New Girlie-Girl Culture*. HarperCollins, 2011.

Orr, Lisa. "Difference That Is Actually Sameness Mass-Reproduced: Barbie Joins the Princess Convergence." *Jeunesse: Young People, Texts, Cultures*, vol. 1, no. 1, 2009, 9–30.

Parke, Maggie Parke, and Natalie Wilson, editors. *Theorizing Twilight*. McFarland, 2011.

Shuster, Simon. "American Ballerina Quits Bolshoi, Accuses Theater of Extortion." *Time*, 13 Nov. 2013, http://world.time.com/2013/11/13/american-ballerina-quits-bolshoi-accuses -theater-of-extortion/. Accessed 10 May 2017.

Shuster, Simon. "Raising the Barre: Moscow's Bolshoi Theatre Gets a $700 Million Makeover." *Time*, 29 Oct. 2011, http://content.time.com/time/magazine/article/0,9171,2097866,00.html. Accessed 10 May 2017.

Stokes, Sally Sims. "Noel Streatfeild's Secret Gardens." *Children's Literature Association Quarterly*, vol. 29, no. 3, 2004, 172–206.

Stoneley, Peter. "Ballet Imperial." *Yearbook of English Studies*, vol. 32, 2002, pp. 140–50.

Streatfeild, Noel. *Ballet Shoes*. 1936. Random House, 1991.

Suma, Nova Ren. *The Walls around Us*. Algonquin, 2016.

Turk, Mariko. "Girlhood, Ballet, and the Cult of the Tutu." *Children's Literature Association Quarterly*, vol. 39, no. 4, 2014, pp. 482–505.

TV Tropes. "Inscrutable Oriental." 15 Dec. 2017. http://tvtropes.org/pmwiki/pmwiki.php/Main /InscrutableOriental.

Woodard, Laurie. "Black Dancers, White Ballets." *New York Times*, 15 July 2015, https://www .nytimes.com/2015/07/15/opinion/black-dancers-white-ballets.html?_r=0. Accessed 7 May 2017.

Further Reading

Bhavati, Robyn. *Dancing in the Dark*. 2010. Flux, 2013.

Bomboy, Erin. *The Piece*. Curtain Call, 2016.

Ferrer, Caridad. *When the Stars Go Blue*. St. Martin's, 2010.

Flack, Sophie. *Bunheads*. Hachette, 2011.

Hewitt, Lauri. *Dancer*. Puffin, 1999.

Hurwin, Davida Wills. *A Time for Dancing*. Penguin, 1995.

Ibbotson, Eva. *A Company of Swans*. Speak, 1985.

Kehoe, Stasia Ward. *Audition*. Penguin, 2011.

Longo, Jennifer. *Up to This Pointe*. Random House, 2016.

McDaniel, Lurlene. *Last Dance*. Darby Creek, 1982.

Meyers, Carolyn. *Marie, Dancing*. Harcourt, 2005.

Rose, Terez Mertes. *Off Balance*. Classical Girl Press, 2015.

Rubin, Sarah. *Someday Dancer*. Scholastic, 2012.

Stevenson, Robin. *Attitude*. Orca, 2012.

Tamar, Erika. *Alphabet City Ballet*. HarperCollins, 1996.

Wenger-Landis, Miriam. *Breaking Pointe*. CreateSpace, 2012.

Williams-Garcia, Rita. *Blue Tights*. Penguin, 1998.

Wilson, Sari. *Girl through Glass*. HarperCollins, 2016.

Yep, Laurence. *Ribbons*. Putnam and Grosset, 1992.

Acknowledgments

We would like to thank our contributors for their hard work and tolerance of our weird email signatures.

We owe Gwen Tarbox an immense debt for her impromptu seminar on Herding Cats 101, advising us from the very start on how to put together a CFP and work with a large group of contributors over a long period of time. This project would have been a lot more complicated without her sage advice.

We send a not-entirely ironic Gator Chomp to Kenneth Kidd, Anastasia Ulanowicz, and the rest of the faculty and graduate students at UF for giving us a false sense of our own importance.

We could not have survived this process without our families, friends, and most importantly our dogs, who supported and snuggled us while we read essay after essay.

We are grateful to the community of Brittain Fellows, especially Monica Miller, Rachel Dean-Ruzicka, and Ruth Yow for putting on a "getting your book published" workshop, and our cohort members for their advice on the book proposal and sample chapters—along with general moral support and encouragement.

We also know that this project would not exist without our delightful editor, Katie Keene, who reminded us that Twitter can do good things when she saw our CFP and invited us to submit to UPM. We are especially appreciative that she didn't laugh at us when we admitted we had no idea how to do that and gently walked us through this process step by step.

Contributors

Megan Brown is an instructor of Early Childhood Literacy at Cedarville University, where she teaches children's literature and early childhood methods courses. She is a doctoral candidate pursuing a PhD in Teaching and Learning from The Ohio State University by May of 2019. Her current research interests include children's literature, preservice teacher education, and disability studies. Her work has been published in *Children's Literature in Education.*

Jill Coste is a doctoral candidate at the University of Florida, where she is specializing in children's and young adult literature. Her research focuses on different forms of feminist resistance and social justice in YA fairy tale retellings. Additional areas of interest include dystopian and speculative fiction, posthuman adolescence, and twentieth-century American youth cultures. She has published on Neil Gaiman and has work forthcoming on diversity in YA dystopian fairy tales.

Sara K. Day is an assistant professor of English at Truman State University, where she teaches classes in young adult literature, children's literature, and popular literature, among others. She is the author of *Reading Like a Girl: Narrative Intimacy in Contemporary American Young Adult Literature* (UP of Mississippi, 2013), the coeditor of two essay collections, and the editor of the *Children's Literature Association Quarterly.* Her research interests include narrative theory, fandom studies, and adaptation.

Rachel Dean-Ruzicka is a lecturer of Writing and Communication in the Literature, Media, and Communication department at Georgia Tech. She received her PhD in American Culture Studies from Bowling Green State University in 2011. She has previously published on Lumberjanes, female engineers in YA dystopian fiction, and YA Holocaust literature. Her book, *Tolerance Discourse and Young Adult Holocaust Literature*, was published by Routledge in 2017 and released in paperback in 2019. She's much more cheerful than the serial killers and Holocaust research might imply.

Rebekah Fitzsimmons is an assistant teaching professor of Professional Communication in the Heinz College of Information Systems and Public Policy of Carnegie Mellon University in Pittsburgh, PA. She previously worked as the Assistant Director of the Writing and Communication Program and a Marion L. Brittain Post-Doctoral Fellow in the School of Language, Media, and Communication at the Georgia Institute of Technology, where she completed a certificate in digital pedagogy. She has a PhD in English from the University of Florida and specializes in children's and young adult literature studies. Her research and teaching interests include popular culture, speculative fiction, the process of canon formation, digital humanities, and bestseller lists. She has published articles in *Children's Literature, The Lion and the Unicorn*, the *Journal of Interactive Technology and Pedagogy*, and the *Journal of the Fantastic in the Arts*. Her work also appears in the edited collections *The Early Reader in Children's Literature and Culture* and the *Prizing Children's Literature Collection*.

Amber Gray is a social sciences and humanities reference librarian at the University of Maine, specializing in the subject areas of children's and young adult literature, education, human development, and psychology. Her interests include fantasy in young adult literature and information literacy.

Roxanne Harde is professor of English at the University of Alberta's Augustana Faculty, where she also serves as associate dean, Research. A McCalla University Professor, Roxanne researches and teaches American literature and culture, focusing on popular culture, women's writing and children's literature, and Indigenous literature. Her most recent books are *The Embodied Child*, coedited with Lydia Kokkola (Routledge, 2017), *Walking the Line: Country Music Lyricists and American Culture*, coedited with Thomas Alan Holmes (Lexington, 2013). Roxanne recently held the Fulbright Canada Visiting Research Chair at Vanderbilt, working on a project entitled, "Still Searching: Singer-Songwriters, Americana Dreams."

Tom Jesse is an assistant professor of English at the University of Wisconsin-La Crosse specializing in 20/21c. American Literature and English Education. His presentations and publications include work in the fields of postwar American poetry (1945–present), modern rhetorical theory, and critical pedagogy in secondary English Language Arts classrooms.

Heidi Jones is a literacy specialist in the School District of La Crosse, where she works with middle school teachers and students to improve literacy teaching and learning. She earned her PhD in 2013 in Curriculum and Instruction, Literacy Education, from the University of Minnesota. She is a former assistant professor of English Education at UW-La Crosse; after four years on the tenure track, she took the leap back into K12. She is enjoying the awesomeness that is middle school after fifteen years of focusing on high school ELA.

Kaylee Jangula Mootz is a doctoral candidate specializing in Native American and African American literatures, as well as Young Adult literature. She is the current graduate student representative for the Society for the Study of Multi-Ethnic Literature of the United States and the former managing editor of the *MELUS* journal. Her current project considers the intertwined relationship between history, temporality, and the speculative in fiction written by Indigenous and African American authors.

Leah Phillips is a sessional lecturer and postdoctoral research associate at the University of Warwick, where she is currently supervising MA Creative Writing students. She is also currently working on a monograph, *Female Heroes in Young Adult Fantasy Fiction: Reframing Myths of Adolescent Girlhood*, which is forthcoming with Bloomsbury. Her research interests include YA fiction, YA genre fiction, adolescence, and embodiment.

Rachel L. Rickard Rebellino is a doctoral candidate specializing in Literature for Children and Young Adults at The Ohio State University. She received her MA in Children's Literature from Eastern Michigan University and has taught courses in composition and children's and young adult literature. Her research focuses on narrative form, digital youth cultures, girlhood studies, and the role of children's and young adult literature in facilitating conversations around equity and social justice. Her work has been published in *The ALAN Review*, *English Journal*, and *The Lion and the Unicorn* as well as in the edited collection *Graphic Novels for Children and Young Adults* (University Press of Mississippi, 2017).

S. R. Toliver is pursuing a PhD in Language and Literacy Education at the University of Georgia. Her current research is based in the critical tradition, analyzing young adult speculative fiction in an effort to promote social justice and equity in the English classroom. Within this research area, she focuses on representations of and responses to people of color in speculative fiction texts to discuss the implications of erasing youth of color from futuristic and imaginative contexts. Toliver's research interests include speculative fiction, narrative analysis, Afrofuturism, and Black girl literacies. Her work has been published in *Research on Diversity in Youth Literature, Journal of Children's Literature, Journal of Adolescent and Adult Literacy*, and *English Journal*.

Jason Vanfosson is an assistant professor at West Chester University, where he teaches courses in children's and young adult literature. His research focuses on the American road trip in young adult novels, queer ruralities, and comic studies. His work has appeared in the *Language Journal of Michigan* and was featured on *Degree of Impact*, a one-hour PBS documentary film by *Roadtrip Nation*.

Sarah E. Whitney is an assistant teaching professor of Women's Studies and English at Penn State University-Erie. Her book *Splattered Ink: Postfeminist Gothic and Gendered Violence* (UP Illinois, 2016) examines how women write stories of traumatic violence, and her current book project focuses upon YA writing sexual assault.

Casey Alane Wilson is an assistant professor of English at Francis Marion University. A former Marion L. Brittain Post-Doctoral Fellow in the Writing and Communication Program at the Georgia Institute of Technology, she completed her MA and PhD at the University of Florida, with a specialization in children's literature and digital media. Her research focuses on trends in young adult literature, social media, and the ways in which the two interact. She is also an author of young adult fiction under the name Casey Alane.

Index

CPSIA information can be obtained
at www.ICGtesting.com
Printed in the USA
LVHW092225021120
670542LV00007B/850